THE
Blooming
GREAT
Gardening
BOOK

THE Blooming GREAT Gardening BOOK

A Guide for All Seasons

Steve Whysall

WHITECAP BOOKS

VANCOUVER/TORONTO

Some of the information in this book appeared previously in
The Vancouver Sun.

"The Fight of the Year" (on page 1) is reprinted by permission of The Peters
Fraser and Dunlop Group Limited on behalf of Roger McGough © 1969 Roger
McGough. "The Red Wheelbarrow" by William Carlos Williams (on page 87)
from COLLECTED POEMS: 1909-1939, VOLUME I. Copyright © 1938 by New
Directions Publishing Corp. Reprinted by permission of New Directions
Publishing Corp. "Tree at My Window" by Robert Frost (on page 137) is from
THE POETRY OF ROBERT FROST; THE COLLECTED POEMS, COMPLETE
AND UNABRIDGED © 1979. Reprinted by permission of Henry Holt & Co.,
LLC. "Faery Songs" by John Keats (on page 173) is reprinted by permission of
Wordsworth Editions Ltd.

Edited by Elaine Jones
Proofread by Elizabeth McLean
Cover design by Susan Greenshields
Interior design and typesetting by Warren Clark

Printed and bound in Canada

Canadian Cataloguing in Publication Data

Whysall, Steve, 1950
     The blooming great gardening book

     Includes index

     ISBN 1-55285-022-6

     1. Gardening. I. Title.
SB450.97.W57.2000   635   C00-910067-9

The publisher acknowledges the support of the Canada Council and the
Cultural Services Branch of the Government of British Columbia in making
this publication possible. We acknowledge the financial support of the
Government of Canada through the Book Publishing Industry Development
Program for our publishing activities.

Acknowledgements

A special word of thanks to the following people for their encouragement, support, inspiration and love.

My wife Loraine's skills as a researcher, proofreader, ideas person and all-round, beautiful, smart, good person were utterly indispensable. Without her love and patience and heart of perpetual self-giving, this book would not have been possible. Thanks to my children Joel, Aimee, and Peter, who I love more than my garden and who I know enjoy the garden more than they realize. I know they each have the talent and knowledge to create marvelous gardens of their own one day. It would be a privilege to lend a hand.

Robert McCullough, director of publishing at Whitecap Books, had confidence, faith and optimism in the success of this project from day one.

Lindsay Davidson of Specimen Trees in Pitt Meadows provided advice on the sections on trees, evergreens and conifers. John Folkerts, of Linnaea Nurseries Ltd. of Langley, was extremely generous with his time and expertise on the section on native plants for coastal gardens. At *The Vancouver Sun*, executive editor Shelley Fralic has always been wonderfully supportive. Colleagues Susan Balcom, Graham Houston and Barbara McQuade have also been enthusiastic supporters of my efforts as a garden writer.

Many dear friends and gardeners have also directly or indirectly had a significant influence on this book. Special thanks to Mary Ballon of West Coast Seeds; Carol Barke-Ashton; Margaret Charlton; Alleyne and Barbara Cook; Terri and Korleen Coward; Fred and Grace Cullingworth; Francisca Darts; Pam Erikson of Erikson Daylilies; the staff at GardenWorks, Burnaby; David Jack of Ferncliffe Gardens; Jens and Carolyn Juhl; Ken and Elke Knechtel of The Perennial Gardens; Barry and Lori Kuypers of Mandeville Garden Centre; Russell and Alice Michaelczuk; Tony Mildbradt of RainForest Nursery; Bernie and Mary Milns; Brian Minter of Minter Country Garden; Betty Murray of Murray's Nursery; Clare Phillips of Phoenix Perennials; John and Kelly Schroeder of Heritage Perennials; Wim Vander Zalm of Art Knapps Nursery; Casey Van Volten of Van Volten Nursery; Carey Van Zanten of Pan American Nursery; Fred Wein of Clearview Horticultural Products; Hart Wellmeire and Tiina Turu of Wrenhaven Nursery; and Ray and Helena Whysall.

Lastly, many thanks to all the faithful readers of my stories in *The Vancouver Sun*, especially to those whose kind words are responsible for inspiring me to do this book. Happy gardening!

Contents

Summer

Fall

Winter

Introduction

Don't sit down and try to read this book from cover to cover. You can if you want, of course, but it is meant to be an eclectic and entertaining package of general gardening information that you can dip into any time you feel like it and find something interesting or practical or inspiring. I think you'll get the most pleasure from this book by simply flipping the pages and waiting for something to catch your eye.

The initial idea for the book came from readers of my weekly gardening column in *The Vancouver Sun*. They repeatedly asked me when I was going to put my stories into a book so they could throw away their folders full of browning newspaper clippings and have all that information in one handy package. Encouraged by their kind words, I looked at the columns and discovered there was indeed a lot of valuable information in them that was worth reclaiming, expanding and reworking into book form.

So that is exactly what I have done here. I went through the more than 1,000 pieces I have written on gardening over the last 10 years and salvaged what I consider the best and most useful bits. Topics have been loosely grouped, in no particular order of importance, around the four seasons. I also thought it would be fun in a book like this to include some of the memorable quotes I have collected over the years from interviewing countless gardeners and horticultural experts.

In the spring chapter, you'll find a great mix of information from a guide to outstanding roses to exciting plant ideas for patios and balconies. Under summer, you'll find stacks of information on everything from how to make the most of containers, vines and shrubs to tips on good gardening practices, pond-building and water plants. Fall is the ideal time to plant bulbs and check out ornamental grasses, so you'll find comprehensive pages on the best bulbs to plant for a beautiful display in spring, as well as an introduction to the best decorative grasses for the late-summer garden.

Much of the material in this book is new. I was surprised to discover in extracting the best information from my newspaper columns that I had written very little about broadleaf evergreens and conifers. Although I had frequently mentioned plants like rhododendrons and azaleas, camellias and boxwood, I had never provided a detailed plant list to give readers clear, usable information on the range and kinds of evergreens and conifers most suitable for the home garden.

But the main aim here is to inform and entertain. You'll find lots of lists. I like lists because they provide me with a great place to start on a journey of discovery. They are not intended to be all-inclusive. They are simply a starting point, a way of getting to grips with horti-culture, which can be a vast and overwhelming subject. A list is a good way to bring plants into a clearer focus so you can get to know them better. There are, for instance, thousands of different roses in cultivation, and most of us find it a daunting experience when we pop down to the garden center to buy one. Where to begin? This is why you'll find lists such as 10 Top Hybrid Teas or 10 Top Floribundas. Rose experts may disagree with some of my choices, but the object here is not to say these are the only good roses in the world, but that they are most certainly some of the best.

You'll also find great information in this book on bulbs (and how to plant them), trees (for all the right places), and beautiful flowering shrubs for the summer garden.

I have included a few stories that have no other purpose than to inspire you or make you think about the garden in a completely different way. For me it is definitely a spiritual place. Whether I'm working in it or just sitting and enjoying the color and fragrance of flowers, the garden is a place where I'm always reminded of the beauty of creation and the creative will behind all that is beautiful in nature. So I hope that as well as finding lots of practical information on a wide variety of topics, you will also find words of enthusiasm and encouragement.

The longer I worked on this book, the more I realized how much more there is to say. My wife, Loraine, had to tear the manuscript away from me to get it to the publisher on time. "There is more to add," I insisted. "There can always be another book," she said. I hope you won't be too disappointed if you don't find the specific reference you are looking for. What I hope most of all is that you have fun dipping into these pages and reading whatever you find there. Every success.

Spring

'The Fight of the Year'

'And there goes the bell for the third month
and Winter comes out of its corner looking groggy
Spring leads with a left to the head
followed by a sharp right to the body
    daffodils
    primroses
    crocuses
    snowdrops
    lilacs
    violets
    pussywillow
Winter can't take much more punishment
and Spring shows no signs of tiring
    tadpoles
    squirrels
    baalambs
    badgers
    bunny rabbits
    mad march hares
    horses and hounds

Spring is merciless
Winter won't go
the full twelve rounds
    bobtail clouds
    scallywaggy winds
    the sun
    a pavement artist
    in every town
A left to the chin
and Winter's down!
1   tomatoes
2   radish
3   cucumber
4   onions
5   beetroot
6   celery
7   and any
8   amount
9   of lettuce
10 for dinner
Winter's out for the count
Spring is the winner!'

—Roger McGough

In the Garden

- Pull weeds before they are overtaken and hidden by emerging perennials. Get the whole root of dandelions and buttercups.

- Keep an eye out for slugs and snails. They will already be chomping on new emerging foliage, especially bleeding hearts, primulas, daylilies and hostas.

- Hunt for slugs after dark. Look for them under rocks and pots. Lure them into "slug saloons" with beer or fermenting yeast.

- Start seeds indoors for onions, eggplants, leeks, asparagus and peppers. Sow seeds for beets, peas, celery, lettuce, Swiss chard, cauliflower and cabbage directly into the soil.

- Prune roses and top-dress rose beds with steer manure. (See How to Plant and Care for Roses, page 65.)

- Aerate and feed lawns. This is the best thing you can do to revitalize grass. Overseed bare spots. Feed the lawn with a slow-release fertilizer with high nitrogen content for lush, green growth.

- Don't cut the grass too short; longer grass has stouter roots and is better able to cope with summer drought.

- This is an excellent time to install a new lawn. If you seed, use good starter fertilizer.

- Prune wisteria and clematis. (See Pruning—The Kindest Cut of All, page 49.)

- Plant away as soon as the soil is workable. Garden centers are now full of new shipments of trees, shrubs, perennials, roses, everything, in fact, except summer bedding plants. Prepare the soil well by adding bonemeal and compost, leaf mold or well-rotted manure.

- Plant gladioli. And plant a second batch in about three weeks to create a sequence of blooms in summer.

- Lift and divide perennials. Have fun putting together new combinations of plants.

- Feed bulbs after flowering with 6-8-6 all-purpose fertilizer.

- Plant lily bulbs.

- Prune forsythia and heathers after they have flowered. Feed rhodos and azaleas after they have bloomed.

- Go shopping for new rhododendrons; many will be in full bloom. In colder climates, ask about hardy rhodos such as those with an H1 or H2 rating. Also ask about the Finnish rhodos ('Peter Tigerstedt', 'Hellikki', 'Elvira') bred specifically for their hardiness. (See Your Guide to Rhododendrons, page 37.)

- Watch for fresh holes in rhododendron leaves. Root weevils will have started their nightly visits. Trap them by applying a band of Tanglefoot around stems; or go out after dark and shake them off the leaves onto a sheet of paper.

- Look out for the first aphids. Their numbers increase very quickly, so try to squish them while there are only a few. Use a strong jet of water to knock them to the ground.

- Plant out bedding plants such as snapdragons, nicotiana, petunias, pelargoniums, pansy and impatiens after May 25.

- Spring dry spells can be deceptive. Don't neglect watering all plants, especially newly planted or pruned trees and shrubs.

- Remove faded flowers from lilacs, rhodos and other shrubs, taking care not to damage the buds below the break point.

- Stake peonies and tall perennials.

3 Projects for Spring

1. Divide perennials. This is the easiest way to double your plant stock. Lift mature clumps of astilbes, hostas, phlox and daylilies, and slice them into two or more pieces. Replant immediately and water with transplant solution. Astilbes especially appreciate being divided and will flower better for it. Hellebores and daylilies will sulk a little, but they'll bounce back. Don't hurt your back.

2. April-May is a good time to plant a new clematis. You'll find a great selection now at the garden centers. Plant where the roots will enjoy cool shade, but the top of the vine will get full sun. Plant deeply—at least 18 inches (45 cm). Pick varieties that will give you a natural sequence of blooms and exciting color contrast. (See Divine Vines, page 98.)

3. Hanging baskets and window boxes are really miniature gardens. They require just as much planning as a flower border. For a lively 16-inch (40-cm) basket, mix the following: 3 dark blue lobelia 'Sapphire'; 3 light blue lobelia 'Cascade'; 3 pink trailing petunias; 1 red pelargonium; 2 white bacopa; 3 ivy geranium; 3 dwarf French marigolds *(Tagetes)*.

Hurrah for the Plant Hunter

You walk into a typical Canadian garden and what do you see? A shrubbery packed with rhododendrons, azaleas, camellias, magnolia, pieris and forsythia. You see arbors or entrances covered with clematis or wisteria or honeysuckle or actinidia or Virginia creeper. There are flower beds full of Japanese anemones, lilies, dicentra, primulas, peonies and chrysanthemums. In one corner you spot the flaking bark of a paperbark maple (*Acer griseum*) or the elegant fanlike branches of a snowbell tree (*Styrax japonica*). In another, the bluish-purple flower cones of a butterfly bush or the myriad pink blooms on a rampant *Clematis montana* catch your eye.

Perhaps you think you are looking at an average Canadian garden with a distinctly European flavor to it. But what you are actually looking at is a Chinese garden. Not a classical Chinese garden, but a garden composed of trees, shrubs and flowers hunted and gathered at great expense over the last two centuries from their native setting in cool temperate forests and subalpine zones of remote regions of China.

There are few native Canadian plants in the average Canadian garden. Most gardens contain an extensive and eclectic collection of plants originating from all over the world: red-hot pokers from Africa, dahlias and fuchsias from South America, the Lenten rose from Greece, and so on. But a huge amount of plant material that is now readily available to Canadian gardeners originated in China. The maple leaf may be Canada's national emblem, but it is not widely known that of 200 kinds in cultivation, China leads with 59, North America follows with 25, Japan comes next with 16 and Europe trails with only 13 species it can call its own. English garden writer Robert Pearson says China's ecological diversity is unrivalled and its estimated 30,000 species of plants make it the third-richest country in the world in terms of plant life, exceeded only by Brazil and Colombia. Thousands of plants were brought out of China by intrepid horticultural hunters-explorers who risked their lives in order to collect seed and bring to the West plant knowledge we now take for granted.

In his book *Plant Hunting in China*, published in 1945, Euan Cox says, "The tale of plant hunting in China is essentially human. It is a tale of trying to kick through the hard brick wall of Chinese ultra-conservatism in the old days; of constant endeavor to bring live plants safely to Europe during the long sea voyage by the Cape of Good Hope; of pertinacity and grit during innumerable hardships while trying to wrest plants and seed from their homes in the fierce climate of the western alps and Tibetan marshes."

The cost of mounting expeditions to China and the cost of bringing seeds back to Europe was an astonishing commitment in its day to the value and importance of horticulture. John Livingstone, chief surgeon with the East India Company in 1819, estimated that every plant in England at that time would have been introduced at the enormous expense of upwards of 300 pounds sterling. That would be several thousand dollars per plant in today's currency.

The first European plant collectors in China were Swedish and French Jesuit missionaries. They were adventurous, educated individuals, skilled in medicine and natural sciences. B.J. Healey, in *The Plant Hunters*, points out: "Like so many more popular fallacies, the concept of the missionary as a narrow and ignorant bigot is merely a literary fantasy." Some of the most successful plant hunters to go to China were Pierre Nicholas le Cheron d'Incarville, William Kerr, John Reeves and John Potts. D'Incarville traded on the appeal of the sensitive plant (*Mimosa sensitiva*) to gain permission to explore the imperial gardens where he found the Chinese tree of heaven (*Ailanthus altissima*) and the China aster (*Callistephus chinensis*). Kerr, a Scots gardener from Kew, found azaleas, chrysanthemums, tree peonies, tiger lilies, dianthus and the shrub kerria, which bears his name. Reeves, a tea inspector with the East India Company, found *Wisteria sinensis*; and Potts brought back camellias, beautyberries and an assortment of primulas.

The two best-known plant hunters, however, are probably Robert Fortune and Ernest Wilson. Between them, they were responsible for sending thousands of new plants to the West, many of which are now commonplace in the Canadian landscape. Fortune found winter jasmine, forsythia, weigela, dicentra, honeysuckle, Japanese anemones (actually Chinese), pompon chrysanthemums, *Campanula grandiflora*, *Platycodon grandiflorum* (Chinese balloon flower), as well as numerous varieties of peony, azalea, camellia and chrysanthemum. Ernest Wilson is credited with finding the paperbark maple, *Viburnum davidii*, *Cotoneaster*, *Buddleia*, *Rosa moyesii*, the popular climbers *Actinidia chinensis*, *Clematis armandii*, *C. montana* and *C. rubens*, and a whole bunch of rhodos, including two of the most famous, *R. augustinii* and *R. williamsianum*. After Fortune, there was George Forrest, who found the pieris which can now be seen in gardens everywhere; J.H. Veitch, the first to spot *Magnolia stellata*; Jean Armand David, who found the pocket handkerchief tree; and Jean Marie Delavay, the first to find the blue poppy (*Meconopsis betonicifolia*).

So next time you see the blue berries on a glossy-leafed viburnum growing at the local gas station or the bright blue flowers of the mophead hydrangea, remember the dozens of plant hunters who risked their lives to bring them out of China.

Plan Now for Summer

Spring's a busy working season in the garden. This is the time to plant new perennials and divide and move old established ones into new exciting combinations. This is also the time to fill planter boxes and window boxes with glorious summer-flowering plants and to make all sorts of new garden plans for your patio and balcony. All the work you do in spring will be rewarded threefold come summer, as containers that initially looked spare and skimpy when first planted fill out to become beautifully artistic works of color and fragrance.

Perennial Favorites: Classics of the Herbaceous Border

Just starting out as a gardener? You won't go wrong with these totally dependable plants for the herbaceous border.

- *Alchemilla mollis* (lady's mantle). All the great gardens of England make bold use of this old-fashioned favorite. It is loved for its seemingly magical ability to display raindrops like diamonds on its rough, hairy leaves. It is also valued for the light lime-green color and the frothy texture of its effervescent flower sprays that first appear in June and last for several weeks. Grows to 12 to 14 inches (30 to 36 cm) in ordinary soil.

- *Aquilegia* (columbine). The bell-shaped flowers of these exquisite woodland plants flourish in the moist, dappled shade of overhanging trees. Look for blue 'Hensol Harebell', green-red 'Nora Barlow', and the maroon-white 'Biedermeier'. Other favorites include the McKana Hybrids, which produce big flowers in pastel and two-tone hues and grow to just over 2 feet (60 cm).

- *Artemisia schmidtiana* 'Silver Mound'. Its delightful, feathery, silver foliage forms a compact, low mound. Drought tolerant and non-invasive, it blends superbly with other plants in the perennial border and makes a nice addition to the rock garden. It grows 12 to 15 inches (30 to 38 cm) high. Also look for *Artemisia ludoviciana* 'Valerie Finnis', which has soft, willow-like silvery leaves on erect stems. It grows to 18 to 24 inches (45 to 60 cm).

- *Astilbe* (false spirea). Thoroughly dependable plants, these send up lovely white, pink or red feather duster–like plumes from spring to late summer and their foliage forms great healthy mounds of leaves. There are literally dozens of cultivars with outstanding flower color. They grow 2 to 3 feet (60 to 90 cm) high and thrive in mostly sunny locations where the soil stays moist.

- *Astrantia major* (masterwort). It has classy greenish-white flowers with light pink centers. Very charming, very elegant. Growing to 30 inches (75 cm) in the shade or light shade of trees or protective shrubs, this plant brings a natural refinement to the garden. *Astrantia major* 'Rubra', popular because of its wine-red flowers, grows to 2 feet (60 cm). *Astrantia maxima* has slightly larger, more pronounced shell-pink flowers with densely clustered pincushion centers, somewhat similar to scabiosa. It grows to 2 feet (60 cm). There is also a variegated form, *Astrantia major* 'Sunningdale Variegated'.

- *Campanula persicifolia* (bellflower). Also known as the peach-leafed bellflower, this is available with either blue or white flowers. It makes a first-rate cut flower. The campanula family is large and serves reliably, year after year, in various parts of the garden. 'Chettle Charm' has pale, china-blue flowers and grows 3 to 4 feet (90 to 120 cm) in full or partial sun in well-drained soil.

- *Cimicifuga* 'Brunette' (bugbane, snakeroot). This has fabulous black-purple foliage and arching stems that bear white bottlebrush flowers with a light purple tint. It is extremely adaptable, flourishing in a variety of situations and performing consistently, with near indifference to soil conditions. It grows 4 to 5 feet (1.2 to 1.5 m).

- *Coreopsis verticillata* 'Moonbeam' (tickseed). It flowers profusely from late spring into summer, growing to about 18 inches (45 cm) and producing hundreds of small, pale yellow flowers that are not at all jarring to the eye. Called a thread-leafed coreopsis because of its lacy foliage, 'Moonbeam' was named perennial plant of the year in 1992 by the Perennial Plant Association of North America.

- *Crocosmia* 'Lucifer' (montbretia). As well as superbly architectural, stiff, gladiola-like leaves, this exceptional perennial produces orangey-red flowers from July to September. Native to South Africa, it grows 4 feet (1.2 m) tall. Other top varieties include 'Vulcan', orange, 2 feet (60 cm); 'Bressingham Beacon', orange and yellow, 40 inches (100 cm); 'Emberglow', orange-red, 30 inches (75 cm); 'Firebird', orange, 32 inches (80 cm); and 'Jenny Bloom', yellow, 40 inches (100 cm).

- *Delphinium* Pacific Hybrids (larkspur). Delphiniums always bring a touch of class to the perennial border. Pacific Hybrids grow 4 to 6 feet (1.2 to 1.8 m) tall in perfect conditions. Many of them are named after

characters in the legend of King Arthur and the Knights of the Round
Table. Names to look for are 'Black Knight' (dark blue), 'Galahad'
(white), 'King Arthur' (purple), 'Guinevere' (lavender-pink), 'Summer
Skies' (light blue), 'Cameliard' (lavender-blue), 'Blue Bird' (blue) and
'Blue Jay' (light blue).

- *Dicentra* (bleeding heart). With its graceful appearance and exquisite
  white or red blooms, it is easy to understand why bleeding heart has
  been a favorite of gardeners worldwide for generations. The heart-
  shaped flowers are suspended along gently arching stems emerging
  from a lush clump of soft green leaves. Some of the best varieties are
  forms of *Dicentra spectabilis*. Also look for cultivars of *D. eximia*. They
  range in size from 2 to 4 feet (60 to 120 cm) and thrive in light shade.

- *Digitalis purpurea* (foxglove). Majestic plants, foxgloves look good as
  solitary sentinels here and there around the garden, or grouped
  together in dense clumps. The pink-purple, drooping tube-shaped
  flowers have a speckled throat and are tightly arranged in layers up the
  sturdy stem. The Excelsior Hybrids are the most impressive. They
  produce spires of white, purple and pink flowers up to 5 feet (1.5 m)
  tall from May to July.

- *Euphorbia* (spurge). Every garden should have at least a couple of kinds
  of euphorbia. You can't go wrong with *E. polychroma* (cushion spurge)
  or *E. dulcis* 'Chameleon' or *E. myrsinites* (donkey-tail spurge) or
  E. griffithii 'Fireglow'. Take time to check them all out. My favorite is
  E. characias wulfenii. It has long sturdy flower stems with large, lime-
  green, multi-eyed flower heads in spring. It grows 4 feet high and wide
  (1.2 by 1.2 m).

- *Geranium* (cranesbill). These are real geraniums. The plants most
  people call geraniums—the multicolor bedding plants you see in
  summer—are really pelargoniums. No garden should be without hardy
  geraniums. My favorites are *G. macrorrhizum*, which has pink flowers in
  early spring and doubles as an extremely good mounding groundcover,
  and *G. cinereum* 'Ballerina', which has exquisite purple-veined pink
  flowers that keep on coming all summer long. There are many other
  kinds worth checking out. They are all hardy and thrive in ordinary,
  well-drained soil in full to partial sun.

- *Helleborus* (Lenten rose). These are robust, reliable plants with
  charming, open, cup-shaped flowers. Once you see them, you'll
  probably grow to love them. Start with the two most popular kinds:
  H. orientalis (Lenten rose), which comes in a range of colors from red
  to pink, maroon to white and flowers from March to June; and

H. niger (Christmas rose), which has flowers ranging from pure white to blush green, and flowers in January. They both grow to 18 to 24 inches (45 to 60 cm).

- *Hemerocallis* (daylily). The daylily has two main assets: superb trumpet-shaped flowers that now come in a grand range of colors, and handsome straplike leaves that rise and fall in cascading mounds. Top of the class is 'Stella de Oro', a long-time favorite, loved for its short 12- to 18-inch (30- to 45-cm) form and its lightly ruffled orange-gold flowers that bloom continuously from spring to fall. 'Catherine Woodbury' and 'Frans Hals' are two other classics.

- *Heuchera* (coral bells). This wasn't always so popular. But over the last few decades, hybridizers have been busy, with the result that today there are many new, outstanding cultivars. One of the best is 'Bressingham Bronze', which grows to 9 inches (23 cm) in full sun to part shade and gets its name from its distinctive, crinkly, bronzy-red foliage. It has tiny white flowers on thin stems in summer. Other top varieties to look for include 'Palace Purple', 'Plum Pudding', 'Chocolate Ruffles' and 'Pewter Moon'.

- *Hosta* (plantain lily). Many gardeners regard hostas as the perfect perennial. They are certainly structural, workhorse plants for the shade garden. They can be large and lush or small and delicate. They come in an impressive diversity of color and form. Most range in size from 2 to 3 feet (60 to 90 cm) and thrive in moist soil in light shade. For all-round beauty and reliability, pick up 'Frances Williams', a long-time favorite with pale lavender flowers and variegated, heart-shaped, blue-green leaves trimmed with gold. Other top variegated hostas are 'Francee', 'Wide Brim', 'Great Expectations', and 'Frosted Jade'. First-rate blues include 'Hadspen Blue', 'Blue Wedgewood', 'Bressingham Blue', 'Halcyon' and 'Big Daddy'. Great yellows are 'Sun Power', 'Midas Touch' and 'August Moon'. Two classy, large-leafed cultivars are 'Sum and Substance' and 'Elegans'.

- *Iris sibirica* (Siberian flag). A marvelous clumping plant with thin, upright but slightly arching leaves and superb purple or blue flower spikes to 3 feet (90 cm) in June to July. Like old garden roses, the beauty of the Siberian iris is in the delicacy of its blooms. Top named cultivars are 'Caesar's Brother' (deep purple), 'Butter and Sugar' (white-yellow), 'Orville Fay' (medium blue), 'Dance Ballerina' (white-purple),

When I started gardening I was inclined to see a plant, say: "Fantastic, got to have it!" and stick it in, instead of saying: "That will look good with that, now how much shoveling and moving of things around do I have to do to get it there?"

—Helen Dillon, Irish gardening writer and lecturer

'Tycoon' (violet), 'Papillon' (light blue) and 'White Swirl' (white). Longer-flowering bearded irises bloom in June and are a lot more showy. The flowers come in a wide range of colors from blue to peach, pink to yellow, purple to black with many bicolor variations. It really all comes down to picking the size and color you like.

- *Kniphofia* (red-hot poker, torch lily). Exotic, architectural plants, these produce mounds of evergreen, daylily-like foliage and send up tall, two-tone yellow flowers tipped with orange-red in May and June. The tops of the stiff, 3-foot-long (90-cm) "poker" stems are composed of dozens of tiny tubular flowers. Kniphofia is a moderately drought-tolerant plant. It will flourish in a hot, sunny border in average soil that is reasonably moisture retentive. Cultivars to look for include 'Alcazar' (orange), 'Bressingham Torch' (orange-yellow), and 'Royal Castle Hybrids'.

- *Lavandula angustifolia* (English lavender). The best two cultivars are 'Hidcote', which has bluish-purple flowers on long stalks, and 'Munstead', which has violet-blue flowers. They both grow to about 18 to 24 inches (45 to 60 cm). Drainage is crucial. Nothing kills lavender faster than boggy, waterlogged soil. It thrives in full sun in well-drained soil. The fragrance is released by brushing the flower stalks or foliage with your hand.

- *Lavatera thuringiaca* 'Barnsley' (tree mallow, Barnsley lavatera). This is an exceptionally lovely plant, but tender in all except the warmest areas of Zone 6. What makes it so desirable is its lovely white-pink hollyhock-like flowers. Grow it in a sunny spot in your garden and it will quickly swell up to become a substantial bush, reaching 6 or even 8 feet (1.8 to 2.4 m). 'Barnsley' gets its name from Barnsley House, the home and garden in Gloucester, England, of one of Britain's most respected garden experts, Rosemary Verey.

- *Liatris spicata* (gayfeather, blazing star). Always a welcome sight in the late summer garden, liatris has slender, poker-like, pinkish-purple flower spikes. They bring a fresh burst of color and provide exciting vertical architecture in the flagging perennial border or cutting garden. The most popular form is the species, which has 2- to 3-foot (60- to 90-cm) spiky-leafed stems with pinkish-purple, bottlebrush flowers. 'Kobold' is a more compact form, growing only 18 to 24 inches (45 to 60 cm), which makes it a good candidate for the front of the border. You can also find a white liatris—'Floristan Violet'—which serves very well in an all-white scheme.

- *Ligularia*. There are two first-rate species for gardeners with lots of room: *Ligularia stenocephala* ('The Rocket') and *L. dentata*

('Desdemona' or 'Othello'). 'The Rocket' has soaring, 4- to 6-foot (1.2- to 1.8-m) yellow-gold flower spikes, similar in shape to foxgloves or foxtail lilies, while 'Othello' and 'Desdemona' grow about 3 feet (90 cm) and have spreading heads of golden-yellow star-shaped flowers. All three have great foliage, but 'Desdemona' and 'Othello' are noted for their exceptional, big, purple-black leaves. They all thrive in moist, semi-shaded sites. Slugs are the biggest problem with growing ligularia. They simply cannot resist the leaves, which have been described as "cheesecake for slugs." The only real defense is to patrol at night with a flashlight and a pair of sharp scissors.

- *Monarda* 'Gardenview Scarlet' (bee balm, bergamot). The main reason to grow this tried-and-tested favorite is because it adds life to the garden in July and August. Its bright scarlet-red flowers are held at the top of sturdy, 3- to 4-foot (90- to 120-cm) stems. The flower clusters first appear in early to mid-July and continue into September. Two other top cultivars are 'Marshall's Delight', with handsome candy-pink flowers, and 'Prairie Night', which has dark purple flowers.

- *Paeonia* (peony). We love peonies for their large, fragrant flowers, which appear from May to June, and for their lush foliage. Your basic garden peony is *Paeonia lactiflora*. It comes in a wide range of colors, including assorted shades and combinations of pink, red, white and yellow. Star performers are 'Karl Rosenfeld' (brilliant, fragrant red), 'Sarah Bernhardt', (apple-blossom pink), 'Bowl of Beauty' (pale pink with pale yellow center), 'Mons Jules Elie' (double pink), 'Shirley Temple' (double white-pink), 'Lady Alexandra Duff' (pale pink) and 'Duchess de Nemours' (pure white). They all grow 3 to 4 feet (90 to 120 cm).

- *Papaver orientale* (oriental poppy). Poppies don't have a lot of substance but they have a special endearing charm. The oriental poppy (*P. orientale*) is one of the most popular kinds with its rough, hairy foliage and soft, satiny flowers that come in a wide range of colors from blood-red to salmon-pink to pure white. The peachy pink 'Mrs. Perry' is an old-fashioned hybrid, especially popular with cottage gardeners. Other great poppies include 'Perry's White' (white with black spot), 'Goliath' (deep red with dark center), 'Allegro' (scarlet), 'Brilliant' (red), 'Carneum' (salmon-pink) and 'Picotee' (salmon-pink with white edges). They all grow 2 to 3 feet (60 to 90 cm) high.

- *Phlox paniculata* (phlox). You know summer is at its peak when you see majestic clumps of *Phlox paniculata* holding up panicles of vivid red, white, pink and purple flowers. It is one of the plants you cannot do without if you want to lift your garden to its best in July and August. A great white form is 'Fujiama', which flowers in mid- to late summer and grows 3 feet (90 cm) tall. Other top performers are 'Nora Leigh' (creamy white variegated foliage and near white flowers with a pink eye), 'Darwin's Joyce' (almost identical to 'Nora Leigh'), 'Starfire' (cherry-red), 'Amethyst' (lavender-violet), 'Elizabeth Arden' (pink), 'Eva Cullum' (pink with a red eye), 'Europa' (white with a pink eye) and 'Bright Eyes' (pink with a cerise eye).

- *Primula* (primrose). The common English primrose (*P. vulgaris*) has simple yellow flowers on 6-inch (15-cm) stems in March to April; the drumstick primrose (*P. denticulata*) is among the first to appear in spring and is also very lovely, growing only 12 inches (30 cm) high

10 Terrific Combos

1. *Euphorbia dulcis* 'Chameleon' has leaves that start out bronze-purple and then fade to purple-green and turn a muted red-yellow in fall. A good companion is star of Persia (*Allium christophii*), a striking member of the ornamental onion family. The flower resembles a space station when it is a fully formed cluster of countless five-point stars, each one a shiny, metallic purple-silver color.

2. *Geranium cinereum* 'Ballerina' (hardy geranium) has exquisite purple-veined pink flowers that keep on coming all summer long. 'Lawrence Flatman' is almost identical to 'Ballerina'. Combine either with *Scabiosa columbaria* 'Butterfly Blue' (pincushion flower), another sun-loving plant with astonishing flower power that produces lilac-blue blooms without pause right through to fall.

3. Pair *Cotinus coggygria* 'Royal Purple' (smoke bush) with Clematis 'Ville de Lyon' or 'Madame Julia Correvon'. Both clematis have reddish-purple flowers that provide a striking partner for the smoke bush's plum foliage.

4. *Sedum* 'Autumn Joy' and *Anaphalis margaritacea* 'Moors Variety' (pearly everlasting) are two great plants that thrive in full sun in poor soil. 'Autumn Joy' provides height and succulent foliage; the pearly everlasting provides soft gray foliage and white flowers.

5. *Clematis x jackmanii* (virgin's bower) is a reliable summer-flowering clematis that produces masses of purple flowers. Grow it with the dependable, disease-resistant pink-flowering climbing rose 'New Dawn' or the white-flowering 'White Dawn'.

6. *Festuca cinerea* 'Elijah Blue', which has powdery blue evergreen leaves, contrasts beautifully with *Carex buchananii*, a very attractive coppery-bronze upright grass.

7. *Euphorbia myrsinites* (donkey-tail spurge) has succulent, evergreen blue-green leaves and chartreuse flowers. Plant it with purple aubrieta tumbling over a sunny rockery wall.

8. *Betula utilis jacquemontii* (Himalayan birch) has brilliant white bark. Contrast it with a lush underplanting of the black leaves of *Ophiopogon planiscapus* 'Nigrescens' (black mondo grass).

9. *Allium aflatunense* has perfectly spherical purple flower heads that resemble cricket balls. Combine it with the pink bottlebrush spikes of *Persicaria bistorta* (knotweed).

10. *Cimicifuga* 'Brunette' (bugbane) has fabulous dark black-purple foliage and arching stems of white bottle-brush flowers with a light purple tinge. It looks great with the carmine-red flowers of the dahlia 'Bishop of Llandaff' or the rich pink flowers of *Geranium endressii* 'Wargrave Pink'.

and coming in a range of subdued colors from blue to lilac, white to pink. But the most classy, to my mind, are the candelabra primulas (*P. japonica*), which hold their flowers in neat tiers (hence candelabra) along stems that can stretch 2 to 3 feet (60 to 90 cm) high. Colors range from white to pink, red to apricot. Even in mass plantings, the colors never jar.

- *Salvia* x *sylvestris* 'May Night' (sage). Voted perennial plant of the year in 1997 by the Perennial Plant Association, this is a beautiful, compact plant that produces striking, indigo-blue flower spikes 18 to 24 inches (45 to 60 cm) high with a slight tinge of purple in early summer. It is very similar to its cousin 'East Friesland', which flowers a little later. When they are planted side by side, it is hard to tell them apart. Both are excellent. The purple-leafed sage (*S. officinalis* 'Purpurascens') is also an excellent plant for foliage contrast. Its soft purple-gray leaves heighten the feathery silver foliage of artemisia or stachys.

- *Scabiosa* (pincushion flower). Scabiosa makes an excellent cut flower and is available in lilac-blue, pink and white. *S. columbaria* 'Butterfly Blue' is one of the best cultivars. It starts flowering in spring and will continue to produce delightful lilac-blue blooms about 1 1/2 inches (4 cm) wide, without pausing to catch a breath, right through to fall. 'Pink Mist' is almost identical, except that it has pale pink rather than blue flowers. *S. caucasica* is also worth getting. It grows to almost 3 feet (90 cm) and has purple-blue flowers. There is also a white form.

- *Sedum* 'Autumn Joy' (stonecrop). This is a plant that has value in the garden from the first moment in spring through to the end of fall. Large perennial borders are often anchored with giant clumps of this plant at either end. It grows 3 feet (90 cm) high and flowers in late summer with clusters of salmon-pink flowers. Similar cultivars include 'Brilliant' and 'Stardust'. There are also some types with bronze-red or purple foliage. Look for 'Atropurpureum', 'Matrona', 'Morchen', 'Vera Jameson', 'Bertram Anderson' and 'Ruby Glow'.

- *Stachys byzantina* 'Silver Carpet' (lamb's ears). A five-star perennial with a wide variety of uses. Its splendid silver foliage makes it most useful as a groundcover or decorative edging plant or simply to provide color and textural contrast. It gets its name from the fact that the soft, silver-gray leaves look and feel rather like the ears of lambs. In mid-June, the plant sends up silvery spikes which, by early July, produce tiny lilac-purple flowers. Of all the cultivars of *S. byzantina*, 'Silver Carpet' is one of the best. It grows 6 to 8 inches (15 to 20 cm) high. 'Primrose Heron', 12 to 18 inches (30 to 45 cm), has pale yellow-green, felty leaves, while 'Countess Helene Von Stein' grows 12 to 18 inches (30 to

45 cm) and is popular because of its large leaves and non-flowering habit.

- *Thymus* (thyme). This popular low-growing perennial is especially useful as a colorful, compact groundcover. It flourishes in sunny rockeries or can be used to fill crevices between paving stones. *Thymus* x *citriodorus* 'Doone Valley' gives off a powerful lemon scent when the leaves are brushed. It grows 4 to 6 inches (10 to 15 cm) high and has dark green aromatic leaves tipped with gold. Other top names include 'Gold Edge', 'E. B. Anderson' and 'Argenteus'. Common thyme (*T. vulgaris*) has aromatic gray-green leaves and tiny, pale lilac flowers in June. Creeping mother of thyme or wild thyme (*T. praecox*) grows 3 or 4 inches (7.5 to 10 cm) high, has purple, red or white flowers, and

Divide and Conquer: How to Double Your Plant Bounty

Division is a quick way to conquer empty spaces and fill your garden with identical plants. It is an excellent and economical way of creating long drifts of the same plant and all that is needed is a little spade work.

You can divide perennials in fall, when plants are starting to go dormant, or in early spring before they get too far ahead and before the really warm days of summer arrive. You are unlikely to kill plants doing this; the worst that can happen is they will put all their energy into growing roots and forget about flowering for a while.

Some species, like clumps of *Geranium macrorrhizum*, just fall apart once they have been lifted and can be easily divvied up to form new colonies. Other plants, such as astilbe and daylilies, need to be split apart with a fork or spade or sharp knife. Here are a few guidelines for dividing and conquering in your garden this spring.

- Your perennial needs dividing if the clump looks very dense and has outgrown its space; the clump has a bare center and busy rims; or you simply want more plants and don't want to go and buy more of the same thing.
- Divide clumps by lifting them out of the ground and splitting them into smaller pieces. As a rule of thumb, try to ensure that each piece is no smaller than what will fit into a gallon-size pot. Each piece of the divided clump should have its own set of roots. If you want to keep the main clump intact but reduce its size, hack chunks off the sides; you can use this technique to keep colonizing groundcover plants like lamb's ears in line when they insist on creeping beyond their boundaries.

- Some perennials, like rudbeckia, helenium, asters, phlox and astilbe, need to be split up every three or four years to keep them healthy. Others, like hostas, peonies, baby's breath and solomon's seal, can be left undisturbed for years to form attractive clumps.
- Not all perennials like being divided. For example, bleeding heart, dianthus, monkshood, balloon flower, globe thistle, lupin and oriental poppy may not return the first season after being broken up.
- Peonies are notorious for sulking after being divided. The best time to divide them is at the end of summer, although many people prefer to do the deed in the spring and let the plants sulk and refuse to flower while they establish themselves in their new spot.
- If you have an ever-expanding clump of mint, the best solution to controlling its rampant, invasive habit is to simply shape up the clump by reducing its size all the way round. The pieces you cut off can be potted up and passed on to friends or thrown out.

spreads to form an attractive mat-like covering. You will sometimes find it in garden centers under the label *Thymus serpyllum*. Good cultivars include 'Purple Carpet' (light purple), 'Coccineus' (red), 'Elfin' (pink) and 'Albus' (white). Wooly thyme (*T. pseudolanuginosus*) has soft silvery foliage and bright pink flowers.

Going to Seed: Starting Bedding Plants and Vegetables

Growing plants from seed is one of the easiest and most satisfying garden projects you can take on in late winter. You don't need any fancy equipment or great expertise to get good results. In fact, many people have great success simply germinating seeds in old egg cartons covered in plastic sandwich wrap and plonked on top of the fridge for a few days. But if you are going to try growing marigolds or snapdragons or nicotiana or any of the dozens of other hardy and half-hardy annuals available, you should decide from the outset that you are doing it strictly for fun, or to grow a few special items not normally available at the garden centers. You are not going to save a lot of money growing your own bedding plants. When you add up the cost of your time and materials, it amounts to only a little less than you would pay for healthy baby bedding plants in May at the local garden center.

The key to growing vegetables and annuals from seed indoors is knowing how to get the seed to germinate properly, which basically means simulating indoors the growing conditions that the seed normally responds to in the garden.

Heat and light are very important. A soil temperature of 64° to 71°F (18° to 22°C) is ideal to start most plants. But there are a lot of exceptions to the rule. Some seed needs the equivalent of a hot summer's day to break out of its dormant state. Petunias, for example, require a soil temperature of 80°F (27°C) and 50°F (10°C) at night to start up, while other seed, such as impatiens, will not get growing at all if the soil is too warm, say more than 82°F (28°C). The same is true of vegetables. While peppers germinate best at 68° to 86°F (20° to 30°C), spinach requires cooler temperatures of 41° to 68°F (5° to 20°C) degrees.

Some seed, like the popular edging plant ageratum, needs light to get growing, while other seed, like the pansy, needs to be kept in the dark to germinate.

Some seed requires special treatment to germinate. Some may need cold or intense heat to break their dormancy, while others need to be scarred, soaked or cracked. You'll find all this basic information printed on the seed packet or in the seed catalog. Most seed packets carry clear instructions on the back about how to achieve a successful germination and Dominion Seed House offers its own Info-leaflets covering a wide variety of plants for a few cents.

When seedlings are big enough to handle or when they get their first true leaves, carefully dig them out of the tray and transplant them into a pot or tray with more space for each individual seedling.

All seedlings started indoors need to be acclimatized gradually to the outdoors before they can be planted in the garden. This process is called hardening off. You do it by moving the new plants outside for a few hours each day and bringing them back inside at night before the temperature drops. Annuals, of course, cannot tolerate any frost, so they cannot be moved outside permanently until all danger of frost has passed.

5 Steps to Success

1. To start, pick up seed, either by sending away to one of the seed companies or by popping into one of the local garden centers, which now carry a wide selection of flower and vegetable seeds in spring.

2. Fill a fairly shallow container, preferably a flat seed tray, with sterilized potting soil or special prepared starter mix. Use seed trays or containers that have been thoroughly sterilized. You can do this by washing them with a weak solution containing 10 percent chlorine bleach to kill any bacteria present. Don't use soil from the garden—it may be too heavy and compact to allow vigorous germination and it may also contain fungi and bacteria. Soilless potting mixes are ideal because they have been sterilized.

3. Sow the seed thinly and evenly on the top of the mix. Gently press the seed into the soil or sprinkle another layer of mix on top. Follow the instructions on the packet about how deep to sow the seed. Amazing but true, seeds are able to determine their depth in the soil by the amount of heat and light they receive and they use this information to decide whether to grow or not.

4. Moisten the soil with a spray bottle, but don't soak it. Too much water is as bad as too little. Cover the container with clear plastic to maintain humidity.

5. Place the container in a place where the soil will get the right amount of heat and light. The top of the fridge works beautifully for many people but heater cables can be used to provide bottom heat. Germination usually takes between 5 and 15 days. Fluorescent lights can be used, but the light needs to be within 6 to 10 inches (15 to 25 cm) of the surface of the soil to be effective. A window sill is often too hot or too cold to get successful germination, but window sills can be ideal for nursing seedlings along. If your seedlings have insufficient light they will be tall, spindly and pale.

How to Grow Vegetables from Seed

If you want to plant a vegetable garden, the most important first piece of information you need to get is the date of the last spring frost in your area. All of the planting you will do in your veggie patch will be determined by that date. Either you'll be sowing seed indoors weeks in advance of the last frost date in order to transplant plants outdoors later in the season or you'll be planting directly into the garden after the danger of frost has passed. Then there are those special cool-season crops like peas and spinach, radishes and lettuce that don't mind if they are planted out a few weeks ahead of the last frost. In any case, most of the planting you do in your food garden will center on the date of the last spring frost. You can get this information from your local weather office or by asking at your local garden center.

Here's an A to Z of basic vegetables and information on when to plant them.

- **Artichokes.** Start seed indoors eight or nine weeks before the last frost. Plant out in fertile, well-drained soil in May.

- **Broad beans.** Also known as fava beans, these are cold tolerant and can be planted directly into the garden as soon as the soil can be worked in spring. They will not be harmed by light frost. In fact, it is better if you plant them a little before the last frost so they can enjoy the cool, moist temperature. In mild-winter gardens (Zone 6 and above), they can be planted in fall for harvest in late spring.

- **Pole and bush beans.** These go by an assortment of names, including runner beans, shell beans, waxy beans, snap beans and string beans. It is a lot simpler to identify them by their growth habit. Some grow into bushes about 18 inches (45 cm) high, while others climb like a vine 6 to 8 feet (1.8 to 2.4 m) up a trellis or around a pole. Sow them directly into the ground after the last frost. Continue sowing every two or three weeks to the middle of June to ensure a steady supply of beans during the harvest season. Bush-type beans are planted in rows; the pole type are planted five or six seeds at a time around a pole or trellis.

- **Beets.** Seed can be sown directly into the ground as soon as the soil can be worked in spring, but the main crop should be sown when the soil has warmed up after last frost. In mild-winter gardens, a crop for winter production can be sown in mid-July, or 10 weeks before the first fall frost.

- **Broccoli.** Start seeds indoors six weeks before the last frost or sow them directly into the ground from May to July. In mild areas, seedlings can be planted into the garden in April provided they are given some cover. Transplant seedlings into the garden at the beginning of May.

- **Brussels sprouts.** Brussels sprouts take about three months to mature, so it pays to get them going early so they mature by the first fall frost. Sow indoors six weeks before the last frost and transplant into the garden in May. In mild climates, you can sow seed directly into the garden a few weeks before the last frost. Some coastal gardeners start Brussels sprouts in June for harvest in October.

- **Cabbage.** Sow seed directly into the ground in early spring. In mild climates, this may be in March; in cooler areas it is usually April. Light frost will not hurt seedlings, so you can start seed indoors and transplant juvenile plants that have been hardened off into the garden before the last frost date. In mild areas, autumn varieties of cabbage can be started in May and transplanted in June for harvest in September and October. Overwinter-type cabbage can be sown in July to mature during winter.

- **Carrots.** Sow seed as soon as the soil can be worked and the danger of hard frost has passed. They grow best in loose, sandy soil that has been deeply tilled and is rich in humus. It is a mistake to add fresh manure, which tends to promote hairy, rough roots. For an extended harvest, sow seeds again in late May and once again in the second week of June.

- **Cauliflower.** Start seed indoors six weeks before the last spring frost and transplant after the danger of frost is past. Early varieties (ones that mature in 50 to 60 days) should be started first between March and June. In mild-winter gardens, the fall-type cauliflowers (bred to mature in the cool days of September and into October) can be sown in May and June. The slow-maturing winter cauliflowers, which take 200 to 265 days, can be sown in June and July and will be ready to harvest in February.

- **Celery.** Since celery needs a long growing season, it is necessary to start it indoors between 7 and 12 weeks before the last frost. Seedlings can be transplanted after the danger of frost in late May. Celery is a heavy feeder and needs to be fertilized and well watered.

- **Corn.** Sow seed when the soil has started to warm up after the last frost date. The second week of May to the middle of June is ideal. Corn will rot if sown too early in cold, wet soil. If you are really keen to produce an early crop, get a head start by sowing seeds indoors three weeks before the last frost and transplanting with care in May.

- **Cucumbers.** Cucumber needs the warm soil of summer to really do well. Sow directly into the garden at the end of May or wait until the soil is even warmer in the second week of June.

- **Eggplant.** This is a warm-season crop that requires a sheltered sunny spot in the garden. Seed can be started indoors five weeks before the last frost and transplanted in the middle of June. They like hot daytime temperatures, 80° to 90°F (27° to 32°C) and warm night temperatures, 70°F (21°C).

- **Garlic.** In mild areas, the best time to plant garlic cloves is in the fall before the first hard frost or in spring after the last hard frost. In cold-climate gardens, garlic is best planted in late August for harvest the following year.

- **Leeks.** Start seeds indoors four or five weeks before the last frost and keep the seedlings clipped to about 4 inches (10 cm) high until it is safe to plant them out in the garden when the danger of frost is past.

- **Lettuce.** Sow seed directly into the soil as soon as the ground can be worked in spring, or start indoors five or six weeks before the last frost and transplant three or four weeks later. Sow every three weeks for a continual crop all summer.

- **Onions.** Onions can be started three ways—indoors from seed and then transplanted into the garden; sown directly into the garden; or grown from sets (small bulbs). Opinions differ about growing onions. Some say starting from seed is difficult, while others say onions are easier to grow from seed than sets. It is probably best to experiment with all three methods. Start seeds indoors 10 weeks before the last frost and transplant about five weeks later. Seedlings can be trimmed if they become too tall before they are planted outdoors. Seed directly into the garden in late April or early May. Onion sets are planted so the pointed tips are just below soil level.

- **Parsnips.** Sow seed directly into the garden as soon as the ground can be worked in spring, from March on. Parsnips need a minimum soil temperature of 36°F (2°C) to germinate and take 110 to 120 days to reach maturity. Don't expect to see seedlings jumping out of the ground until about three weeks after sowing. Keep the soil moist. Some gardeners sow radish seeds with the parsnip seed so the radish sprouts will open the way for the emerging parsnip shoots.

- **Peas.** Plant peas four weeks before the last spring frost or as soon as the soil can be worked. They prefer cool soil temperatures and do not germinate well once the soil has warmed up in late May and June. The enation virus is spread by aphids, so it is recommended that only enation-resistant varieties are planted in late spring or in areas where soil temperatures warm up rapidly in spring.

- **Peppers.** Start indoors at the same time as eggplants—at least five weeks before last spring frost—and transplant into the garden in June. They germinate at about 80°F (27°C) and need night-time temperatures no cooler than 55°F (13°C). They thrive in sunny, sheltered sites in the garden.

- **Potatoes.** Potatoes are grown from seed potatoes, which are specifically developed and certified as disease free. They are sold at garden centers in early spring. Each seed potato can be planted whole or cut into pieces, each with two or three "eyes"—tiny indentations from which sprouts will grow. Plant them four to five weeks before the last spring frost.

- **Pumpkins.** Most pumpkins take from 90 to 120 days to reach maturity. If you want them in time for Halloween, it is best to start them indoors and transplant them into the garden once the danger of frost is past. You can plant the faster-maturing varieties directly into the garden.

- **Radishes.** Perhaps the easiest and fastest-growing vegetable, these can be sown directly into the garden any time after the last spring frost. They grow quickly, so fresh crops can be sown every two weeks throughout the growing season.

- **Spinach.** Sow directly into the garden six weeks before the last frost. It thrives best in soils with a high nitrogen content. If your spinach does not turn out big-leafed and succulent, it is probably due to a lack of nitrogen. In mild-winter gardens, spinach can be sown in early fall to provide greens in spring.

- **Swiss chard.** Sow directly into the garden as soon as the soil can be worked from mid-April up to July. Plants reach maturity about 60 days after sowing.

- **Tomatoes.** Start from seed indoors six to eight weeks before the last spring frost. Transplant into the garden after the danger of frost has passed in early May, if you protect the seedlings with a cloche. Coastal gardeners have to learn to deal with late blight (*Phytopthera infestans*), which decimates many promising crops each year. Tactics for dealing with the problem include selecting resistant heirloom varieties, spraying with a fixed copper spray, maintaining good air circulation and healthy spacing, and planting in a site that offers protection from rain, heavy dew and condensation. The experts at West Coast Seeds say: "The best advice we can offer discouraged tomato growers is to concentrate on the varieties which can be easily grown in attractive pots and planters up under the house eaves. There is less trouble with staking and covering. Determinates ripen much earlier than the indeterminate varieties, so they are ready for summer salads simultaneously with other salad ingredients."

No-Problem Summer Staples

If you're looking for reliable, high-performance annuals or tender perennials—for pots or the open garden—here are a few recommendations.

Old Favorites

- *Nicotiana* (tobacco plant). If you don't know this plant, you're in for a real treat. Not only are the pink, white or lime-green flowers lovely to look at, they are also very fragrant, especially at sunset. An extremely useful, uncomplaining, perpetual flowering, half-hardy annual. Grow it in a pot or in the open garden in full sun or light shade. Place it next to a door or under a window to enjoy its fragrance.

- *Pelargonium*. Most people call them "geraniums," but whatever name we use, everyone recognizes these immensely popular and useful plants. Drought-busters, they love sunshine and sulk if they get overwatered. Summer wouldn't be the same without a pot of two of them on the steps or in the window box. They never let you down. If you can't bear to part with them at the end of summer, you can always take cuttings.

- *Petunia*. Another sun-loving summer favorite, but the excitement these days is over the new trailing hybrids, Surfinias and Supertunias (both *P. axillaris* hybrids), which can swell and easily fill a half-barrel tub or sizable hanging basket. Straight single colors are easier to work with than some of the more dazzling bi-color mixes. Pinch-prune (snip back the flower stems) to get a bushier, more prolific flowering plant.

- Other reliable summer standards are French marigolds, ageratum (blue), snapdragons, alyssum (white), cineraria (silver), impatiens, salvia (red, blue) and verbena (blue, violet, lavender).

Something Different

- *Bacopa*. A relatively new bedding plant, this forms a large, lush-leafed ball or low mound of tiny white flowers. In a hanging basket, window box or container, it will spill over the sides and trail its flowers. It thrives in sun or partial shade.

- *Cerinthe major purpurascens*. Described by the Thompson & Morgan seed company as a "highly versatile, aristocratic border plant," this is being tested out by hundreds of gardeners. It has blue-green foliage and nodding, purple-blue, tube-shaped flowers.

- **Scented geraniums.** Grown for their aromatic leaves, which release their scent when touched or brushed, these collectible geraniums offer a variety of smells including lemon, apple, rose, mint, nutmeg or lime. Most won't overwinter outdoors.

- **Scented mints.** You can have wonderful smells at your fingertips: spearmint, pineapple mint, butter mint, apple mint, chocolate mint. Instant aromatherapy.

- *Cuphea*. This is sometimes called the Mexican cigar plant because the tips of the red, tube-shaped flowers have white and dark purple "ash." Looks best when combined with things like agyranthemum and mimulus in a pot or window box.

- *Heliotrope* (cherry pie plant). This is a subtropical shrub with deep green, corrugated leaves and deep mauve to purple flowers with a slight fragrance of licorice.

For the Connoisseur

- *Cosmos atrosanguineus* (chocolate cosmos). This tender perennial is best grown in a pot so it can be overwintered in a frost-free place. The rich maroon flowers clearly smell of chocolate.

- *Melianthus major*. With striking gray foliage of deeply cut leaves, this has the odd distinction of giving off a smell not unlike peanut butter when the leaves are rubbed. A fine plant on its own in a pot, or to contrast with other plants.

- *Nicotiana sylvestris*. Its fragrant white, pendant flowers look exceptionally good alongside phlox, Chinese balloon flowers, hardy geraniums or veronica.

- *Osteospermum*. This daisy from South Africa should be more popular but we are still learning how to get the best out of it. Look for 'Buttermilk' or, for novelty, 'Whirligig', but don't be surprised if all you find is 'Silver Sparkler', a very attractive white form.

- *Rhodochiton atrosanguineus*. The purple bell-vine is actually a climber, but if left unsupported in a hanging basket it will trail beautifully.

Great in Pots

- *Datura* (angel's trumpet). Stunningly fragrant, this wildly exotic plant produces large, floppy, down-facing, yellow trumpet flowers that can reach up to 16 inches (40 cm) long. Be careful not to rub your eyes after touching the plant—a member of the deadly nightshade family, the blooms contain atropine, which can make your pupils dilate.

- *Festuca glauca.* You can plunk all kinds of ornamental grasses in pots and they all look terrific, but this small, clump-forming blue grass performs exceptionally well in a container.

- *Fuchsia.* The tender summer varieties really give their best when they have a deep, moist root run in a large container.

- *Nemesia* 'Confetti'. Immensely popular in Britain a few years ago, this South African plant with dainty pale-pink flowers is catching on in a big way. It performs well in pots but is being used more and more in hanging baskets.

- **Parsley.** Fill each of the openings in a terracotta strawberry pot with parsley. You'll be surprised at how striking it looks. Chives, basil and fennel also look good in containers.

- *Phormium tenax.* For a truly exotic, tropical look, put this with some bright red pelargoniums in a pot and add some drama to your backyard. Its iris-like leaves will thrust like swords out of the container.

- *Salvia argentea.* This is a floppy, furry, silver-leafed plant that will thrive happily for years in a terracotta pot. In a pot it will need some winter protection.

Best Use of Bedding Plants

Before the 1990s, few people had heard of bacopa. Today it is one of the most popular plants for the summer garden. With tiny, snow-white flowers and attractive green foliage, bacopa now easily ranks alongside such long-established favorites as petunias, pansies and geraniums as a top-seller. It thrives in full sun or light shade and is the perfect low-maintenance plant for stuffing into hanging baskets or for trailing over the sides of window boxes and containers. Bacopa is just one of the many great bedding plants available to gardeners. When the danger of frost is gone, it's time to start packing flower beds full of annuals and tender perennials to create vibrant splashes of color for summer. Think of yourself as an artist with a rich palette of colors at your disposal and have fun mixing and matching plants in all sorts of daring and imaginative combinations.

For sunny locations, plant drifts of sweet-scented nicotiana along with old-fashioned snappy-jawed snapdragons and fragrant cherry-pie plant

(*Heliotrope*), which some people think smells like baby powder. These all combine very well with the soft grays of dusty miller (*Cineraria maritima*) and low-growing blues of *Ageratum*.

There are some outstanding varieties of verbena available. Look for 'Soft Pink', 'Powder Blue', 'Pink', 'Lavender', and 'Blue Violet', all of which are totally drought resistant, but also consider *Verbena canadensis* 'Homestead Purple', which is sold as a perennial but is best grown as a bedding plant. In a sunny, well-drained spot, it will carpet the ground with bright, deep purple flowers all summer.

For truly exotic colors, check out the spectacular daisy-like flowers of osteospermum, arctotis and gazania, but don't miss some of the newer varieties of Paris daisies (*Argyranthemum frutescens*) such as 'Summer Melody' (soft pink), 'Butterfly' (yellow), 'Sugar Baby' (white with a yellow center) and 'Summer Pink' (rosy pink with a yellow center). You'll find

Colorful Coleus: Shades of Exotica

With the increased popularity of bright, bold colors in the garden, there has been a revival of interest in the more fiery forms of coleus. 'Burgundy Sun', 'Volcano', 'Rainbow' and 'Black Dragon' are four of the most striking forms available at garden centers. 'Volcano' has startling, plum-scarlet foliage, while 'Burgundy Sun' has slightly more subdued, deep wine-red leaves. The leaves of 'Rainbow' contain a sensational mix of red, yellow, copper and pink, while 'Black Dragon' has curly red leaves with serrated, blackish-purple edges.

Coleus fever swept Britain at the end of the 19th century when wealthy gardeners were prepared to pay a small fortune to own the latest and most outrageously colorful varieties. The former darling of Victorian gardeners, coleus is also known as flame nettle. But coleus have tended to be dismissed as houseplants, useful perhaps for including in a hanging basket or window box, but not considered desirable for mass planting or as feature items in the open garden. All that has changed. Ian and Joy Cooke, of Brocking Exotics in Nottingham, have collected almost 100 varieties and are busily hybridizing them to create all sorts of weird and wonderful new splashes of color.

There has been an awakening to the potential and usefulness of coleus as a brightener in the shade garden along with, or instead of, the more traditional staple of the shade border, impatiens. More gardeners are discovering that coleus not only comes in a wide variety of dazzling colors and forms, but some varieties flourish quite happily in full-sun situations, provided they are not exposed to too much scorching afternoon heat.

Foliage ranges from brilliant burgundy with yellow edges to bright green with wine-red centers to shocking neon green with maroon splotches. The secret to getting your coleus to maintain its marvelous leaf color is not allowing the plant to produce its pale purple flowers. The flower heads should be snipped or pinched off the moment they appear. Pinching out the central stem will also make the plant bushier, which in turn will produce more cuttings that can be harvested in summer.

Coleus is easy to propagate. Take a tip cutting about 3 inches (7.5 cm) long with two or three leaves. Fill a glass with water, cover the top with plastic wrap, make a hole in the plastic, and poke the cutting into the water. Within a few weeks, the cutting will form white roots. The plant can then be potted up and overwintered indoors or in a frost-free environment.

some of these under the label Cobbitty daisies. Osteospermum perform better when planted in slightly cooler spots where temperatures don't soar so high that they cause the plant to cease flowering.

Bidens is another one of the new generation of bedding plants that has quickly gained popularity, mainly because of its cheerful yellow flowers, ferny foliage and apparent indifference to poor soil and drought conditions.

Salvia is always a good choice and they all have so much more impact when planted in dense drifts. The hot reds make a startling contrast intermingled with deep blue.

In shady areas, impatiens and both fibrous and tuberous begonias do a reliable job, but for something different try the new varieties of *Torenia* now available, notably 'Summer Wave', which covers the ground with a mass of large, dark blue, snapdragon-type florets.

Spring Bulbs for Summer Color

Think back to your summer garden last year. Was it missing a little pizzazz? Did the color run out in August? Was there a distinct lack of exotic foliage, seductive fragrance, special interest? Well, spring is the time to take action if you want to save your garden from the perpetual blahs of summer.

All you need to know are the following magic words: "Spring-planted, summer-flowering bulbs." Practice this phrase the next time you enter the portals of your local garden center and watch how quickly your arms fill up with bags full of exciting bulbs, corms and tubers. Here, then, are six ways to fill your garden with color and spice and everything nice for summer.

Zero in on Zantedeschia

This is better known as the calla lily or arum lily and it develops from a tuber with a skin that resembles a new potato. Many gardeners grow the common white calla (*Z. aethiopica*), but there are now all sorts of wonderfully colorful new hybrids such as 'Flame' (fiery red), 'Gem' (rosy mauve) and 'Mango' (orangey-peach). There is also the buttery yellow species, *Z. elliottiana*; ivory white *Z. albomaculata*; and, what is regarded by some as the prettiest of the pink callas, *Z. rehmannii superba*.

Callas thrive in full sun to light shade, produce their delightfully sculptural, vase-shaped spathes from June to July, and demand moist soil. Grow them in the ground or in containers and remember to water with half-strength water-soluble fertilizer. It pays to start your callas indoors in February in a 6-inch (15-cm) pot and transplant them into the garden or outside container after the last frost in May.

Go Lavish with Lilies

Pick the right kinds and you'll have flowers from June to October. Lilies can be used to bring vibrant color, architectural interest and delicious fragrance to the summer garden. There are almost as many types as there are roses. It is an enormous family with at least 100 species. Making a selection usually comes down to a matter of color preference and desired blooming time.

With a little careful planning, you can have a sequence of blooms from early summer right through to fall. Hardy in all Canadian gardens, the secret to success is to plant properly and then never allow them to go hungry.

Here are some top early to midsummer bloomers.

- The Asiatic hybrids are the first to bloom from early to midsummer. They mostly grow 3 to 4 feet (90 to 120 cm) high, rarely need staking, are good naturalizers in the perennial border, and come in an impressive range of colors. Outstanding cultivars include 'Stargazer' (fragrant, strawberry-pink throat with a creamy white edge), 'Affinity' (rose-pink with an apple-green center), 'Enchantment' (orange-red), 'Connecticut King' (yellow) 'Côte d'Azur' (pink), 'Mont Blanc' (white with spots) and 'Citronella' (yellow).

- The Martagon lilies are also known as turk's-cap lilies because of the distinctive shape of their heavily reflexed, pendulous, turban-shaped flowers. *Lilium martagon* has deep rose blooms with purple freckles. There is also a rarer all-white form. They both flower from June to July.

- *Lilium longiflorum* is the fragrant Easter lily. This has given birth to a number of excellent hybrids, including 'Camelot' (pink), 'Kiss me Kate' (scarlet) and 'Royal Highness' (ivory-white). These are more often grown in planters and containers on a patio than in the open garden.

- *Lilium candidum* is the traditional, extremely fragrant Madonna lily with waxy white flowers on 4-foot (1.2-m) stems. These need to be planted very early with no more than an inch (2.5 cm) of soil over them in order to bloom in midsummer.

You can add some excitement to your garden with these mid- to late summer bloomers.

- The Oriental hybrid lilies provide spectacular color from August to September. They grow 4 to 5 feet (1.2 to 1.5 m) tall and are delightfully fragrant. Top names are 'Casa Blanca' (pure white), 'Crimson Elegance' (crimson), 'Marco Polo' (pink), 'Montreal' (white with yellow stripes) and 'Seduction' (orchid pink).

- Trumpet lilies are the giant midsummer bloomers, with large flowers that can easily stretch to 8 inches (20 cm) long. One of the best is 'African Queen' (apricot-orange). Other quality performers include 'Black Dragon' (deep burgundy), 'Pink Perfection' (pink) and 'Golden Splendor' (pure yellow).

- *Lilium regale.* One of the most fragrant lilies you can plant, this has long, trumpet-shaped flowers that go from white inside to a soft pink-purple on the outside. It comes into bloom in mid- to late July.

- *Lilium lancifolium.* Better known as tiger lilies, these have orange petals with black spots. They grow 4 feet (1.2 m) high and bloom from August to September. There are now yellow, white and red hybrids in cultivation.

Be Creative With Cannas

Native to the tropics, these plants have brilliantly colorful flowers and equally attractive exotic foliage. It remains a mystery why we still mostly tend to see them in municipal landscapes rather than home gardens, but that is slowly changing as more gardeners have success growing them. The secret is to start tubers on a sunny window sill or in a heated greenhouse in March, then move them out to their permanent location in the garden or in containers after the last frost. Cannas thrive best in full sun and they look most effective when planted in groups rather than as solitary specimens. Three sizes of cannas are available.

- There are varieties that grow 3 to 5 feet (90 cm to 1.5 m) tall, such as 'City of Portland' (coral), 'Red King Humbert' (red with bronze foliage), 'Yellow King Humbert' (yellow), and 'Pretoria' (melon-colored flowers with yellow-green striped foliage).

How to Grow Lilies Perfectly

- Plant lily bulbs in early spring or fall in well-drained soil in full sun. Martagon and Oriental lilies like a little shade but the Asiatics generally prefer as much light as they can get. If you plant in early fall, the bulbs will have time to establish their anchor roots before winter and this will give them a jump on the season in spring.

- It is important to get the planting depth correct. Many gardeners don't have the success they are seeking because bulbs are planted too shallow. The majority of lilies form stem roots above the bulb and must be planted at the proper depth to develop, a factor many new gardeners are not aware of. As a rule of thumb, lilies should be planted three to four times the height of the bulb, or about 6 to 9 inches (15 to 23 cm) deep. Soil type can make a difference. Plant bulbs deeper in warmer, sandy soils than in heavier, clay-type soils.

- Like clematis, lilies love to have their heads in the sun and feet in the shade. They like a cool root run. In the perennial border, lilies don't mind if they are surrounded by low-growing, non-competitive neighbors that provide some shade for their roots. Mulch is another good way to create cooler temperatures for the lily's "feet."

- Don't starve your lilies. Enrich the soil with well-rotted compost or a balanced fertilizer. Lilies are fairly heavy feeders and they respond impressively when they are well fed.

- Taller lilies, such as the giant trumpet varieties, will need to be staked or they will flop over when the flowers appear.

- The stalks can be cut when they have finished flowering.

- Semi-dwarf varieties include 'Los Angeles' (pink), 'The President' (red) and 'Harvest Yellow' (yellow), all of which grow to 3 feet (90 cm).

- Dwarf varieties such as 'Lucifer' (red and yellow), 'Crimson Beauty' (red) and 'Salmon Pink' (salmon) grow to only 18 inches (45 cm).

- There are also some new hybrids that are considered superior because the flowers fall away cleanly when they wither. Look for 'Shining Pink' (soft pink with burgundy foliage), 'Angel Pink' (apricot and peach with a yellow throat) and 'North Star' (red). They all grow to 30 inches (75 cm).

Plant Glads All Over

If you are careful in your color and size selection, you'll be pleasantly surprised how useful and effective the gladiolus can be throughout the summer garden. There are now three sizes available—tall varieties that soar to 4 to 5 feet (1.2 to 1.5 m); landscape varieties that grow to only 42 inches (105 cm) and stand up by themselves; and dwarf varieties that grow to 2 feet (60 cm).

The key to success is to plant in clumps every couple of weeks through spring. This will guarantee a natural sequence of blooms to the end of summer. You can use glads like fireworks to add bright bursts of color here and there.

- In the tall varieties, look for 'Flevo Safari' (deep crimson), 'Victor Borge' (deep red), 'Semerang' (golden yellow) and 'Tout a Toi' (pink with yellow throat).

- In the no-staking landscape varieties, look for 'White Wings' and 'White Friendship' (pure white), 'Award' (pink), and 'Norsman' (brilliant red).

- In the dwarf category, outstanding varieties include 'Charming Beauty' (cerise pink), 'Elvira' (soft peach and ivory), and 'Prins Claus' (white with peppermint red blotches).

Don't Ignore Dahlias

If your garden lacked color in late summer through to fall, it was probably because you forgot to use dahlias—the saviors of the end-of-summer garden. To get the best from dahlias, pick a sunny spot. Plant after the danger of frost has passed and stake carefully. Plant groups of two or three of the same kind for impact. Think about height and color in relation to neighboring plants. If you are nervous about color clashes, grow the dahlias in a pot so you can move them around. Dwarf varieties perform perfectly on sunny balconies.

Take the time to pick the right color and form and you can create elegant schemes. There are waterlily types, giant dinner-plate varieties, and small pompom kinds. For your white garden, look for 'White Wonder,' 'My Love,' 'Cheam Ice,' 'Sneezy' or 'Tsuki Yori'. For your hot-red border, there's 'Deutschland' and 'Barbarossa'.

Try Something Special

- *Acidanthera bicolor* (peacock gladiolus) will produce 30-inch (75-cm) stalks of fragrant white flowers with chocolate-brown centers at the end of summer.

- *Galtonia candicans* (summer hyacinth) produces even taller stalks of white flowers, up to 4 feet (1.2 m), in summer. Mix them into your sunny perennial border or white garden for special interest. Again, planting in clumps will give you a more dramatic show.

- *Eucomis bicolor* (pineapple lily) is a fun bulb to grow in a pot or in the ground. It produces purple-spotted foliage and a pineapple-shaped flower.

- For something truly outstanding, how about big-leaf elephant ears (*Colocasia esculenta*)? It has giant heart-shaped leaves and makes an impressive jungle-like specimen for a pot or moist corner in light shade. You could also give upright elephant ears (*Alocasia macrorrhiza*) a try. These grow 6 feet (1.8 m) tall in an ideal location. A dwarf form grows only to 3 feet (90 cm). The bigger the bulb, the bigger the plant you get.

Winter Care Tip

Dahlias, cannas, gladioli, and the majority of the more exotic calla lilies are all tender plants in Canadian gardens. They need to be lifted after the first frost when the leaves have turned black. Store the tubers and corms in a box of peat moss or newspaper in a frost-free place. Lilies can be left in the ground but benefit from the protection of a mulch over winter.

Contain Your Enthusiasm: Create a Lush Container Garden

Take a few small pots of pure white marguerite daisies (*Argyranthemum frutescens*) and sink them into a large terracotta or glazed ceramic pot. Or create a slightly more sophisticated display by marrying up the chocolate-colored and chocolate-scented flowers of *Cosmos atrosanguineus* with the gray leaves of *Melianthus major* or with the feathery silver leaves of *Artemisia* 'Powis Castle'.

These are just two ways to put a great show on your patio, balcony or deck using plants in containers. You don't want to plant before the threat of frost has passed at the end of May, but late spring is the time to let your imagination fly and combine some plants for a few sizzling displays of summer flowers. There's no shortage of choice. You'll find a marvelous array of virtually every summer-flowering plant imaginable at your local garden center: petunias, marigolds, impatiens, fuchsias, lobelia, snapdragons, lovely pink, white and blue trailing verbenas, and a grand selection of pelargoniums. There are plants for growing in full sun, like the deliciously scented nicotiana or purple-leafed heliotrope, and flowers for the shade, like impatiens, coleus and begonias. Here's how to make your summer plantings more successful.

Patio Practicalities

- **Don't use only small pots and containers.** It's better to have two or three large containers than a whole bunch of little pots. Small containers are not only harder to keep watered, they lack visual impact.

- **Keep it light.** The weight of containers is always an important consideration in a balcony garden, but you can find lightweight stone and terracotta lookalikes, and lightweight soil mixes can be enriched with slow-release granular fertilizers.

- **Roses can be a lot of work.** If you aren't keen on doing a fair amount of maintenance work, give roses a miss. Consider simpler plantings such as *Acacia baileyana* underplanted with black mondo grass, or *Carex buchananii* and *Salvia bicolor*. And don't forget to make good use of easy-care shrubs such as photinia, boxwood, euonymus, waxleaf privet, evergreen azaleas, nandina, pieris, skimmia and viburnum.

- **Think about the breeze factor.** The higher up you are in a highrise the colder and windier it gets. Choose plant material that's structurally capable of coping with gusts of wind.

- **Be prepared to change plants often.** You are closer to the plant material in a container garden. Decay and deterioration are far more visible. To keep it looking fresh and healthy, be prepared to change the plants more often than you would in the open garden.

- **Container gardening isn't inexpensive.** People are always shocked at how much it costs to do a container garden on a patio or balcony. Containers are not cheap and even a small space can consume a lot of plant material. But remember that good-quality pots will last for years.

Pot Principles

- **Jumbles can be jolly.** Don't be afraid to stuff your pots with more than one kind of plant. Annuals like to have their roots in compact spaces, and they often look better when pressed together in a jumble of color. The rules of the color wheel don't apply. Want to put orange and blue or pink and yellow together for fun? Go for it.

- **Asymmetry is important.** Don't try to balance your planting too precisely. Strive to create drifts or groups of plants and see if you can achieve contrasts, such as burgundy coleus with a line of hot pink stock.

- **Don't plant only annuals in pots.** Consider such perennials as hostas, astilbe or heuchera; herbs like parsley, sage and rosemary; and shrubs like choisya, ceanothus or hydrangea. They all look terrific in pots. You can also grow trees like the green- or burgundy-leafed maple (*Acer palmatum dissectum*) in a pot on a patio, along with standard fuchsia or euryops. Conifers like *Chamaecyparis obtusa* or the densely conical *Juniperus chinensis* also look very attractive in pots on patios.

- **Don't starve your plants to death.** Mix in some slow-release fertilizer (14-14-14) at planting time. This also applies to window boxes and hanging baskets. Many gardeners feed their annuals by spraying them twice a week with a half-strength solution of 20-20-20.

- **Watering is the most crucial factor.** In full sun, a pot will dry out very quickly. One solution is to mix polymer crystals into the soil at the time of planting. The crystals swell up to 400 times their own weight as they absorb water, then slowly release it back into the soil. But for most people, routine watering is really the key to success.

- **Protect plants from direct sun.** Move pots out of the direct sun and into a shadier spot (or create temporary shade by moving a sun chair or angling a patio umbrella) to protect sun-sensitive plants during the hottest times of the day. It will make a big difference.

Hanging Baskets

- The truth about hanging baskets is that you can buy them for only a few dollars more than they cost you to make. But then you don't have the creative fun of doing it yourself. And you may not like the plants on sale. A 16-inch (40-cm) moss basket with seven or eight plants will cost $50 or more. But remember, most of the work was done a month or more ago. The plants have matured since then into more expensive specimens and the entire basket has been carefully looked after in a greenhouse to bring it to perfection for the May market. Garden centers are certainly not gouging customers by charging a few dollars extra to cover the cost of all the work, time and cost of materials.

- Contrary to what some people think, growing plants in containers is not less work. When you add up the cost of plants, fertilizer, moss and other materials plus the work involved, a hanging basket can easily take as much work, effort and expenditure as a small flower bed.

- The most important issue with hanging baskets is getting the location right. Most disappointment stems from putting a basket full of shade-loving plants in full sun and vice versa.

- You can't go wrong with impatiens or begonias or fuchsias in the shade and petunias (especially trailing Surfinias and Supertunias) in the sun. Also consider 'Million Bells' varieties of *Calibrachoe*, with their small, petunia-like flowers. There are four key cultivars to look for— 'Cherry Pink' (hot pink), 'Trailing Blue' (purple-blue), 'Trailing Pink' (lavender-pink) and 'Trailing White' (white with yellow center). These are also all great plants for using as groundcover in the flower border.

- Other top-performing plants for hanging baskets include creeping jenny (*Lysimachia nummularia*), trailing snapdragons, pansies, trailing Kingfisher daisy (*Felicia*), nasturtiums, potato vine (*Solanum jasminoides*), strawflower (*Helichrysum bracteatum* 'Golden Beauty' or 'Blushing Beauty'), lady's slipper (*Calceolaria*), *Nemesia* 'Confetti', Swan River daisy (*Brachycome*), ivy geraniums, and the silvery feathery foliage and exotic red flowers of lotus vine (*Lotus berthelotii*).

- For special foliage interest, add the variegated foliage of Swedish ivy (*Plectranthus*), or the silver-gray leaves of *Lamiastrum galeobdolon* or *Lamium maculatum*.

- Always striking is the combination of the dark purple foliage of the sweet potato vine *Ipomoea* 'Blackie' next to the chartreuse leaves of *I.* 'Marguerite'. For a rich shade of blue, pick up some *Anagalis* 'Sky Lover' or the bush violet (*Browallia*) or lobelia.

- For something a little different, make a hanging herb garden, using a hanging box instead of a basket and filling it with interesting herbs such as curry plant, golden sage and pineapple mint.

- The best location for a mixed basket is where it will get plenty of morning sunshine but protection from hot, direct sunlight in the afternoon.

- Begonias and impatiens can be planted en masse in a basket to create a very dramatic effect. Look for begonia varieties such as 'Gin' or 'Vodka', which have burgundy leaves and, like the double-flowered varieties of impatiens, look much like miniature roses.

- Watering is critical. A great labor-saving idea is to install a wick—a short piece of rope that runs through the center of the basket and out the bottom into an attached water tray. This allows plants to suck up water into the basket when it starts to dry out. In Britain, many gardeners also use a pulley system so that baskets can be lowered for watering, then raised back into position. Watering wands with angled nozzles are useful for "raining" water into baskets.

- Some plants, such as verbena, nasturtium, petunia, impatiens and brachycome, will sulk if you forget to water them, but they will surprise you by bouncing back once watered, with no lasting ill-effects.

- Sweet-scented tobacco plant (*Nicotiana*) always looks good in containers, as do Paris daisies and the fragrant *Heliotropium*. But more gardeners are trying new bedding plants in containers, such as the Temari hybrid verbenas from Japan, which produce amazing flower balls of violet, bright pink, red or burgundy.

Window Boxes

Think of a window box as a miniature garden and you won't go wrong. Plan it the way you would a regular flower bed. You want to create balance from one end to the other, back to front. Which means not putting tall plants at one end and short ones at the other, but creating an even, structured planting all the way along.

The biggest problem with planting in a window box is that if it is done badly you end up blocking the window with plants that are too big. Or you may pick plants that don't behave themselves when confined and end up in a tangled mess.

In a sunny spot, a single row of plain red geraniums (*Pelargonium*) looks very classy. Trailing lobelia and petunias always go well together. For a shady window sill, a trough full of begonias, pansies and impatiens can look very elegant.

10 Rules for Containers

1. Use lightweight, free-draining potting mix. Add sand or pumice to improve the soil's drainage.
2. Always add slow-release fertilizer to ensure plants don't starve.
3. Add water crystals to reduce need for watering.
4. Use large gravel, stones or broken terracotta at the bottom of pots for good drainage.
5. Put pots on bricks or special ceramic legs to allow free drainage and prevent ants, slugs and sowbugs from lurking underneath.
6. Pick the right plants. For sun, pelargoniums, petunias, brachycome, verbena, marigolds, zinnias, salvia, nemesia, nicotiana, lobelia, argyranthemum. For shade, impatiens, browallia, fuchsia, pansy, begonia and mimulus. Most situations call for a mixture of sun- and shade-loving plants.
7. Pots, window boxes and hanging baskets that are located in full sun should be watered once or twice a day.
8. Feed bedding plants in containers with a half-strength solution of 20-20-20 liquid fertilizer once a week.
9. Deadhead every few days to prolong flowering and maintain appearance.
10. Be prepared to refresh your pots with new plants from mid- to late summer.

For added contrast, mix in the gray leaves of *Helichrysum petiolare*, ivy geranium, some trailing variegated bird's-foot ivies, or Swedish ivy (*Plectranthus*).

One-Plant Simplicity: Effortless Patio Elegance

A jumble of plants in a pot can look wonderful on your patio, but it can also look like a big mess. Mixing and matching flower colors and picking the right blend of plants for sun and shade can be a headache. The answer is to do what many top garden designers know works very well: stick to one-plant simplicity. This means you take one large, beautiful ceramic or terracotta pot and fill it with one kind of plant. You'll be surprised how elegant this will make your patio look and how versatile this concept can be. For instance, instead of mixing pink verbena, white marguerite daisies, red geraniums and blue lobelia, reduce your planting to one color and one type of plant. Instead of four different plants, fill the pot with three or four white marguerite daisies (*Argyranthemum frutescens*) and you'll end up with a display that looks a lot more sophisticated and has far more dramatic impact.

When plants are isolated in this way they often end up being more appreciated. People suddenly start to notice the quality of the flowers or the beauty of the foliage. Red pelargoniums, for example, always seem to look more exceptional when seen in a solitary pot. This is also true of such commonplace and frequently taken-for-granted shrubs as euonymus, pieris, hydrangea and rhododendron. Most people never think of making a special show of them in this way. When they do, they are surprised how exciting they look. It can be equally stylish to plant a simple green or red cutleaf maple (*Acer palmatum dissectum*) in a large blue or green ceramic pot and display it as a solo feature in a semi-shady corner of the patio. You can heighten the sense of drama by raising the pot on a pedestal where the maple's graceful cascading leaves are even more visible.

All sorts of perennials look marvelous when they are pulled out of the clamoring herbaceous border and exhibited on their own in a pot. Hostas are certainly a prime candidate. They have outstanding foliage and any of the big-leaf varieties, such as 'Kossa Regal', 'Sum and Substance' or 'Frances Williams', add a lush, tropical look to any patio.

For the sunny patio, a white or pink 'Flower Carpet' rose will grow very happily in a deep urn or large vase. Since it is the habit of this extremely floriferous groundcover rose to expand at least 2 or 3 feet (60 to 90 cm) sideways in a single season, it will be forced to send cascades of blooms over the sides of the pot.

New Zealand flax (*Phormium tenax*) is another plant that makes an excellent solitary container specimen for the sunny patio. The upward-thrusting sword-like leaves can be a startling sight and are useful to add interest to dull spaces.

Ornamental grasses—especially purple fountain grass (*Pennisetum setaceum* 'Rubrum') and the golden yellow blades of *Hakonechloa macra* 'Aureola'—are also natural candidates for single-pot planting. Bold *Miscanthus* species can also be grown successfully in big pots to create a privacy screen or special feature, and blue grasses are particularly eye-catching when displayed separately.

Patio trees are made to stand alone, but they also seem to look better when they are not cluttered up with a whole bunch of other plants in pots. *Lantana camara* has lovely orange-yellow verbena-like flowers; *Tibouchina urvilleana* has fragrant purple flowers; and *Euryops* has yellow marigold-like flowers. But you can also find fuchsias, laurel, boxwood, photinia, lavatera, buddleia and roses trained as standards (sometimes called patio trees). Another delightful potted tree for the patio is *Salix integra* 'Hakuro Nishiki', a small willow with reddish stems and white-splashed leaves.

For shady patios, hanging baskets composed entirely of sizzling red impatiens, pink fuchsias or purple-leafed begonias are always striking. A window box stuffed with a single color scheme of pansies or browallia also makes a good impression. For more dense shade, the silver variegated foliage of Swedish ivy (*Plectranthus*) and lamiums can be used to fill containers.

For a novelty touch, you could make a hanging ivy ball out of two hanging baskets. After lining them with moss, filling them with soil and fastening the baskets together, you plant one variety of ivy (*Hedera helix*) all around the outside. The ivy ball can then be hung from a chain or displayed on a column or pedestal. Three ivy balls suspended in ascending order can make an intriguing decoration.

If you don't like the single-plant scheme, you might find it easier to stick with a single-color scheme. Fill a window box with purple petunias underscored by purple lobelia and verbena. Or limit your plant palette to blues or whites. Simplicity is the key. An all-white scheme of roses, lilies and petunias still gives the impression of a simple, restrained planting. When it comes to patio elegance, less usually adds up to more when you keep the planting simple.

 Shrubs

Shrubs help to give a garden its basic shape and structure. They are as important as paths and walls in not only defining the garden's fundamental look but also its style and atmosphere. Picking the right shrubs is an essential step in designing a great garden. And spring is the perfect time to buy and plant them. Rhododendrons are enormously popular for their evergreen foliage and lilacs never fail to please with their fragrant blooms. Here's your chance to discover some of the best shrubs for the garden and how to care for them.

For the Love of Lilacs

You won't fall in love with lilacs for their foliage, but once you have caught a whiff of the exquisite perfume of their flowers in late spring you will be hooked. They have a multitude of uses. You can grow them in containers, although they will need to be repotted regularly and well watered in summer months. Or you can use lilac to build small sweet-scented hedges. Taller-growing varieties are ideal for screening out eyesores. The most effective use of lilacs, however, is next to a gate or arbor to provide heady fragrance in your garden in late spring. The big question is which kind of lilac to grow. They come in a wide range of sizes and colors, from white and purple to pink and red.

Once upon a time there wasn't much choice. You either had the common lilac (*Syringa vulgaris*) or nothing at all. Then French hybridizer Victor Lemoine entered the scene with a new exciting set of plants. These are still known as the French lilacs. They grow to 8 to 10 feet (2.4 to 3 m), require minimal maintenance and can be relied upon to put on an impressive display of perfumed blooms every spring. Star performers are 'Charles Joly' (magenta), 'Sensation' (lilac-blue), 'Madame Lemoine' (creamy yellow to white), 'Monge' (single red), 'Belle de Nancy' (double pink), 'President Grevy' (lilac-blue), 'Olivier de Serres' (lavender-blue) and 'Montaigne' (light pink).

Another excellent lilac is 'Krasavitsa Moskvy', which was first bred by a Russian hybridizer named Kolesnikov. It has pink buds turning a waxy white with a frilly, dense petaled look that is rather similar to noisette roses. In North America, this lilac goes by the name 'Beauty of Moscow'.

Here's a guide to other star performers.

- *Syringa patula* 'Miss Kim' ('Miss Kim' dwarf lilac). This is very popular for one main reason—it grows only 6 feet high (1.8 m), which means it can fit without much trouble into gardens where space is tight. The fragrant flowers of icy purple appear from May to June. In fall, the foliage turns a warm burgundy color. In cold areas, where temperatures drop to –30°F (–34°C), it is important to wrap 'Miss Kim' in burlap to keep off the chill.

- *Syringa prestoniae* (Preston lilacs). Developed by Isabella Preston of Ottawa, this group of lilacs is exceptionally disease resistant and hardy. Look for 'Donald Wyman' (mauve), 'James McFarlane' (clear pink), 'Minuet' (pale pink), 'Isabella' (purple-pink) and 'Nocturne' (purple-pink).

- *Syringa reticulata* 'Ivory Silk' (Japanese tree lilac). This is a tree rather than a shrub but if you are checking out lilacs you might like it better than all the rest. It grows to 25 feet (7.5 m) and produces large clusters of creamy white flowers in June. Best of all, it fits very comfortably into the small garden.

- *Syringa meyeri* 'Palibin' (dwarf lilac). If you are considering making a low lilac hedge, this is the kind to buy. It is compact, grows only to 5 feet (1.5 m) and has purple-pink flowers in June. You can often find it for sale trained as a standard patio tree.

Lilacs flourish in full sun or light shade. They prefer soil that is more limey (alkaline) than acidic, or neutral but tending towards the alkaline end of the spectrum. You can use lilac as a specimen plant to provide color and fragrance from May to June or you can plant a row of them to create an informal hedge or windbreak. There are now some excellent dwarf varieties available for growing as low hedges or in containers or borders where space in limited. The key to keeping your lilac happy and flowering year after year is to do three things. Always deadhead, making sure to remove the flower heads the moment they are finished. Never allow brushes to become choked by dead or unproductive branches; prune out all the old and weak stems to make room for strong, new shoots. And remember to nourish the soil by top-dressing every few years with compost or cow manure.

Your Guide to Rhododendrons

Every garden should have at least two or three rhododendrons. Without doubt, they are one of the most important flowering shrubs, especially for coastal gardens where they grow like weeds. They are evergreen, they give the garden year-round structure, and they flower reliably and beautifully every spring. 'Unique', 'Virginia Richards', 'Cunningham's White', 'Christmas Cheer', 'PJM', 'Jean Marie de Montague' and 'Taurus' are all favorites with home gardeners and landscapers.

And then, of course, there's poor old *R. ponticum* 'Variegatum', the strikingly variegated rhodo, still popular with many gardeners and yet so

disparaged by rhodo experts. You'll find 'Variegatum' on sale (without fuss
or fanfare) at local garden centers. It is a perfectly fine plant, so if you like
it don't be put off buying it. What do rhodo connoisseurs have against it?
Well, they regard it as just too common. "It's the scourge of Britain, it's a
weed," they will tell you. They say this mainly because in the British Isles,
R. ponticum, also known as the "common rhodo," has been left to
naturalize without interference for hundreds of years. The result is that it
has seeded itself with almost wilful abandon everywhere and acquired a
reputation as a relentless colonizer. It is a "weed" in the sense of being
commonplace, tending to crop up where it is not welcome. However, even
the British have at least one kind word to say about this most maligned of
rhodos. "It is excellent for hedging and as a shelter belt," according to
Hillier's, one of England's top nurseries.

Having said all that, however, it is a fact that there are many other
superb rhododendrons that deserve your attention and a place of honor in
your garden far more than *R. ponticum*. If you do go looking for new
rhodos to buy, you'll find hundreds of varieties from which to choose. You
won't go wrong if you pick one of the following. The majority of rhodos
are hardy to around –5°F (–21°C). A few are tender and will not tolerate
any long cold spells without protection. Others are extremely hardy, even
to –25°F (–31°C).

Rhodos for New Gardeners

If you're a novice gardener just beginning to build a garden, these are good
varieties to start with.

- 'Dora Amateis'. Low-growing and mounding, this is extremely
  floriferous, producing white blooms that are slightly fragrant and tend
  to cascade to the ground. It is a favorite of both rhodo growers and
  gardeners because it so easy to grow and visually rewarding. Size: 2 feet
  (60 cm). Hardy to –15°F (–26°C).

- *R. impeditum*. A dwarf species, this has tiny bluish-green foliage and
  intense purple flowers. Size: 1 foot (30 cm). Hardy to –15°F (–26°C).

- 'Maureen'. There are many low-growing rhodos available, but
  'Maureen' and 'Polaris' stand out from the rest. Maureen is an *R.
  williamsianum* hybrid with cute round leaves (typical of that species)
  that emerge with the coppery hue of brand-new pennies. The flowers
  are clear pink. Size: 2 feet (60 cm). Hardy to 0°F (–17°C).

- 'PJM'. This old-fashioned favorite flowers in early spring, producing
  plenty of vivid rosy-purple flowers. It is an extremely hardy variety
  with scented leaves that turn purplish-brown in winter. Size: 4 feet
  (1.2 m). Hardy to –25°F (–31°C).

- 'The Honorable Jean Marie de Montague' (also known as 'Jean Marie de Montague'). With big, bright red trusses and long, dark green leaves, this is sun tolerant and very dependable. These characteristics may seem unremarkable, but perhaps it is its image as a typical rhododendron—vigorous, uncomplicated and bold—that has maintained an ongoing affection for 'Montague' among gardeners throughout most of this century. Size: 5 feet (1.5 m). Hardy to –5°F (–21°C).

- 'Trude Webster'. A vigorous, healthy variety that has medium pink flowers in large, tight trusses. A very reliable performer. Size: 4.5 feet (1.4 m). Hardy to –10°F (–23°C).

- 'Unique'. This is another popular rhodo that has proven its worth in the garden over many years. Its warm pink buds open to lovely, translucent, buttery cream flowers of great delicacy and charm. Size: 4 feet (1.2 m). Hardy to –5°F (–21°C).

Rhodos for Intermediate Gardeners

If you already have a few rhodos and are looking for one or two unusual varieties to add to your collection, you won't go wrong with these.

- 'Azurika'. This is an attractive dwarf hybrid with small leaves and terrific blue blooms when young, which is a definite asset when you consider that some varieties are a tad lazy and you could wait a good dozen years before seeing a single flower. It is the profusion of intense blue-purple flowers that makes 'Azurika' so charming. Size: 1 1/2 feet (45 cm). Hardy to –10°F (–23°C).

- 'Blue Bird'. A dwarf variety, this has striking blue flowers with a magenta accent and finely textured, bright green foliage. Size: 2 feet (60 cm). Hardy to 0°F (–17°C).

- 'Buketta'. One of the best of the low-growing red-flowered varieties. A fairly new hybrid from Germany, this can tolerate growing in the sun and is very hardy. The buds open black-red and end up a dark velvety crimson—an uncommonly luxurious shade. Size: 2 1/2 feet (75 cm). Hardy to –10°F (–23°C).

- 'Goldflimmer'. Since the bloom time of rhododendrons is relatively short, foliage plays an important role. Variegated leaves are always attractive. The better known 'President Roosevelt' is sometimes too tender even for coastal gardens. But 'Goldflimmer' is very reliable, with dark green leaves that are buttery yellow towards the center. The mauve flowers appear in June. Size: 4 feet (1.2 m). Hardy to –15°F (–26°C).

- 'Hotei'. Loved mainly for the beauty of its clean, true yellow flowers, this has other winning characteristics, including its medium size and compact growth habit and the soft sheen of its foliage. Size: 3 feet (90 cm). Hardy to −5°F (−21°C).

- 'Point Defiance'. The large leathery leaves of this variety are attractive enough, but then there is the added bonus of lovely white flowers edged with strong pink that are displayed in huge, lush trusses. Size: 5 feet (1.5 m). Hardy to −5°F (−21°C).

- 'Redwood'. This has much more to offer than just pretty flowers. Translucent and crinkled, the mauve-pink blossoms give off a delicate fresh scent, but it's the cranberry-red stems that make it so special. Size: 4 feet (1.2 m). Hardy to −5°F (−21°C).

- 'Royal Pink'. A first-rate, hardy hybrid of *R. williamsianum*, this has pretty, ice-pink bell-shaped flowers. It will grow to a modest-sized shrub with handsome heart-shaped leaves. Size: 3 feet (90 cm). Hardy to −15°F (−26°C).

Rhodos for Connoisseurs

These varieties are not for everyone. But rhodo enthusiasts will appreciate the characteristics that set them apart.

- *R. augustinii*. In terms of spectacular color, the electric blue of this rhodo is without equal. At twilight, as red and green colors outside recede, the blue flowers come to life with a luminous glow. An unmistakable standout in the garden. Size: 5 feet (1.5 m). Hardy to −5°F (−21°C).

- 'Goldstrike'. The buds open chartreuse and turn a strong golden yellow. The waxy flowers open in April and last a long time. It is a nice complement to the blues and purple dwarf varieties that bloom about the same time. Size: 4 feet (1.2 m). Hardy to 0°F (−17°C).

- 'Morgenrote'. Suitable for the small garden, this is a compact, low-growing variety that has glossy, olive-green leaves that are fawn colored underneath. The flowers open a radiant light red and become a little lighter in the center. Size: 2 1/2 feet (75 cm). Hardy to −15°F (−26°C).

- *R. obtusum* 'Amoenum'. A dwarf variety with exceptional bright magenta flowers. Its free-flowering habit makes it a very desirable specimen. Size: 1 1/2 feet (45 cm). Hardy to −5°F (−21°C).

- 'Ptarmigan'. With dark gray-green foliage, this forms a low bush. It covers itself with pure white flowers with chocolate-colored anthers in early spring. Size: 1 foot (30 cm). Hardy to −5°F (−21°C).

- *R. yakushimanum* 'Ken Janeck'. There are several desirable "yaks," all of which are slow growing and provide structural elegance in the garden. 'Ken Janeck' is special because of its blooms: strong pink turning white with a pink edge and yellow speckling inside. The underside of the leaves also has a buff-colored indumentum. Size: 2 1/2 feet (75 cm). Hardy to –25°F (–31°C).

- *R. yunnanense*. This is another species with wonderful characteristics. An "ugly duckling" in youth, it develops into a large, rambling shrub with narrow leaves and masses of white flowers speckled with orange. Most notable, however, is the sweet vanilla fragrance that fills the air around the mature plants when in bloom. Size: 6 feet (1.8 m). Hardy to –5°F (–21°C).

For Gardeners in Super-Cold Areas

It is a challenge to grow rhododendrons and azaleas successfully in cold-climate gardens. Some prairie gardeners have had success with rhodos by building burlap boxes around them in winter and allowing the snow to fill them. There are, however, some rhododendrons that have been specifically bred to flourish very nicely in colder climates.

To enjoy gardening you have to have the courage to say, "Well, I'm going to try this, it is a really weird thing to do, but if it fails, to hell with it, I'll live with the results, but if it succeeds it will be so exciting."

—Nigel Colborn, British broadcaster and gardening writer, on buying plants

- The Northern Lights azaleas. These top-performance hybrids were developed at the University of Minnesota specially for growing in the coldest areas of Canada and the United States. There are seven popular cultivars in the series: 'Golden Lights' (reddish-orange buds, highly fragrant yellow flowers); 'Hi-Light' (white flowers with yellow blotch); 'Orchid Lights' (orchid-pink flowers); 'Spicy Lights' (apricot and peach blooms); 'White Lights' (milk-white flowers); 'Rosy Lights' (purplish-red with rose-red shadings); and 'Mandarin Lights' (lightly fragrant bright red-orange blooms). They are all hardy, even in chilly Zone 4 and 5 areas, flower in late May and grow between 5 and 6 feet (1.5 to 1.8 m) high, except for 'Orchid Lights', which is more compact, growing only 20 inches (50 cm) high.

- The Finnish rhododendrons were developed at the University of Helsinki to withstand winter temperatures of –25°F (–31°C). Varieties to look for are 'Hellikki', which grows about 5 feet (1.5 m) tall and has dark violet-red trusses; and 'Peter Tigerstedt', which grows 5 feet (1.5 m) high and has white flowers with violet specks.

- Other reliable, hardy performers include: 'P.J.M.' (bright lavender-pink); *R. catawbiense* 'Album' (pure white); *R. catawbiense* 'Boursault' (lavender-violet); 'Olga Mezitt' (phlox pink); *R. ponticum* 'Variegatum' (green and white foliage); 'Party Pink' (purple-pink); 'Nova Zembla' (striking red); 'Cotton Candy' (pastel pink); 'Casanova' (pink and yellow); 'Black Satin' (red-purple). They bloom from late April to mid-May and grow 4 to 6 feet (1.2 to 1.8 m) high.

How to Plant and Care for Rhododendrons

- Plant your rhodo in the right place. Most thrive in light shade in well-drained, acidic soil that is fairly rich in organic matter. Generally, the smaller the leaves, the more sun the plant can take. The bigger the leaves the more likely it is a woodland specimen that thrives only in shade.

- The planting hole should be wider than the rootball, but only slightly deeper. Check the drainage before planting. Rhodos hate to sit in waterlogged soil.

- Rhodos can be moved easily since they have compact, shallow roots, even when they are quite large. The best time is in autumn or spring. Transplanting is often a better idea than severe pruning.

- Remember to lightly water rhodos and azaleas in hot summer months, as well as during dry spring and fall periods.

- Heavy, wet snow can bend and snap branches. With a broom handle or other long stick, gently tap the branches so that the snow falls off. In areas where snow accumulates over winter, the increasing depth of the snow will eventually support the branches of larger rhodos.

What Kills Most Rhodos?

Here's what the American Rhododendron Society says does most of the damage.

- **Too much water.** It kills about 75 percent of all rhodos. They are fibrous, shallow-rooted plants that need good drainage to perform well. In planting a rhodo, gardeners are often told to dig a hole twice as wide and twice as deep as the rootball and then put the plant in the hole and backfill with a mixture of peat, soil and other amendments. Many rhodos die from being planted this way. It amounts to putting the plant in a bathtub that holds excessive water. Rhodos grow best in shallow, well-drained beds rich in organic matter.

- **Too little water.** Rhodos do not have tap roots like trees. Their roots grow very near the surface, which means they need frequent watering. New plants just planted in spring need to be watered at least twice a week for the first couple of years. As time goes by and the plants increase in size and root development, less frequent watering works well. Sunburned leaves are often the result of inadequate watering.

- **Too much fertilizer.** Don't apply fertilizer directly to the base of the trunk. A good rule of thumb—fertilize more frequently with smaller amounts, rather than one large dose.

- **Planting too deeply.** If they are placed too deep in the ground, rhodos stop growing and ultimately die because the soil smothers the root system.

- If you want to rejuvenate an old rhododendron, try to do it over a period of a few years. Start by fertilizing the plants the year before starting to prune. In late winter of the first year, thin out the old growth, choosing the oldest, weakest stems. Cut these back to 6 to 12 inches (15 to 30 cm) above the ground. Remove another third of the old growth in late winter of the second year. Complete the job in the winter of the third year. The new growth that sprouts from these stubs will become the new plant.

- Pruning in early March instead of after blooming in May will produce the best results, because the season for new growth will be extended by up to six weeks. Be brave. Rhododendrons are resilient shrubs and, unless diseased or weak, tend to flush back with amazing vigor.

- Deciding how much to prune should be based on how soon you want the plant to attain its original size. Taking off up to half is considered safe. Using a pruning saw or loppers, cut just above a fork or above an obvious growth line. Shape the plant into a rough outline of the way you wish it to grow.

- Rhodos like acidic soil. Maintain a permanent mulch of oak leaves, pine needles or ground bark under them.

- Even established plants benefit from a feeding and top-dressing in the early spring. A mixture of peat and garden compost or leaf mold spread in a thin layer at the base of the plant will certainly help to maintain the acidity and nutrient level of the soil. Take care not to pile this around the stem, or apply it too thickly—rhododendron and azalea roots are particularly touchy about having their oxygen supply cut off underneath too much earth.

- Fertilize before and after flowering or feed them every two months from mid-November until July with a light sprinkling of 10-8-6.

- Careful removal of dead flowers will not only make the plant look tidy but encourage new flowers buds to develop.

Versatile Viburnums

Viburnums have a major role in gardens of all sizes. From the utilitarian usefulness of a groundcover like *Viburnum davidii* to the layered splendor of *Viburnum* 'Mariesii', the viburnum family offers a rich and diverse range of outstanding plants. Here are some of the best for the home garden.

- *Viburnum* x *bodnantense* 'Pink Dawn'. Ideal for the winter garden because its very fragrant pink blooms appear on bare branches in January and February. It grows 8 to 10 feet (2.4 to 3 m) high. Hardy to Zone 7.

- *Viburnum burkwoodii* (Burkwood viburnum). This is a semi-evergreen shrub with white flowers in May and shiny green leaves that turn bronze-brown in fall. It grows 7 to 10 feet (2.1 to 3 m). Hardy to Zone 5.

- *Viburnum carlcephalum* (fragrant snowball). This is a compact shrub with very fragrant dense clusters of waxy white "snowball" flowers in May. It grows 6 to 8 feet (1.8 to 2.4 m). Hardy to Zone 5.

- *Viburnum carlesii* (Korean spice viburnum). An outstanding spring-flowering shrub. It grows into a rounded, 4- by 4-foot (1.2- by 1.2-m) bush with white, heavily scented clusters of flowers in March and April. Hardy to Zone 6.

6 Great Shrubs for the Mixed Border

Gardeners are always in a quandary about what shrubs to choose when building a new mixed border. Here are six that give flower or foliage interest to a border throughout the seasons. They are all hardy, reliable peformers.

1. *Aronia melanocarpa* 'Autumn Magic' (eastern chokeberry). A deciduous shrub that grows to 6 to 8 feet (1.8 to 2.4 m), it has dark green glossy leaves and fragrant white flowers in May followed by attractive clusters of shiny black berries in fall. The foliage turns a brilliant mixture of red and purple in autumn. It flourishes in neutral to acidic soil in full sun to partial shade. Hardy to Zone 3.

2. *Cornus alba* 'Elegantissima'. For feature foliage that can brighten shady corners and provide long-lasting color and contrast, you can't beat the silverleaf dogwood. This has been a popular and reliable performer for years and has established itself as one of the mainstays of a mixed border and an integral part of the botanical bones of many outstanding home gardens. Hardy to Zone 2.

3. *Cotinus coggygria* 'Royal Purple' (smoke bush). This is a most attractive and useful foliage shrub for gardens of any size. The distinctive plum-purple, oval-shaped leaves are exceptional when contrasted against the dark green background of a cedar or yew hedge.

Native to southern Europe and eastward to China, the shrub gets its common name from its delicate, feathery panicles of pinkish-purple flowers that form in summer and give the impression of puffs of smoke. Grows 10 feet (3 m) or more. Hardy to Zone 5.

4. *Forsythia* x *intermedia* 'Lynwood Gold'. One of the most well-known harbingers of spring, forsythia is not only a welcome sight when its golden-yellow flowers appear in early spring, it also acts as a reminder to get busy giving roses their spring pruning. Grows 25 feet (7.5 m) and taller if allowed. Hardy to Zone 5.

5. *Philadelphus coronarius* 'Aureus' (mock orange). The great value of having a mock orange in the garden is that it has masses of white flowers in July. This helps to bridge the midsummer gap and provides a smooth transition in the shrub border between spring and autumn. 'Aureus' has golden-yellow leaves that provide excellent foliage contrast, especially alongside the purple leaves of smoke bush. 'Aureus' grows about 6 to 8 feet (1.8 to 2.4 m) high. Hardy to Zone 3.

6. *Ribes sanguineum* 'White Icicle' (flowering currant). This deciduous shrub grows 10 feet high by 6 feet (3 by 1.8 m) wide, and produces drooping, pure white flowers in early spring. It grows well in full sun to light shade in average, well-drained soil. Hardy to Zone 4.

- *Viburnum davidii*. A first-rate groundcover with glossy, evergreen leaves and metallic-blue berries, it grows to 2 feet (60 cm). Hardy to Zone 7.

- *Viburnum juddii*. A mounding shrub with fragrant white flowers in May. The lush green foliage turns an attractive shade of purple-red in October. Hardy to Zone 5.

- *Viburnum opulus* 'Roseum' (European snowball). Commonly called the snowball bush, it is possibly the best-known viburnum because of its spectacular June display of dazzling creamy white, globular flower heads that look like snowballs. It grows to 10 feet (3 m). *V. opulus* 'Compactum' (compact highbush cranberry) produces white flowers and has green leaves that turn purple-red in October. Hardy to Zone 4.

- *Viburnum plicatum* 'Summer Snowflake'. Introduced by the University of B.C. Botanical Garden, this is an ideal shrub for a low-maintenance garden. It covers itself in April to May with a full flush of white, clover-shaped flowers. The rate of flowering slows in June and continues at a more modest tempo all summer. 'Summer Snowflake' has a compact form and slow-growing habit, making it very manageable and a good shrub for the small- or medium-sized city garden. Grows to 8 feet (2.4 m). Hardy to Zone 4.

- *Viburnum plicatum tomentosum* 'Mariesii'. This is a spectacular shrub if you have space. It grows to 8 feet (2.4 m) and in spring its pure white, flat, lacecap flowers are elegantly displayed along the entire length of the bush's long, horizontal, tiered branches. It has been planted to dramatic effect as the feature at the end of a large lawn, or as one of the stars of the shrub border. Hardy to Zone 4.

- *Viburnum tinus*. Evergreen in mild areas, this grows ultimately to a 10-foot (3-m) bush in ideal conditions, and produces clusters of fragrant white flowers followed by blue-black berries. Hardy to Zone 7.

Best of the Broadleaf Evergreens

"Is it evergreen?" It's the first question a lot of people ask when buying a new shrub for the garden. The appeal of evergreen plants is that they provide color and structure all year round. Broadleaf evergreens can have wide leaves, such as rhododendrons, holly, aucuba and camellia, or small narrow leaves, like boxwood, pieris, azaleas, leucothoe and sarcococca. Here's an A to Z of the most useful broadleaf evergreens for the home garden.

- *Aucuba*. This has blotchy, shiny, yellow-green leaves, grows 7 feet (2.1 m) high and thrives in full or partial shade. A popular cultivar is 'Gold Dust'. Zone 6.

- *Azalea*. There is a wide selection of popular varieties, all thriving in partial shade and flowering from mid- to late spring. Top varieties include 'Blue Danube' (bluish-violet), 'Girard's Fuchsia' (reddish-purple), 'Herbert' (lavender), 'Hino Crimson' (deep crimson), 'Hino White' (bright white), 'Rosebud' (rose-pink), 'Purple Splendour' (red-violet), 'Macrantha' (pink) and 'Red Fountain' (red flowers and noted for being a late bloomer, sometimes into July). Zone 6.

- *Berberis* (barberry). Useful for burglar-proofing a window, this shrub has thorny stems and prickly foliage and is mostly used for low hedging. The most popular species is *B. darwinii*, which grows to 6 to 8 feet (1.8 to 2.4 m). Thrives in full sun to part shade. Zone 6.

- *Buxus* (boxwood). Common boxwood, also known as English boxwood, is *Buxus sempervirens*. This is perfect for making neatly clipped parterres or for creating decorative topiary cones, balls and pyramids in pots. The dwarf variety, 'Suffruticosa', is more compact and a slow grower, which makes it ideal for enclosing a formal rose or herb garden. *B. sempervirens* is a good choice for mild-winter gardens, but for colder, drier areas the Korean boxwood (*B. microphylla*) is a better choice. Popular varieties are 'Winter Beauty', 'Green Velvet' and 'Winter Gem'. Zone 5.

- *Camellia*. There are two kinds—the ones that flower in the spring (*C. japonica, C. williamsii*) and the kind that flower in the fall and winter (*C. sasanqua*). For spring flowering, the *C. williamsii* varieties tend to do better in coastal gardens than the *C. japonica* cultivars. Look for 'Donation' (orchid-pink), 'Anticipation' (pink), 'Elsie Jury' (pink), 'Jury's Yellow' (yellow stamens surrounded by white petals) and 'Daintiness' (salmon-pink). In less wet areas, top *C. japonica* varieties include 'Nuccio's Pearl' (orchid-pink), 'Bob Hope' (red), 'Tom Knudsen' (dark red) and 'Debbie' (deep rose). Top *C. sasanqua* cultivars include 'Yuletide' (fragrant deep red flower), 'Appleblossom' (white tinged with pink) and 'Chansonette' (bright pink). Zones 7 to 8.

- *Ceanothus thyrsiflorus* 'Victoria' (California lilac). Evergreen when planted where it is protected from extreme cold and severe frost, this grows 6 to 10 feet (1.8 to 3 m) high and produces deep blue flowers in spring. Zone 7.

- *Choisya ternata* (Mexican orange). This has wonderful aromatic foliage and, in spring, fragrant clusters of white flowers resembling orange blossoms. 'Aztec Pearl' is an excellent cultivar, while 'Sundance' is more compact and has bright golden foliage. Zone 7.

- *Cotoneaster*. There are two key kinds: the low-growing groundcover *C. dammeri*, which has glossy leaves, white flowers and red berries in fall, and the taller-growing *C. franchetii*, which grows to 7 feet (2.1 m), has silvery green foliage and produces bright orange-red berries in winter. Zone 5.

- *Daphne odora*. This has soft, slender evergreen leaves and extremely fragrant purple-pink flowers in January through to March. It grows about 4 feet (1.2 m) high. *Daphne* x *burkwoodii* 'Carol Mackie' is semi-evergreen, also has pink flowers and grows to about 5 feet (1.5 m). Zones 6 to 7.

- *Elaeagnus pungens* 'Maculata' (oleaster). This has green leaves with a striking golden-yellow blotch in the center. It grows to 4 to 6 feet (1.2 to 1.8 m). Zones 6 to 7.

- *Euonymus fortunei* 'Emerald Gaiety'. This dependable evergreen has crisp, gray-green and creamy white variegated foliage and grows into a compact bush, 3 to 5 feet (90 cm to 1.5 m) high. Another popular cultivar is 'Emerald 'n' Gold', which has bright yellow and green variegated leaves and grows 1 to 2 feet (30 to 60 cm) high. Zone 5.

- *Fatsia japonica* (fatsia). A beautiful, big-leafed plant, admired for its architectural stature, this only has one drawback—it is tender in all but the warmest part of Zone 7. It is used as an indoor plant in colder climates, but if you have a warm, protected temperate zone spot in your garden that gets shade from the hot sun in summer, you can grow fatsia as an evergreen. This is what many West Coast gardeners manage to do. In the perfect location, it can grow 7 to 10 feet (2.1 to 3 m) high with very little effort. Zones 7 to 8.

- *Gaultheria procumbens* (wintergreen). A well-behaved groundcover with shiny green foliage, this has small white flowers followed by scarlet berries in fall. Excellent also for use in containers for winter interest. Thrives in partial shade and grows to 6 inches (15 cm). Zone 5.

- *Ilex* (holly). Classic English holly is *Ilex aquifolium*. Best varieties for the garden are 'Hedgehog', 'J.C. Van Tol', and 'Argentea-marginata'. 'Siberia' is one of the hardiest, thriving very happily in Zone 5. Also consider the blue hollies—*I. meserveae* 'Blue Boy', 'Blue Prince', and 'Blue Princess', all of which have blue-green leaves. Zones 6 to 7.

Before we go buying new plants, we should go into the garden, look each plant in the face and ask it: "Do you pay your rent? What do I get out of you? A fortnight's color and 50 weeks of boredom?" And if you don't get an answer you like, the plant should come out and be replaced by one that does pay the rent.

—Nigel Colborn, British broadcaster and gardening writer

- *Kalmia latifolia* (mountain laurel). A good plant for light shade in acidic soil, this has shiny, leathery leaves and pink flowers and grows to 4 to 5 feet (1.2 to 1.5 m). Top varieties are 'Snowdrift' (pure white), 'Minute' (light pink), 'Heart of Fire' (red), 'Olympic Wedding' (pink) and 'Ostbo Red' (deep red). Zones 4 to 5.

- *Leucothoe*. The all-green *L. axillaris* has lance-shaped leaves, while the more colorful 'Rainbow' has dark green foliage splashed with yellow, pink and cream. Both grow 2 to 3 feet (60 to 90 cm) high and thrive in light shade in acidic soil. Zone 5.

- *Mahonia aquifolium* (Oregon grape). With holly-like leaves and yellow flowers in spring followed by clusters of tiny blue, grape-like berries, this has a lot going for it. Some consider it indispensable in the shrubbery. The common *M. aquifolium* grows 6 to 8 feet (1.8 to 2.4 m) high, but the dwarf variety (*M. aquifolium compacta*) grows to only 2 to 3 feet (60 to 90 cm). 'Charity' grows 6 to 8 feet (1.8 to 2.4 m) and has fragrant yellow flowers. Zone 4.

- *Nandina domestica* (heavenly bamboo). This plant has bamboo-like foliage with stiff, upright stems to about 7 feet (2.1 m). There are two excellent dwarf varieties, 'Harbour Dwarf' and 'Gulf Stream', both of which grow 2 to 3 feet (60 to 90 cm) high. It thrives in full sun and the foliage turns orange to wine-red in fall. Zone 6.

- *Photinia*. This has a multitude of uses—as a low or high hedge or as a small tree. Its main appeal is the attractive ruby-red new foliage in spring, which contrasts with the existing evergreen leaves. Zone 7.

- *Pieris japonica* (lily-of-the-valley bush). A very popular shrub found in many gardens, the most famous cultivar is 'Forest Flame', which has red-orange new foliage and white flowers in spring. Other top varieties are 'Mountain Fire', 'Flamingo' and 'Cavatine'. There is also a variegated form, *P. japonica* 'Variegata', which has silver-green leaves. All thrive in sun or shade. Zone 5.

- *Pyracantha* (firethorn). Ideal for espaliering against a wall or fence or as a thorny barrier under a window, it has bright red, orange or yellow berries, depending on the variety, and clusters of white flowers in spring. 'Orange Glow' is popular because of its hardiness and disease resistance, but other worthy cultivars include 'Cherri Berri', 'Soleil D'or', 'Teton' and 'Golden Charm', all of which can be trained to reach 6 to 10 feet (1.8 to 3 m). Zone 6.

- *Rhododendron*. There are hundreds of varieties to choose from. The secret is to pick the one you want when it is in bloom and to know whether it is a small-, medium- or large-growing specimen in order to get it in a spot where it can grow to maturity. (See Your Guide to Rhododendrons, page 37.)

- *Sarcococca* (sweet box). One of the most heavenly scented evergreens, there are two main types—*S. hookeriana humilis* (Himalayan sweet box), which grows to 1 1/2 to 2 feet (45 to 60 cm) and *S. ruscifolia* (fragrant sweet box), which grows 5 to 6 feet (1.5 to 1.8 m). They both produce fragrant white flowers in early spring. *S. hookeriana* has black berries, *S. ruscifolia* has red berries. Zone 6.

- *Skimmia japonica*. A great shrub for including in a winter container as well as an evergreen component in mixed shrubbery. It thrives in full shade or partial sun and produces red berries in fall and winter and slightly fragrant reddish flowers in winter. One of the best varieties is 'Rubinetta', which grows to 2 to 3 feet (60 to 90 cm) and has vivid red flower buds in winter. Zone 7.

- *Viburnum*. There are two excellent evergreen forms ideal for the home garden—*V. tinus* 'Spring Bouquet', which grows to 5 feet (1.5 m) and has fragrant white flowers in early spring, and *V. davidii*, which grows to 3 feet (90 cm) and has leathery-veined leaves and blue berries in fall and winter. Both thrive in sun or light shade. *V. tinus* is hardy to Zone 7 and *V. davidii* is hardy to Zone 5.

- *Yucca* (Adam's needle). Like it or hate it, this shrub has become a familiar feature in the garden landscape. The tropical-looking foliage can add an exotic touch to a hot sunny area and the large clusters of white flowers are held up high on 4- to 6-foot (1.2- to 1.8-m) stalks. It combines well with windmill palms (*Trachycarpus*) and hardy banana trees to create a neo-tropical landscape. Zones 3 to 4.

Pruning: The Kindest Cut of All

Pruning is the kindest cut of all, but there is a little more to it than simply lopping dead and diseased branches off trees and shrubs. You should follow some basic rules or you can do more harm than good. Here are a few simple tips.

- **Stay focused.** Remember your main goal is to remove dead, diseased or damaged wood. Crossing branches that rub and damage other branches should come out, but also prune intelligently to create a pleasant framework. Before you start to slice away, take time to examine the plant carefully. Wander and ponder before pruning. It is so easy to get carried away and prune off perfectly healthy branches.

- **Use the right equipment.** Don't try to chomp through a thick tree branch with a pair of hand-pruners. You'll end up leaving ragged edges, which can lead to disease. Some of the secateurs and loppers being sold at garden centers are no good for the job. Don't use those that have a blade that cuts down on a flat surface. They tend to crush branches or stems and leave a nasty, ragged cut. Use pruners with blades that bypass each other, guaranteeing a clean, crisp cut.

- **Prune at the right time.** If you don't know when this is, you need to do a little homework on the habits of the specific plant. As a general rule, the best time to prune most plants is at the end of their dormant season, usually in late winter/early spring, just before they start to grow again. Nature is a very good teacher. It does most of its pruning in winter using ice, snow and winds to break off dead and diseased branches. If you watch the plants in your garden you will notice the cycle they go through each year. Some trees (maples, birches, walnuts) are "bleeders." Cut them when the sap is running and you will have a sticky mess on your hands. The general rule is prune when the tree is dormant, before the sap rises in the spring.

  But to prune shrubs or vines with confidence, you need to find out when and how they flower. Plants that bloom in summer on new growth are generally pruned hard in early spring, while plants that flower on growth produced the previous year are pruned after they flower in summer or fall. The reasoning is simple enough: prune, say, a magnolia, witch hazel or forsythia in the spring, and you end up lopping off all your flowers before they've bloomed. On the other hand, neglect to prune a *Buddleia davidii* hard in the spring and you end up with a tangled mess of new growth on top of last year's old woody stems.

- **Cut to a healthy bud.** Always cut back to an outward-facing bud. This promotes healthy new growth that will go in the right direction and not interfere with other branches. Make a crisp cut not too far away, not too close, not too slanted, but just above the outward-facing bud at a 45-degree angle. If you cut between two buds, the stub of the branch that is left will turn black and decay, a process called dieback.

- **Watch the collar.** When cutting a branch, make sure you don't cut into the collar, the slightly thicker bulge where the branch joins the main trunk. There are chemicals in the collar that help heal the wound.

- **Use three cuts to remove large branches.** It is a common mistake to attempt to remove a large branch of a tree by making one cut. This never works. The weight of the branch usually tears the limb away from the trunk of the tree. The right method is to make three cuts. The first is a partial upward cut, about 12 to 18 inches (30 to 45 cm) out from the branch collar. This is done from the bottom up and about a quarter of the way into the branch. The second is a complete cut all the way through the branch a few inches out from the undercut. This takes off most of the branch. The undercut will prevent it ripping away by providing a weak spot for a clean break. The third cut removes the remaining stub of branch from the trunk. This is done by making a clean, downward cut next to the collar.

- **Forget about wound paint.** Experts disagree about how effective it is to seal a wound with tar or paint after pruning. Studies have shown that, far from helping, wound paint can actually cause disease by sealing in moisture and inhibiting the tree's natural healing mechanisms.

- **Resist the urge to top a tree.** Topping a tree that seems too tall or is blocking your view may seem like the perfect solution, but it's not. Topping—chopping off the tree's main leader at the top—not only opens the tree to all sorts of disease, it also destabilizes it. It encourages unstable multiple new leaders (all vying for top position), destroys the fundamental shape of the tree, and basically tells the whole neighborhood how stupid you are. It is far better to remove carefully selected branches in order to thin out the tree and create views through the tree. Consult an arborist.

The Two Most-Asked Pruning Questions

- **When and how do I prune my wisteria?**
Wisteria can be pruned twice a year to keep it in good shape and promote blooming. Cut back lateral and side stems in late winter or early spring to within a few inches (8 to 10 cm) of two or three buds. This removes weak and wispy growth from the previous summer and makes the vine look cleaner and healthier. Two months after flowering—usually in July or August—again snip back lateral and side stems to within four or five buds of the main branch. If your wisteria is not blooming, it is either because it is still maturing—new wisteria can take up to seven years to bloom—or it is lacking sunlight, receiving too much nitrogen and not enough phosphorus, or is recovering from ill-timed pruning.

- **When and how do I prune my clematis?**
It all depends what kind of clematis it is. If it is an early spring bloomer, such as *C. montana*, *C. armandii* or *C. macropetala*, it will bloom on stems that grew the previous year (old wood). Prune these early-flowering clematis after they have bloomed. Usually, this calls for a light touch. The summer-flowering types such as *C. x jackmanii* flower on new growth. Prune them back to within about 2 feet (60 cm) of the ground in spring. This promotes vigorous new growth on which flowers will appear in summer. Some clematis bloom twice, on old wood in spring and new wood in fall. Prune these types lightly for appearance and size after blooming. (For more information on clematis, see page 98.)

- **Go with the flow.** A key concept to grasp about pruning is that it is a way of redirecting nature's central energy. Sap flows up through trees and shrubs with immense vigor in spring, producing astonishing new growth. When you prune, you are directly interfering with that energy. A simple cut can send sap rushing in an entirely different direction. The pruning process is like playing at being nature's traffic cop, stopping sap here, waving it on there, slowing it down this side street, allowing it to speed unimpeded along this highway. It's no wonder once gardeners grasp the creative potential in all this that they quickly move on to doing topiary and espaliers, pollarding and pleaching—all artistic refinements of the basic pruning techniques.

- **Don't overextend yourself.** If you're looking at a major thinning of a tree's whole canopy, or the removal of large lower limbs to open space and lift the crown of the tree, hire a professional arborist.

- **Think about the roots/shoots ratio.** There is a proportional relationship between the amount of root below ground and the quantity of growth the plant produces above. Whatever you prune off, the plant will attempt to grow back somehow to restore the balance of roots to shoots. So don't think what you prune off will stay off—it won't, unless you are smart enough to root-prune, which is a lot more tricky.

- **Relieve the stress.** Since it relies on its foliage to provide nutrients, you can't remove a lot of foliage without causing stress to the plant. If you do any substantial pruning, remember to feed the plant afterwards with a balanced fertilizer to help make up for lost nutrients.

- **Don't sweat root suckers.** Some trees (poplars, cherries, ailanthus, robinia) are notorious for "suckering"—sending up vertical shoots from under the tree. They don't do any harm, but they do look messy. Cut them out as soon as they appear. By digging or pulling them up you may unwittingly stimulate them to grow more vigorously.

- **Cut canes with care.** Some plants thrive by producing new canes from their base. These include shrub dogwoods, forsythia, hydrangea, roses, buddleia, kerria, weigela, Oregon grape and bamboo—all virtually indestructible. Prune them by completely removing dead, old or weak stems, rather than cutting them back. This also allows more room for new canes to develop.

- **Take some shrubs in hand and slice them back.** Perfect candidates include escallonia, abelia, spirea, honeysuckle, holly, cistus, aucuba, evergreen azaleas, boxwood, Japanese holly, choisya, potentilla and evergreen viburnums. Grab a handful of overgrown branches and snip them back closer to the center of the bush until the shrub looks tidy.

- **Don't do it all at once.** If you want to reduce the size of a tree or large shrub such as a rhododendron, resist the temptation to go too far too fast. It is better to reduce the size of a tree or shrub gradually over a few years than hack away at it and leave it looking a mess. As a rule, it is best not to prune a tree or shrub by more than a third of its size in one year. (See How to Plant and Care for Rhododendrons, page 42.)

Roses

What's a garden without roses? The queen of flowers, roses are as indispensible to the total garden picture as birds and butterflies. The range of roses available to gardeners today is extraordinary. More than 10,000 different roses in a wide range of colors and sizes are now sold at nurseries worldwide. Finding the right one for your garden can be a challenge. Here you'll find some helpful recommendations of top roses in all the key categories—hybrid teas, floribundas, climbers, shrub roses, groundcovers, patio roses and English roses, as well as all the information you need to grow and care for them.

10 Top Hybrid Teas

The most popular type of rose, hybrid teas outsell all others. Most hybrid teas produce large or medium-sized blooms with five petals or more on long stems. The first hybrid tea, 'La France', was introduced in 1867. A cross between a hybrid perpetual and a tea-scented China rose, the hybrid tea got beauty, fragrance and repeat-flowering habit from the China roses and energy, vigor and winter hardiness from the hybrid perpetuals. Here are 10 of the best.

1. 'Chrysler Imperial'. A classic that has stood the test of time. This has large, deep crimson flowers and glossy foliage and grows into a bushy shrub. First introduced in 1952, it is considered an outstanding exhibition rose. Size 2 1/2 to 4 feet (75 cm to 1.2 m). Fragrance: 4 stars.

2. 'Double Delight'. Named the world's favorite rose in 1985 by the World Federation of Rose Societies, this is one of the best of the two-tone roses. It has distinctive creamy white and raspberry-pink blooms. The memory of its perfume will linger with you all winter. Excellent cut flower. Size: 3 feet (90 cm). Fragrance: 4 stars.

3. 'Fragrant Cloud'. This rose has it all—outstanding color, excellent fragrance and a great name. Introduced in 1964, it has won consistent praise for its intoxicating perfume and the beauty of its coral-red to dusty-scarlet blooms. It makes a splendid spectacle when mass planted. Size: 30 inches (75 cm). Fragrance: 4 stars.

4. 'Freedom'. A marvelous yellow rose, this won the Award of Garden Merit from the Royal Horticultural Society but has never achieved the same level of popularity in North America as it enjoys in Britain. Considered the best yellow rose for difficult conditions, it is a good choice for gardeners who want quality results with minimal effort. Size: 30 inches (75 cm). Fragrance: 3 stars.

5. 'Fulton Mackay'. Sturdy and disease-resistant, this striking Scottish-bred rose has unusual apricot-yellow flowers that have a strong scent. Introduced in 1998, one of its parents is 'Silver Jubilee', another exceptional rose. Size: 3 feet (90 cm). Fragrance: 3 stars.

6. 'Paul Shirville'. Also known as the "heart-throb" rose, this is one of the best varieties ever introduced by the famous English rose company, Harkness. The salmon-pink flowers have a beautiful scent. One of its parents is the equally impressive 'Compassion'. Size: 3 feet (90 cm). Fragrance: 4 stars.

7. 'Peace'. Its cheerful, primrose-yellow flowers have a touch of soft pink in them. Perhaps the world's most famous rose, 'Peace' was hybridized in France and named at the end of the Second World War. Healthy, vigorous, and always reliable, it is easy to grow. Size: 4 feet (1.2 m). Fragrance: 2 stars.

8. 'Pristine'. With its large, elegant, creamy white flowers with blush pink on the edges of the petals, this is a super vigorous rose that scored a 9.2 (outstanding) rating from the American Rose Society. It has a light fragrance and is a good choice for an informal rose hedge. Size: 3 to 4 feet (90 cm to 1.2 m). Fragrance: 2 stars.

9. 'Rosemary Harkness'. The color is very hard to capture in a photograph since the mixture of salmon-pink, yellow and orange is very subtle and deceptive. A favorite rose for cutting and useful as a table decoration, it has won awards for its delicious perfume. Size: 40 inches (1 m). Fragrance: 2 stars.

10. 'Savoy Hotel'. One of my personal favorites, this rose looks exceptional when planted in groups of three or five. Easy to grow, it produces lovely, light pink, highly scented blooms. It also goes by the name 'Integrity' and has been recognized as an outstanding rose by the Royal Horticultural Society. Size: 3 feet (90 cm). Fragrance: 3 stars.

10 Top Floribundas

The word "floribunda" was invented by rose growers in the 1940s to describe a new class of roses, originally developed by a Danish hybridist. Floribundas produce abundant blooms in clusters or trusses. Although the flowers are sometimes dismissed as technically inferior to hybrid teas, floribundas are extremely popular with home gardeners who love them for their fragrance, fabulous range of colors and energetic blooming habit. So much hybridizing has now been done between floribundas and hybrid teas, experts often disagree over which is which. Here are 10 of the best.

1. 'Angel Face'. Not terribly well known but certainly a rose that deserves more attention with an 8.1 (excellent) rating from the American Rose Society. The ruffled flowers are lavender with a slight blush of ruby. As well as the striking color, the blooms are noticeably fragrant. This lovely package of qualities is all contained in a low-growing bush with dark glossy foliage. Size: under 3 feet (90 cm). Fragrance: 4 stars.

2. 'City of London'. You could do an entire rose bed on a city theme—'City of Leeds', 'City of Belfast', 'Southampton', 'Canterbury'—but 'City of London' is particularly worth having because of its highly perfumed clusters of white blooms with a slight pink blush. Some think the flowers have the look of an old-fashioned, cottage garden bourbon rose. One other curious thing is that if lightly pruned, 'City of London' is apt to turn into a small, shrub-like climbing rose. Size: 3 to 6 feet (90 cm to 1.8 m). Fragrance: 4 stars.

3. 'Europeana'. This offers a superb combination of long-lasting, deep crimson blooms and dense reddish-green foliage. It forms a medium-sized, rounded bush, which also makes it useful as a low-maintenance landscape rose. Rated "outstanding" by the American Rose Society, 'Europeana' is celebrated for its ability to produce flowers all summer. Size: under 3 feet (90 cm). Fragrance: 1 star.

4. 'Fellowship'. Vigorous and reliable, this produces wide clusters of deep coppery-orange blooms all summer. It looks exceptional when planted in small groups and has a subtle fragrance that manages to hang in the air long into fall. Good disease resistance makes it an easy rose to care for. The color is particularly striking when backed by blue or white delphiniums. Size: 30 inches (75 cm). Fragrance: 2 stars.

5. 'Iceberg'. Many rose-lovers regard this as the best of all the white floribundas. English rose grower Jack Harkness once said, "What a pity we don't have 'Iceberg' in every color. There would be no need to grow a long list of floribundas." It is certainly one of the most popular roses ever. Disease resistant, vigorous and free-flowering, it has pinkish buds that open to pure white blooms. Easy to care for, it only requires light pruning. Size: 3 to 4 feet (90 cm to 1.2 m). Fragrance: 2 stars.

6. 'Margaret Merril'. The main challenge for Iceberg's crown as queen of the white floribundas, this has very impressive credentials, winning all kinds of top awards. It does not produce as many flowers as 'Iceberg', but its blooms are considered more perfect and they have a delicious

Most gardeners are basically show-offs. After all, it's pointless to do all this work if you're not going to show the world—or at least the gardening cognoscenti—what you have created.

—Jill Stewart-Bowen, former president of Victoria Horticultural Society, British Columbia scent. It is perhaps disappointing to learn that the rose is not named after a real person: the name Margaret Merril was dreamed up by the makers of Oil of Olay, who commissioned the rose. Size: 3 feet (90 cm). Fragrance: 4 stars.

7. 'Sheila's Perfume'. A rival to the popular hybrid tea 'Double Delight', this has equally attractive red and yellow blooms, as well as a knockout fragrance. 'Sheila's Perfume' has a good reputation for disease resistance and vigorous, healthy growth. The story goes that amateur rose-lover John Sheridan accomplished in 1985 what countless professional rose growers around the world were trying to achieve when he succeeded in raising the first seedlings of this two-tone beauty on his window sill in London. Size: 3 feet (90 cm). Fragrance: 4 stars.

8. 'Showbiz'. This gets its name from its long-lasting, fire engine–red flowers, which are produced in extravagant sprays. With glossy green leaves, 'Showbiz' scores high points for disease resistance. It looks good in a rose garden or can be used to great effect in a sunny mixed flower border. Size: 3 to 4 feet (90 cm to 1.2 m). Fragrance: 1 star.

9. 'Sunset Boulevard'. British rose of the year in 1997, this has scored top marks from rose growers on both sides of the Atlantic. It has coppery-orange blooms and performs reliably in ordinary garden settings. It came through eight years of trials with flying colors for disease resistance. A good pick for a garden or patio where space is limited. Size: 3 feet (90 cm). Fragrance: 2 stars.

10. 'The Fairy'. Technically a polyantha shrub rose, this is most often listed as a floribunda at garden centers. A compact plant, it produces a wonderful profusion of dainty, rosette-shaped, pink blooms in clusters. Extremely hardy and disease resistant, the only negative thing you'll hear about it is that it blooms late, usually around the middle of July. But it continues until late frost. Size: under 3 feet (90 cm). Fragrance: 1 star.

10 Top Climbers and Ramblers

It's not worth getting too concerned about the difference between climbers and ramblers since they are basically both used for the same purposes. It can be hard to tell which is which, but climbers generally have stiffer stems and produce larger flowers than ramblers, which have more wiry, flexible stems. Climbers are usually repeat-flowering (meaning they continue to produce occasional blooms after the main flush), while ramblers usually produce one great flush of flowers in midsummer. A vigorous rambling rose can cover an entire garden shed or fill the wall of a house. Since these types of roses are often planted next to walls and fences or in fast-draining, exposed sites, it is important to remember to keep them well watered, especially during the first few years when they are getting established.

Top Climbers

1. 'Compassion'. A lovely, highly fragrant rose with pink- to salmon-colored blooms, this is one of the best from the Harkness Rose Company of England. It is ideal for walls and fences. Grows to 12 feet (3.6 m). Fragrance: 4 stars.

2. 'Dublin Bay'. This is one of the best repeat-bloomers, producing a generous flush of deep red flowers from June to July, and then producing more intermittently through the summer. It lacks the vigor to reach the top of an arch or pergola, but it can provide a bright backdrop or be effective for creating a spot of eye-catching color. Grows to 10 feet (3 m). Fragrance: 2 stars.

3. 'Madame Alfred Carrière'. Vigorous and shade-tolerant, this old-fashioned rose has the ability to cover a north-facing wall or fence with masses of beautiful, fragrant, white, gardenia-like flowers. It traces its roots back to a nursery in France in 1879 and was named after a passionate rosarian. Grows to 18 feet (5.5 m). Fragrance: 4 stars.

4. 'New Dawn'. One of the most dependable and disease-resistant climbing roses, 'New Dawn' can be relied upon to cover fences or walls and produce an outstanding flush of slightly fragrant, shell-pink blooms in early June. First introduced in 1930 as the offspring of the famous rambling rose 'Doctor W. Van Fleet', it is less vigorous than its parent but is still considered by many to be the yardstick by which all other climbing roses are judged. The leaves have a healthy, shiny look and the light pink, 3-inch-wide (7.5-cm) flowers are small, somewhat fragile, but plentiful. Grows to 15 to 20 feet (4.5 to 6 m). Fragrance: 2 stars.

5. 'Zéphirine Drouhin'. This thornless climber is popular with British garden designers, who often use it to cover arches along paths. It has vivid, crimson-pink blooms that have been described as expressive of the "warmth of some old remembered days of summer, when roses innocently quartered their centers, and were expected to breathe a gentle fragrance into the air." Grows to 10 feet (3 m). Fragrance: 3 stars.

Top Ramblers

1. 'Albertine'. Introduced in 1921, this has highly fragrant, pale coppery-pink blooms. It is a fairly rampant rambler capable of covering a long fence or pergola. Grows to 15 feet (4.5 m). Fragrance: 3 stars.

2. 'American Pillar'. This flowers profusely in July and rates as one of the best climbers of all time. You do, however, need to plant it where the air circulates freely, because in stagnant air this rose is prone to mildew. They are not noticeably fragrant. The flowers are deep pink with a white center. Grows to 15 feet (4.5 m). Fragrance: 1 star.

3. 'Félicité Perpétue'. This has fragrant, creamy white flowers and will happily clamber into trees. It belongs to the "evergreen" group of ramblers (sempervirens hybrids), which means it will retain its leaves in all but severe winters. Grows to 15 feet (4.5 m). Fragrance: 2 stars.

4. 'François Juranville'. This has fragrant, pale salmon-pink flowers in June and will easily scramble 20 feet (6 m). It is perfect for rose pillars, arches and arbors. It is a lot more pliable than other climbers, making it a little easier to bend it into place over structures. Fragrance: 2 stars.

5. 'Rambling Rector'. An outstanding rambler, capable of covering large fences, reaching up into trees, and hiding eyesores in the garden. It produces masses of fragrant clusters of white flowers in midsummer. Grows to 20 feet (6 m). Fragrance: 2 stars.

10 Top English Roses

English rose breeder David Austin made a name for himself internationally by combining the exquisite, multi-petaled beauty of famous old garden roses with the prolific flowering power of top-performing modern hybrid teas and floribundas. The result is a new class of roses called "English roses." 'Constance Spry' (soft pink) was the first to be introduced in 1961. There are now dozens of English roses in cultivation. Not all of them are star performers. Austin himself is a fairly hard critic of his own roses, ruthlessly rating them with a star from 1 (below average) to 4 (outstanding). Here are 10 of the best that also happen to have received a 4-star rating from Austin.

1. 'Abraham Darby'. The large, beautiful apricot blooms with a touch of yellow have a strong, fruity fragrance. The bush grows into a fairly dense shrub with dark green leaves and thorny stems. It has the desirable old-world rose look with its showy, cup-shaped flowers. A good choice for growing in the mixed border or against a fence or wall, but it needs a little special protection in colder areas. Size: 5 feet (1.5 m). Fragrance: 3 stars.

2. 'Evelyn'. The flowers of this excellent, upright shrub rose are mainly apricot but they also contain delicious tints of yellow and pink. With another successful English rose, 'Graham Thomas', as one of its parents, 'Evelyn' is regarded as having the most fragrant flowers of any

of the Austin hybrids. It was selected by the perfumers Crabtree and Evelyn as the rose for their company. Size: 4 feet (1.2 m). Fragrance: 3 stars.

3. 'Gertrude Jekyll'. Named after the famous nineteenth-century English grand dame of gardening, this is one of Austin's best-selling roses because of its health and vigor and exceptionally attractive blooms. The large, deep pink flowers have a distinct and powerful antique-rose perfume. Size: 4 feet (1.2 m). Fragrance: 3 stars.

4. 'Glamis Castle'. Austin has produced a few good white roses, including 'Fair Bianca', 'Winchester Cathedral' and 'The Nun', but one of the most dependable whites is 'Glamis Castle'. It has deeply cupped blooms with a clean myrrh fragrance and grows into a small bush easily accommodated in a garden where space is limited. Size: 3 feet (90 cm). Fragrance: 3 stars.

5. 'Graham Thomas'. First introduced at the Chelsea Flower Show in 1983, this lovely golden-yellow rose now probably ranks as the most popular of all the English roses. The reason? The multi-petaled blooms have an old-world charm and a modern tea-rose fragrance. The bush is a vigorous grower with an impressive ability to produce flowers throughout the summer. But it is perhaps the rich yellow color of the blooms that has warmed and captivated the hearts of gardeners all over the world. Size: 5 feet (1.5 m). Fragrance: 3 stars.

6. 'Heritage'. Gardeners love the name, but this vigorous, bushy rose has two other winning qualities—exquisite, cup-shaped, blush-pink flowers and a strong fragrance which has been described as both honeyed and lemony. A tall rose, it is ideal for growing at the back of the border. Some of the attractive characteristics of 'Heritage' undoubtedly come from its parent, 'Iceberg', a world-class floribunda acclaimed for its disease resistance and free-flowering nature. Size: 5 feet (1.5 m). Fragrance: 3 stars.

7. 'L.D. Braithwaite'. Austin has produced a number of excellent red roses. 'The Prince', 'The Dark Lady' and 'Wenlock' are three of the most impressive, but 'L.D. Braithwaite' is the best of the bunch with exquisite bright crimson flowers with a subtle old-world perfume. The offspring of two other top English roses ('Mary Rose' and 'The Squire'), it can be relied upon to produce flowers of a consistent quality throughout summer. Size: 42 inches (1 m). Fragrance: 1 star.

8. 'Leander'. You can grow this tall rose as a shrub in the mixed border for nodding over walls and fences. The deep apricot blooms have a strong fruity aroma and grow in sprays, which can make an interesting change

of pace in the garden. 'Leander' has a reputation for blooming in one lovely flush, but it will repeat-bloom once established. Size: 6 feet (1.8 m). Fragrance: 2 stars.

9.   'Mary Rose'. Everyone has his or her favorite English rose. 'Mary Rose' is mine. It has cheerful, fragrant, rose-pink blooms that start to appear in early June and continue sporadically to the end of summer. Austin describes the rose's growth habit as "near to ideal—bushy, twiggy and vigorous without being unruly." The American Rose Society gave it an 8.7 rating out of 10. Size: 4 feet (1.2 m). Fragrance: 1 star.

10. 'St. Swithun'. The flowers are large and soft pink with a myrrh-like fragrance. Named after the patron saint of Winchester Cathedral, 'St. Swithun' has a good reputation for vigorous, upright growth and disease resistance. Introduced in 1993, it is one of the best roses to play a supporting role in the border. Size: 3 feet (90 cm). Fragrance: 3 stars.

10 Top Shrub Roses

This is a diverse group containing old-fashioned roses that have been popular for centuries, as well as modern roses that combine the beauty of the roses of the past with the color and performance of modern hybrid teas and floribundas. Shrub roses are versatile enough that they can be used to create informal hedges or slotted into the sunny mixed border or used as a feature plant. Some bloom only once, while others are repeat-flowering. Most are fragrant. Here are 10 of the best.

1.   'Anna Zinkeisen'. The clusters of creamy white flowers with yellow centers have a distinct cinnamon fragrance. They are borne on a bushy, rounded shrub with handsome semi-glossy foliage. A reliable repeat bloomer, 'Anna Zinkeisen' is useful for adding a cool white balance to all the shades of pink in the summer garden. Size: 4 to 5 feet (1.2 to 1.5 m). Fragrance: 4 stars.

2.   'Armada'. Extremely cold resistant, this has large trusses of soft pink blooms that linger a long time before fading. The Harkness Rose Company rates it as "the most effective shrub rose in this pink, bearing out the theory that highly disease-resistant varieties are often also the best for flower production." Good choice for an informal hedge. Size: 4 to 5 feet (1.2 to 1.5 m). Fragrance: 2 stars.

3.   'Ballerina'. I love this rose so much I have planted two in my back garden, one either side of a Victorian-style rose arbor supporting two climbing roses, 'Blossomtime' and 'Swan Lake'. 'Ballerina' forms a low hedge and produces abundant trusses of pink flowers with a soft white

center. The flowers resemble the skirt of a ballerina. It grows 4 to 5 feet (1.2 to 1.5 m) high and has bright orange hips in fall. Fragrance: 2 stars.

4. 'Fru Dagmar Hastrup'. Also spelled 'Frau Dagmar Hartopp', this rose is exceptionally healthy and has lovely clear pink flowers which are modestly scented. It forms a compact bush with fresh green foliage that looks great in the mixed border, in a mass planting or as an informal hedge. Size: 3 to 4 feet (90 cm to 1.2 m). Fragrance: 3 stars.

5. 'Golden Wings'. Popular since its introduction in 1956, this has the largest yellow flowers of any shrub rose. These elegant, saucer-shaped blooms—actually pale-primrose with amber stamens—are produced in loose clusters and have a light, orange-blossom fragrance. Indifferent to rain, the flowers hold their color for a long time and keep coming, provided the old blooms are regularly deadheaded. Size 5 feet (1.5 m). Fragrance: 2 stars.

6 Great Rose Standards

Tree or standard roses have a slim, erect stem on top of which a rose is grafted, usually a hybrid tea or floribunda, although you can get them with shrub and old-world roses. Tree roses are trained on stems 3 1/2 feet (1 m) high. Half standards are on stems 1 1/2 feet (45 cm) high. Here are six of the best.

1. 'Flower Carpet' (pink). There are four forms of 'Flower Carpet'—yellow, white, apple-blossom pink and red. But pink 'Flower Carpet' is still the most popular and makes a sensational patio tree. Black spot and mildew resistant, it requires minimal care and is an unstoppable bloomer. Fragrance: 1 star.

2. 'Gene Boerner'. With beautiful, pure pink blooms that have a perfect hybrid-tea form, this rose is super-vigorous, forming a large bushy head of foliage and flowers. It scored an 8.5 (excellent) rating from the American Rose Society. Fragrance: 1 star.

3. 'Mister Lincoln'. A favorite, highly fragrant hybrid tea for many years, it is only natural that people would also enjoy this as a rose standard on their patio or deck. The deep velvety red roses make excellent cut flowers and the dark green leaves make the plant even more handsome. Fragrance: 4 stars.

4. 'Pascali'. A top-notch hybrid tea, this has soft white flowers and a light refreshing fragrance. It has a better resistance to mildew than many roses, which makes it a good choice as a patio tree for growing in a planter box or container. Fragrance: 2 stars.

5. 'Red Gold'. Its golden-yellow flowers are edged with scarlet, making for a very striking and cheerful summer display. Able to handle rain showers without ending up looking bedraggled, 'Red Gold' has a fine reputation for its long-lasting blooms. Fragrance: 1 star.

6. 'Sunsprite'. Considered by some to be the best of all the yellow roses, it has deep yellow, super-fragrant flowers and healthy, deep green leaves. Rated excellent by the American Rose Society, it scored high marks for disease resistance and its prolific flowering habit. Fragrance: 4 stars.

6. 'Hansa'. Like all rugosa roses, 'Hansa' is extremely hardy and disease resistant, with leathery dark green foliage and scented reddish-violet blooms. An excellent shrub rose, it can also be used to create a short, informal hedge. 'Hansa' thrives in a wide variety of conditions, including light shade. It can also be grown in a container. Size: 3 to 4 feet (90 cm to 1.2 m). Fragrance: 4 stars.

7. 'Jacqueline du Pré'. Named after the famous cellist, this rose is noted for its lengthy blooming period. The first blush-white flowers, which have subtle orange stamens in the center, appear in May and keep coming all summer and into fall. The flowers also have a delicious lemon-musk perfume. Good for making a barrier hedge. Size: 4 to 5 feet (1.2 to 1.5 m). Fragrance: 4 stars.

8. 'Lambert Close'. The perfect shrub rose for cold climates, this is one of the famous Explorer series (see page 64). It produces masses of tea rose–like pink blooms in clusters of three. Size: 3 to 4 feet (90 cm to 1.2 m). Fragrance: 4 stars.

9. 'Morden Blush'. One of the best of the Parkland roses (see page 64). A proven performer, 'Morden Blush' is extremely floriferous, producing masses of peachy-pink, old-fashioned blooms that slowly fade to a soft shade of ivory. Compact, with gray-green foliage, it has a reputation for having a long and impressive bloom period. Size: 3 to 4 feet (90 cm to 1.2 m). Fragrance: 2 stars.

10. 'Queen of Denmark'. Albas are one of the oldest races of roses. They are noted for their old-fashioned flowers, disease resistance, and gray-green foliage. 'Queen of Denmark' is one of the most beautiful with its sweet-smelling bright pink blooms borne on a tall, elegant bush of arching canes. It is best used as a supporting shrub in the sunny border. Size: 5 feet (1.5 m). Fragrance: 4 stars.

10 Top Groundcover Roses

Groundcover or landscape roses are low-maintenance, disease-resistant roses that can be mass-planted to cover sizable open areas. There are two basic types: prostrate, creeping groundcovers and taller, bushy kinds that spread sideways. Prized for their versatility in most any landscape situation, these roses grow broader than tall and are useful as groundcovers, trailing out of containers and hanging baskets, cascading over walls, edging borders, forming low hedges, or for underplanting shrubs. Here are 10 of the best.

1. 'Baroque'. Suitable for planters as well as a groundcover, 'Baroque' has deep pink blooms with yellow stamens. It will grow happily in a wide

range of conditions and demands virtually no attention, save for the lightest of pruning. Size: 2 by 4 feet (60 cm by 1.2 m). Fragrance: 2 stars.

2. 'Bonica'. The first shrub rose to win the All America Rose Society top award in 1987 and to get an "outstanding" rating, 'Bonica' has good disease resistance and is a vigorous grower. The soft pink flowers are lightly fragrant. Once established, it will form a dome-shaped bush. Size: 3 by 6 feet (90 cm by 1.8 m). Fragrance: 2 stars.

3. 'Carefree Wonder'. This gets its name from its excellent record for immunity to disease. It is also a very easy rose to grow and requires minimal care. The flowers are pinkish-white with a light perfume. Size: 3 by 6 feet (90 cm by 1.8 m). Fragrance: 2 stars.

4. 'Flower Carpet' (yellow). More fragrant than the pink, white and apple-blossom varieties of 'Flower Carpet', this has primrose-yellow flowers and requires minimal maintenance. Size: 30 by 40 inches (75 cm by 1 m). Fragrance: 3 stars.

5. 'Magic Carpet'. An ideal rose for planters and containers, 'Magic Carpet' was the first groundcover rose to receive serious recognition when it was named rose of the year in Britain in 1996. The lavender blooms are slightly fragrant and look lovely trailing over the sides of a large container. Size: 18 inches by 4 feet (45 cm by 1.2 m) Fragrance: 2 stars.

6. 'Nozomi'. This is really a miniature pink rose with a propensity for climbing. This makes it a very useful groundcover, especially for sweeping down banks or for tumbling out of containers and over low walls. Size: 18 inches by 3 feet (45 by 90 cm). Fragrance: None.

7. 'Royal Bonica'. Considered an improvement on the original 'Bonica', this is really an equally excellent groundcover rose. The blooms are a more vivid pink than 'Bonica' and are a little showier, being displayed in clusters on long arching canes, but like 'Bonica' it is also very hardy, vigorous and disease resistant. Size: 3 by 6 feet (90 cm by 1.8 m). Fragrance: 2 stars.

8. 'Suma'. An offspring of 'Nozomi', this has all its parent's good characteristics—low-growing, creeping habit, vigor and healthiness—as well as exceptionally attractive ruby-red flowers that are produced in generous profusion from midsummer to fall. The perfect partner for 'Nozomi'. Size: 18 inches by 10 feet (45 cm by 3 m). Fragrance: 1 star.

9. 'Surrey'. This rose tumbles out of a pot in the most delightfully carefree manner. A reliable and vigorous rose, 'Surrey' has rose-pink flowers in clusters with about 20 petals per bloom. As a groundcover, it is a little

Roses for Super-Cold Areas

- The Parkland Series. These are extremely hardy, disease-resistant, long-blooming roses, specifically developed for cool, northern gardens. They all came out over the last 30 years as the result of a breeding program that began in Morden, Manitoba, in the 1940s. A proven winner, 'Morden Blush' is one of the most popular (see page 62). There are stories of gardeners discovering this rose and then rushing back to the garden center to buy more once they have seen it in action. Other outstanding Parkland roses include 'Morden Centennial' (medium pink), 'Morden Fireglow' (flaming orange-red), 'Morden Ruby' (ruby red), 'Winnipeg Parks' (scarlet-red) and 'Morden Amorette' (bright red).

- The Explorer Series. These roses came out of a breeding program started at the Ottawa Experimental Farm in the 1960s. Seedlings were tested in Prince George, B.C., and Kapuskasing, Ontario, and amazed everyone by surviving temperatures of $-30°F$ ($-35°C$) with minimal winter-kill. Named after Canadian explorers, the roses are mostly hybrids of rugosa roses, which have always been noted for their hardiness and immunity to pests and diseases. Popular hybrids include the neat, low-growing, white-flowering 'Henry Hudson', which scored a 9.1 out of 10 rating (outstanding) from the America Rose Society, and the fragrant red 'John Cabot', which scored 8.2. Other dependable Explorer roses include 'Martin Frobisher' (light pink), 'Alexander Mackenzie' (red), 'Frontenac' (deep pink), 'Champlain' (bright red), 'Charles Albanel' (red), 'Jens Munk' (clear pink) and 'Simon Fraser' (dark pink); and climbers 'John Davis' (pink), 'William Baffin' (pink), 'Henry Kelsey' (red), 'Captain Samuel Holland' (medium red) and 'Louis Jolliet' (medium pink).

- Two special climbers for super-cold climates, both in the Explorer series, are 'Henry Kelsey' and 'John Cabot'. 'Henry Kelsey' has spicy-scented red flowers. It grows 6 to 8 feet (1.8 to 2.4 m) high and is resistant to powdery mildew and moderately resistant to black spot. 'John Cabot' has fragrant red flowers and a vigorous, upright growth habit. It flowers freely in June and July and sporadically in late summer. Grows 8 to 10 feet (2.4 to 3 m).

- Pavement roses. Compact, low-growing shrubs of 6 to 9 feet (1.8 to 2.7 m), these extremely hardy and disease-resistant roses were developed in Germany. The name "pavement" makes them perhaps sound a little unattractive to our ear, but they have proven popular with both novice and expert rose growers for lining sidewalks and boulevards. There are 7 varieties in the series: 'Scarlet Pavement' (fuchsia-red), 'Snow Pavement' (apple-blossom pink), 'Pierrette Pavement' (dark pink, exceptional fragrance), 'Showy Pavement' (pink), ' Foxi Pavement' (purple-pink), 'Dwarf Pavement' (bright pink') and 'Purple Pavement' (purplish-red).

- Many old-fashioned roses are extremely hardy. Alba, centifolia, damask, gallica and moss roses are all hardy in cool climates. Great roses to consider include 'Maiden's Blush' (pink, alba), 'Fantin Latour' (pink, centifolia), 'Madame Hardy' (white, damask), 'Cardinal de Richelieu' (purple, gallica) and 'Henri Martin' (crimson, moss).

- Meidiland Series. The Meidiland roses, of California, have gained a lot of respect over the years as "landscape roses" because of their dependable flower power and resistance to mildew and black spot. Six top varieties, all hardy to Zone 4, include 'Bonica Meidiland' (pastel pink), 'Carefree Delight' (vivid pink), 'Fuchsia Meidiland' (mauve-pink), 'Sevillana' (scarlet-red), 'Pink Meidiland' (clear pink) and 'White Meidiland' (pure white).

taller than most, becoming a small, mounding shrub rather than a prostrate creeper. It also looks terrific as a standard, if you're lucky enough to find one. Size: 3 by 5 feet (90 cm by 1.5 m). Fragrance: 1 star.

10. 'Sussex'. What makes this rose special is its unusual apricot color. While the blooms have no fragrance, they do a great job of brightening up the dreary dead space under shrubs in sunny locations. 'Sussex' is also a good rose for growing in planters and urns or with annuals in the flower border. Size: 18 inches by 3 feet (45 by 90 cm). Fragrance: None.

How to Plant and Care for Roses

Roses will grow in a wide variety of soils and situations but they thrive best in open, sunny locations with fertile, slightly acidic soil. They do best when they get at least six hours of sun a day. Good drainage is essential, although it is important for the soil to be moisture retentive. Roses require regular watering in summer.

A month before planting, dig the ground to 18 inches (45 cm) and work in about a third of humus-rich material such as compost, peat moss, leaf mold or well-rotted manure. Don't add commercial fertilizer. Leave the topsoil untrampled so it is loose and air can circulate. In mild areas, roses can be planted any time the soil is workable, but spring is still traditionally the most popular time. In cold areas, the best time to plant roses is early spring so roots have time to establish before top growth begins. Fall planting is riskier, especially in cold areas where plants need to be protected over winter.

If you are replacing an existing rose with a new one, always take the time to replace the soil in the planting hole. Roses seem prone to a mysterious condition called "specific replant disease." Some experts believe roses infect the soil in which they are growing to deter root competition from other roses. This is sometimes thought to be the reason some roses do not do well when they are added to existing rose beds and the soil is not changed.

The following distances between roses are recommended: 18 inches to 2 feet (45 to 60 cm) for hybrid teas and floribundas; 5 feet (1.5 m) for shrub roses; 7 feet (2.1 m) for climbers; 3 feet (90 cm) for standard tree roses. Plant your roses as soon as possible after you get them. Try to plant them at least 15 inches (38 cm) from any path or lawn. Dig a hole deep and wide enough to accommodate the roots so they are not crowded when they are spread out.

Instructions often call for planting the roses on a mound of soil with roots spread down the sides, but unless this is done carefully it can lead to planting at an improper depth. Spread out the roots and comb them out with your fingers to keep them from crossing. Lay a stake across the hole to mark the level of the soil. Use this to establish the correct planting depth. There is controversy over how deep to plant the bud union, the nobbly point above the root system where a hybrid variety has been budded to the rootstock. Some say in climates where the temperatures drop below 45°F (7°C) for most of the winter, the bud union should be set 1 to 2 inches (2.5 to 5 cm) below soil level to protect it from injury. Others insist that it should be 1 inch (2.5 cm) above and then protected by a mound of fresh soil or thick mulch in winter. Still others think the bud union is best positioned level with the surface and protected by mounding in cold areas.

All roses need firm planting. When the hole is two-thirds filled, firm the soil around the outside of the roots. Slowly add water to fill the hole and let it soak in before adding more soil. This helps to eliminate air pockets. Finish filling the hole and make a shallow ditch around the edge of the planting to hold water in the root area.

Pruning

The best time to prune roses is at the end of the dormant period just as the buds begin to swell, before new growth begins. One old garden rule is to prune roses when you see forsythia in bloom. In mild areas this could be as early as February or March. In colder areas it may be as late as April. It is best to wait until the danger of hard frost is past.

First prune out all dead, diseased or damaged stems. Then remove thin, wiry stems that look unlikely to produce flowers. Prune out stems that rub against each other or cross one another. Keep in mind the overall shape of the bush.

To promote good roots and healthy new growth in hybrid teas, prune healthy stems to about 18 inches (45 cm) from the ground. If you are still nervous, follow the "easy care method" devised by Britain's Royal National Rose Society. Prune your rose bush to half its height and then take out any dead wood. The society conducted experiments and found, in most cases, this worked as well as more complicated methods.

To make a proper pruning cut, use sharp pruning shears to cut the stem cleanly, leaving no ragged edges. Cut no more than a quarter-inch (.6 cm) above an outward-facing bud. If the cut is made too far away from the bud, the stem may die back. Angle the cut so that it slopes back and away from the bud, which encourages moisture to drain away. The bud should face outward to allow growth to spread outward from the center; this encourages the bush to develop an open center, which promotes better air circulation. When removing a complete stem, cut as close as possible to the parent stem with pruning shears, then trim the stump flush with the stem using a sharp knife.

There is so much talk about how to prune, when to prune and what to prune, the average gardener ends up too confused and scared to do anything. At the end of summer, hybrid teas and floribundas can be lightly pruned back by about a third so they are not damaged or uprooted by strong winds over winter. More serious pruning should be done at the end of winter.

Climbers are best given a light pruning when they finish flowering and again in early spring. To encourage maximum flower production, canes need to be trained to grow horizontally. The stems that grow up from the horizontal canes are called *laterals*. The laterals are where all the roses are produced. Laterals can be pruned in spring right back to the stem or to a couple of sets of leaves. Main canes can be pruned back for length or if they show signs of winter dieback. On varieties that bloom just once, some of the older canes can be cut back to the base each spring. On all other climbers, remove old canes only when necessary to shape the plant and to prevent overcrowding.

Weeping standards are pruned lightly after flowering. Prune out all dead or weak wood in spring. In summer, as soon as the flowers have faded, cut back the laterals on which they were borne to within two or three buds of the main canes.

Shrub roses, which include many old garden varieties and the latest English roses from David Austin, as well as popular groundcover and landscape roses, are pruned in early spring for size and shape. The Austin roses can be treated almost like floribundas and pruned by at least a third into a rounded dome shape. Groundcovers should be lightly sheared back. It is worth remembering here that roses are rarely killed by pruning mistakes.

Basic Care

Air circulation helps to keep foliage healthy, so don't overcrowd your roses. Always keep an eye open for problems and act quickly if you see any. Don't leave old foliage or prunings on the soil around your roses. Mildew is promoted when roses are dry at their roots and the air is cool. Black spot is promoted when moisture stays on the leaves overnight. Watch for shoots that come from below ground level. These suckers grow from the rootstock below the bud union. They can usually be identified by leaves and thorns that are different from those of the top growth. The leaflets of suckers are narrower than those of the rose and the thorns are needle-like. Wrench suckers off at their point of origin, popping them out of the sockets. Don't cut them: it only encourages additional suckers to grow.

Deadhead hybrid teas as soon as each bloom withers. Prune just above a strong shoot or an outward-facing leaf bud to encourage a second flowering. Deadhead more lightly toward the end of the season as you don't want to encourage young growth that won't have time to harden before winter. With floribundas, deadheading must be ruthless. There are no leaf buds on the blossom stems, so cut the whole flower truss back to the leaflet below it. Seed heads should not be allowed to form unless they are wanted for decoration or seed and even then not until the rose is two years old.

It is best to water roses only around the roots. Overhead watering can damage roses in full flower. When the roses are not in bloom, a sprinkler that gives a fine mist-like spray can be used. Do not use a coarse stream of water that will splash soil on the leaves since this can spread soil-borne diseases. A gentle soaking is best. To prevent mildew, water early in the day so that the plants will be dry by nightfall.

Do not feed roses in the first year after planting. In subsequent years begin feeding as soon as the frost has gone and new growth begins. As one blooming period ends, feed the plant to stimulate the next bloom. In cold areas, do not feed roses after August. Scratch superphosphate with bone or blood meal or a commercial rose fertilizer lightly into the soil around the plants. As soon as the ground warms up in spring, apply a 2- to 4-inch (5- to 10-cm) cover of mulch to conserve moisture, improve soil and suppress weeds. Good mulches include well-rotted compost, ground corncobs, shredded leaves, sawdust, straw and shredded bark. Well-rotted cow or horse manure is good mulch but it can contain weed seeds and is often not readily available.

In cold winter zones, it is important to insulate the crown of the plant to enable buds (which will form the following year) to survive. Mound garden soil up the crown to a depth of 9 to 12 inches (23 to 30 cm). Take the soil from a separate location: digging soil from between plants may damage the surface feeder roots. Leaves or straw packed into a wire collar can also be used. In Zones 6 and colder, climbing roses should be wrapped with burlap to protect the canes from freezing winds or they can be removed entirely each fall from the fence or trellis to which they are attached, laid on the ground and protected with soil or straw. Snow is an excellent insulator.

Fuchsia magellanica
'Riccartonii': The easiest to grow of the hardy fuchsias, it flowers from mid-summer to fall in full sun to light shade and makes a great backdrop to *Sedum* 'Autumn Joy'.
(See pages 13, 23)

Acer japonicum
'Acontifolium': The deeply cut leaves of this outstanding Japanese maple are an attractive green all summer and turn brilliant flame red in fall. (See pages 158-162)

Tulipa 'Allegretto': This lightly scented peony-like tulip is one of the last to flower in May. (See pages 145-150)

Ligularia 'Othello': Above handsome purple leaves are sturdy stalks of bright orange-yellow daisy-like flowers for a striking end of summer display. (See pages 10-11)

International Flower Bulb Centre

Steve Whysall

International Flower Bulb Centre

Steve Whysall

Spring glory: Masses of tulips and grape hyacinths provide a splash of vibrant color in the garden in early spring. (See pages 144, 145)

Windmill palm (*Trachycarpus fortunei*): An essential and dependable tree for creating a jungle-like subtropical garden along with hardy bananas and bamboo. (See page 76)

Pan American Nursery Products Inc.

Rosa 'Flower Carpet' (pink): An exceptionally floriferous groundcover rose noted for its disease resistance and versatility in the garden. (See page 61)

Clematis 'Nelly Moser': A classic performer for more than 100 years. (See page 100)

Clearview Horticultural Products

Clearview Horticultural Products

Clematis montana:
Wonderful spring-flowering
vine ideal for growing into
a sturdy tree. (See page 99)

Rhododendrons and tulips
team up to bring spring
color to the "sunken
garden" at Butchart
Gardens. (See pages 37-43,
145-150)

Butchart Gardens Ltd.

Riot of color in the late spring garden prepares the senses for the sizzle of summer. (See pages 21-29)

Proven Winners

Argyranthemum frutescens 'Summer Pink': One of the sensational new breed of marguerite daisies in the Proven Winners collection. (See page 24)

Steve Whysall

Rhododendron 'Temple Belle': A delightful hybrid of the classy species *R. williamsianum*, which many experts feel is incapable of producing an inferior plant. (See pages 37-43)

Into the rustic:
Wooden baskets become elegant containers for a sunny patio when filled with an artistic mix of colorful bedding plants.
(See pages 29-31)

VanDusen Botanical Garden

Persicaria bistorta
'Superba': The soft pink, poker-like flower spikes combine perfectly with the purple, spherical flower heads of the ornamental onion, *Allium aflatunense*, in late spring.
(See page 151)

Steve Whysall

Rosa 'Elina': A popular hybrid tea with a delicate scent and impressive disease resistance. It scored 8.6 out of 10 with the American Rose Society. (See pages 53-54)

Rosa 'Sunset Boulevard': This is a good pick for a garden or patio where space is limited. (See page 56)

Rosa 'Dream' (orange): The iridescent blooms of this member of the Dream rose collection combines beautifully with the blue flowers of delphiniums, nepeta or lavender. (See pages 53-68)

Rosa 'Dublin Bay': One of the best repeat-blooming climbers for creating a splash of eye-catching color. (See page 57)

Rosa 'Sheila's Perfume'. The sensational fragrance of this famous floribunda completes the beauty of its exceptional two-tone blooms. (See page 56)

Rosa 'Gertrude Jekyll': One of David Austin's best selling English roses, primarily because of its health, vigor and genuine old-world charm. (See page 59)

Happy together: Winter flowering heather (*Erica carnea*) backed by the blue ornanmental grass (*Festuca glauca*) and *Spiraea* 'Goldflame'. (See pages 187, 108, 97)

Gaillardia 'Painter's Palette': Brilliantly colored blanket flower, perfect for growing in full sun in containers and flower beds. (See pages 29-33)

Hick's Yew (*Taxus* x *media* 'Hicksii'): A cross between English and Japanese yews, this makes a classy, dark green hedge. (See page 192)

Steve Whysall

Passiflora caerulea (blue passionflower): A sun-loving vine with unique flowers and glossy foliage. It grows best on a white, south-facing wall. (See page 102)

VanDusen Botanical Garden

You're welcome: Good gardens use benches to send a clear invitation to visitors that they are welcome to come and sit and stay awhile. (See page 204)

Celosia 'Cramer's Amazon': Colorful novelty plant for brightening the summer flower bed. Discovered in Peru by Ralph Cramer, this unusual form thrives in a sunny location and rivals coleus for its dramatic foliage.

Rubus calycinoides 'Emerald Carpet': Fast-growing, evergreen groundcover for full sun or part shade that produces edible, golden berries at the end of summer. (See pages 69-71)

Allium aflatunense (purple ornamental onion): Indispensable summer-flowering bulb that looks terrific under the cascading yellow blooms of laburnum trees or scattered throughout a sunny perennial border. (See pages 150-151)

Erythronium 'Pagoda': This popular dog's-tooth violet flowers in early spring and disappears completely during summer making it ideal for growing in light shade in sequence with such perennials such as hostas and astilbes. (See page 145)

Fringed and parrot tulips, loved for their ruffled petals and striking colors, offer a little novelty and surprise in the late spring garden. (See page 150)

International Flower Bulb Centre

International Flower Bulb Centre

Down to Earth

Whenever asked to solve a garden problem—diseased rose, blighted tree, infected shrub—the late great English garden guru Percy Thower always used to say, "The answer lies in the soil." Within this answer are all the tenets of good gardening: protect the soil, enrich the soil, and get the right plant in the right place. All the best gardeners get down to ground level to know their gardens. This is how to locate weeds and discover new seedlings and find bugs and slugs lurking in the leaf litter. Plants at ground level protect the soil, shielding it from harsh weather conditions and erosion, and also form the first layer of interest in the many levels of the garden. Spring is the perfect time to get down to earth and open your heart to new insights.

Best of the Groundcovers

One of the basic rules of gardening is that all soil should be covered, especially in summer when the sun can suck the life-giving moisture from the ground and put your plants under stress. The answer is to plant a groundcover—a low-growing, tightly structured plant that not only covers the ground but suppresses weeds and reduces moisture loss. Here are some of the best. Most are extremely hardy, to Zone 2; those that are not are noted.

- *Ajuga reptans* 'Bronze Beauty' (common bugleweed). A sturdy creeping plant with shiny, rounded bronze leaves and 4- to 6-inch (10- to 15-cm) spikes of blue flowers from May to June, it thrives in full to part sun in moist but well-drained soil. Other cultivars include 'Burgundy Glow', 'Braunherz', 'Mini Crisp Red' and 'Catlin's Giant'.

- *Arctostaphylos uva-ursi* (bearberry, kinnikinnick). A first-rate evergreen groundcover that will thrive in sun or partial shade. The glossy leaves are decorated by pink bell-shaped flowers in spring followed by bright red berries. Grows 4 to 6 inches (10 to 15 cm) high. Thrives in the harshest climates.

- *Artemisia stelleriana* 'Silver Brocade'. Low-growing, compact plant with soft gray foliage similar to dusty miller. A first-rate rockery edging and can also be used in hanging baskets.

- *Asarum* (wild ginger). With dark green, glossy, evergreen, heart- or kidney-shaped leaves on thin stems, this plant gets its name from its ginger-like fragrance. Look for *A. canadense* or *A. europaeum*. It thrives best in moist, acidic soil in deep shade under rhododendrons or hydrangeas.

- *Bergenia cordifolia* (giant rockfoil). This has large, leathery, bright green leaves that turn coppery-red in fall. It thrives in sun or shade and sends up striking pink, red, white or purple flower heads in spring.

- *Cerastium tomentosum* (snow in summer). The soft gray leaves of this popular groundcover will rapidly form a low carpet of foliage on a sunny bank. Some gardeners use it to simulate a stream running over rocks. The white flowers that give it its common name are an added bonus. It grows 6 to 12 inches (15 to 30 cm) high.

- *Convallaria majalis* (lily-of-the-valley). Not the most original groundcover, but it is one of the most dependable and hardy. In spring, it puts out sweetly scented, white, bell-like flowers.

- *Cornus canadensis* (bunchberry). Native to North America, this is slower than other groundcovers to get established, but has attractive, broad foliage and white flowers in late spring followed by red berries in late summer. Grows best in light shade with lily-of-the-valley, epimedium or sweet woodruff. Hardy to Zone 5.

- *Cotoneaster dammeri*. This has glossy evergreen foliage and white flowers with small red berries in fall. An excellent groundcover for covering banks or trailing over low walls in full sun or partial shade.

- *Epimedium* (bishop's hat or barrenwort). Grown for its leaves, which are heart-shaped and held up on delicate, wiry stems, this also flowers, producing tiny pink or white blooms in spring. Its folk name, barrenwort, comes from the belief that it was supposed to be able to prevent conception. Hardy to Zone 4.

- *Galium odoratum* (sweet woodruff). This has nice white flowers and lacy foliage in spring and is the perfect choice for underscoring boxwood hedges or shrubs in the shady woodland border. It is a notorious colonizer. If planted in an unrestricted area, it will self-sow freely and spread rapidly. But perhaps that is precisely what you want.

- *Gaultheria procumbens* (wintergreen). A short evergreen plant with shiny green foliage, this produces small white flowers followed by scarlet berries. Excellent also for use in containers for winter interest. Thrives in partial shade.

- *Hedera helix* (English ivy). The easy answer to many cover-up problems, ivy will quickly clamber into trees, over walls and fences and cover large areas under shrubs. Evergreen, it forms a thick, leafy carpet, and it is indifferent to whether it is grown in sun or shade. While acknowledging its tremendous value as a woodland plant, critics tend to see ivy as a boring, monotonous choice for the home garden. But it does have its uses. Hardy to Zone 5.

- *Houttuynia cordata* 'Chameleon'. This has small, showy, heart-shaped leaves with yellow, green, bronze and pink coloring. It is a vigorous grower, especially in moist soil, and produces white flowers in summer. It grows 2 to 3 inches (5 to 7.5 cm) high. Hardy to Zone 4.

- *Hypericum calycinum* (St. John's wort). Too common for the taste of some gardeners, but very reliable, producing attractive leaves on low arching stems, and distinct yellow flowers for great summer color. Look for *H. calycinum*, which is not bothered about the quality of soil in which it is planted and flourishes in both sun or part shade. Hardy to Zone 5.

- *Lamium maculatum* (spotted dead nettle). The soft, green leaves have a greenish-white mottle or stripe and purple flowers. It will quickly form a mat of foliage in sun or light shade.

- *Lysimachia nummularia* (creeping jenny). One of the prettier groundcovers, this has soft yellow-green leaves and tiny, bright yellow flowers. Ideal for brightening up a dampish, semi-shady corner in summer, the trailing stems should be snipped to make the plant thicken up. It is also known by other names—moneywort, two penny grass, meadow runagates, string of sovereigns and wandering tailor.

- *Pachysandra terminalis* (Japanese spurge). Will do as thorough a job as ivy at covering ground with a thick carpet of handsome, evergreen foliage, only it will take longer to do it. Hardy and drought tolerant, Japanese spurge has creamy white flowers in late spring. It is especially useful in areas where nothing else will grow.

- *Vinca minor* (periwinkle). Probably the most widely grown groundcover and for a good reason—it does a steady, dependable job and requires minimal attention. Flourishing in shade or part sun, it spreads rapidly, rooting its trailing stems as it goes. The dainty, five-petal, lilac-blue flowers are not unattractive either.

Roses are a mess. They have not been bred for hardiness or healthiness. My goal is to put some hybrid vigor and disease resistance back into them. I hope for a nice flower, but the healthiness of the plant is always my first consideration.

—Jerry Twomey, Canadian breeder of such popular roses as 'All That Jazz', 'Sheer Elegance' and the 'Dream Series'

Fabulous Ferns

You may think a fern is a fern is a fern. Not so. It can come as a bit of a shock to discover just how many kinds of ferns are being commercially cultivated today. There's an ostrich fern, parsley fern, shield fern and

Japanese lady fern, as well as Korean rock fern, licorice fern, oak fern and champion's wood fern. Actually, there are no fewer than 132 kinds in commercial cultivation. Fabulous foliage plants for the shade, ferns, along with hostas, are the royalty of shade plants. The main role of ferns in the garden is to provide architectural form and foliage texture and contrast. We don't expect them to have colorful flowers, although some have patterned fronds. We mainly appreciate them for their reliable, long-lasting greenness and dependable structure. Where to begin? Here's a great list of proven winners to start with.

- *Adiantum aleuticum* (maidenhair fern). Sometimes sold as *Adiantum pedatum*, this has delicate, fan-shaped fronds and thin, black-ribbed stems. A supremely elegant plant, it is indispensable for adding a light, airy, romantic touch to the shade under trees. It grows about 2 feet tall (60 cm).

- *Athyrium nipponicum* 'Pictum' (Japanese painted fern). Sometimes listed as 'Metallicum', this has attractive, deep green fronds with decorative gray-pink markings that give the plant an almost metallic sheen. It grows to 1 to 2 feet (30 to 60 cm).

- *Dicksonia antarctica* (Tasmanian tree fern). This exotic specimen has huge fronds that make it look rather like a palm tree. Slow growing, it can eventually reach 15 feet (4.5 m), with a thick tree-like trunk 3 feet (90 cm) around. It is designated Zone 8, which means it needs to be brought into a frost-free environment over winter. Gardeners in mild areas can wrap their tree fern with burlap stuffed with straw.

- *Dryopteris*. Any of the durable workhorse *Dryopteris* ferns tend to define what the word "fern" means for most people. Notable ones include the marginal wood fern (*D. marginalis*), which has bright blue-green fronds, and the lacy crested broad buckler fern (*D. dilatata* 'Lepidota Cristata'). They grow to 18 to 24 inches (45 to 60 cm).

- *Matteuccia struthiopteris* (ostrich fern). Grows 3 to 4 feet (90 cm to 1.2 m) tall and gets its common name because the fronds look rather like the plumes of an ostrich. Also look for the deciduous cinnamon fern (*Osmunda cinnamonea*), which is somewhat similar to the ostrich fern but has cinnamon-colored fronds.

- *Osmunda regalis* (royal fern). Will ultimately reach 4 feet (1.2 m) and makes a very bold feature plant that provides structure in the garden.

- *Polystichum arcostichoides* (Christmas fern). The dark green fronds were once used for Christmas decorations, hence the name. It is still one of the most useful evergreen ferns. It grows to 18 inches (45 cm).

Pointers on Primulas

Primroses can be maddeningly perverse when you attempt to cultivate them in the garden. There are, however, ways to get some of the better forms of the more than 425 species of primula to take root in your garden. The hardy outdoor garden primrose is happiest growing in shaded places where the soil is fertile and dampish. There are some marvelous varieties available: drumsticks (*Primula denticulata*), dainty *P. auricula*, Asiatic primroses or the candelabra and giant cowslip types.

Primula seed is notoriously tricky, either losing its viability quickly or refusing to germinate until it has gone through the cold of winter. Here's a good tip: soak the seed on a wet tissue for 24 hours, put the whole thing in the refrigerator for two or three days, and then sow it in a heated propagator. Seems to work every time. Here are some other pointers on primulas.

- If I could grow only one kind of primula, it would have to be one of the candelabras (*Primula japonica*). These are the classiest of all the primulas to my mind. They are also fairly easy to grow, although you may have to be patient to develop an entire colony in a creekbed or on the banks of a stream or pond. This is where they flourish best, in moist soil cooled by the dappled shade of overhead trees. The candelabra primula gets its name from the way its flowers are beautifully arranged in neat tiers along stems that can stretch 18 to 24 inches (45 to 60 cm) high. Colors range from white to pink, red and apricot.
- The old-fashioned, double English primroses have multi-petaled, rose-like flowers. They thrive in moist, rich soil and must be protected from scorching sun. Look for popular cultivars such as 'Alan Robb' (pale apricot), 'April Rose' (deep red), 'Dawn Ansel' (white), 'Lilian Harvey' (rose-pink), 'Sunshine Susie' (golden yellow), 'Sue Jervis' (muted peach), 'Miss Indigo' (purple with white edges) and 'Quaker's Bonnet' (lavender-violet).
- Primula grows in a variety of conditions. Some prefer wet, boggy ground; others like growing in cool rockeries. The best location to grow the majority of primulas in a typical home garden is on the east side of the house. Rich soil in a cool, shady spot seems to suit most kinds. A spot under rhododendrons or deciduous trees is ideal. This gives the flowers plenty of warm sunlight in spring and protection from the hot sun in summer.
- To get your primulas off to a good start in spring, give them a shot of 20-20-20 liquid fertilizer, and 0-10-10 fertilizer in fall. It pays to dig in sand or crushed rock or peat moss at planting time to improve

drainage. Coastal gardeners need to be wary of making the soil too rich in organic matter, for it can become compact and soggy in winter and your primulas will rot. Watch for slugs, snails, cutworms, weevils and aphids—they can all be a problem.

- The auricula primulas (*P. auricula*) are considered by some experts to be the aristocrat of the primula family because of the intricate design of the flowers. They are more drought and cold resistant than other primulas and they thrive in slightly alkaline soil. Victorian gardeners used to construct special shelves in the garden—auricula theatres—to protect the flowers from weather and to showcase them better. Top hybrids to look for include 'Camelot' (purple), 'The Baron' (bright yellow with white center), 'Chorister' (white) and 'Matthew Yates' (deep red).

- If you're lucky enough to have a garden with a brook or pond, you could grow the giant cowslip (*Primula florindae*). This produces large, fragrant yellow blooms on stems 2 to 3 feet (60 to 90 cm) in summer.

- A primula everyone seems to fall in love with the moment they see it is the Chinese pagoda primrose (*Primula vialii*). This has short pink bottlebrush flower spikes with a distinctive red cone on top. Unfortunately, it does self-seed, but if you get it in the right spot you can enjoy it for years.

Magic Moments

You are sitting in the garden, not thinking of much, when all of a sudden, everything looks fantastic. The bluebells under the magnolia are phenomenal. The rhododendrons never looked lovelier. The dogwood is absolutely breathtaking. You feel the urge to rush to the phone. You want to call someone to invite them over to see this marvelous sight. Not to boast but to share the magic of the moment.

This kind of thing happens to gardeners all the time. Magic moments. A hushed interlude when the garden is suddenly, beautifully, spectacularly transformed into paradise. Call it a trick of the mind or a subtle change in light. Whatever it is, it is a marvelous thing that touches the heart. In my spring garden I am always slain by the awesome sight of late-afternoon sunlight streaming through the fresh green leaves of a maple, underscored by a dense carpet of deep blue grape hyacinths. And I can never get enough of how charming the

tiny purple flowers of aubrieta look as they mingle with the lime-green flowers of donkey-tail spurge.

May is such a magnificent month in the garden. June and July are superb with their luxurious, extravagant flushes of roses and clematis, but May is always so fresh and full of promise as herbaceous borders leaf out and tall banks of Solomon's seal rise up and the ripe buds on peonies begin to pop. Magic moments in the garden always make me want to call neighbors over to come and see. But it's a curious thing— they often don't see things the same way. Perhaps these moments in the garden are not just a case of seeing something beautiful, but more a personal recognition and response to beauty. If, as the late English cleric J.B. Phillips believed, God brings himself into focus through beauty, then the garden is certainly the place to have a close encounter with the divine.

Garden Design

Not everyone wants an English cottage garden with a cheerful jumble of flowers or a sweeping herbaceous border. Some long for a tropical paradise, a place of big, lush leaves and a taste of the exotic. Subtropical gardening is growing in popularity as more and more people realize that they can achieve the look they are after by using clumping bamboos, hardy ferns and palms, big-leafed perennials and all sorts of tender exotics in pots.

But no matter what style of gardening you choose, the basic premise always applies—match your planting to your site. One of the best ways to do this is to use plants native to your area, a growing trend in gardening, and this section includes a good working list of plants for West Coast gardeners.

Going Bananas: A Touch of the Tropics

Growing bananas is one of the easiest and fastest ways to turn your backyard into a tropical paradise. Hard to believe, perhaps, but tall, giant-leafed banana trees are no more difficult to grow in mild-winter gardens than most popular perennials such as hosta, daylilies and astilbe. In fact, in a sheltered Zone 7 garden, banana trees perform almost exactly like herbaceous perennials—growing rigorously in spring and summer and dying down to the ground in winter. Gardeners with a love for the exotic jungle look of tropical foliage have been growing banana trees successfully for years. Yet, while there are hundreds of varieties of banana trees, only one has proved hardy enough to tough it through winter and reliable enough to always put on a great show in summer—*Musa basjoo*, from southern Japan. If protected over winter, this will quickly grow to 12 to 14 feet (3.6 to 4.3 m) with minimal effort. Left unprotected, it will die down to the ground, but revive again in spring to grow to a modest height.

Don't expect to fill your fruit bowl with great bunches of delicious bananas from *Musa basjoo*. It does produce fruit once every four years, depending on how happily it is located, but the fruit doesn't taste very good. A few gardeners have tried their hand at growing another highly rated banana tree, the Abyssinian banana (*Ensete ventricosum*), which was particularly popular with green thumbs in England at the turn of the century. William Robinson, one of the most influential gardening advocates of the day, described the tree as the "greatest and noblest of all plants for the flower garden." Unfortunately, although it makes a spectacular feature plant, the Abyssinian banana is challenging to overwinter even in mild climates, primarily because of the shortage of sunlight. While it can be protected from the cold and damp, the lack of sunshine ultimately causes it to lose vigor and the tree invariably ends up rotting. For this reason, if it is grown it is usually planted as a bedding plant and treated like an annual.

What is not widely known about banana trees is that they are technically not a tree—they do not have a woody trunk like a regular tree, they just have a thick set of leaves that overlap each other to form a stiff stem. To get your banana tree safely through winter, build a cage of chicken wire around it and fill the cage with leaves or straw. Cover the top of the tree with plastic to keep it dry. This is the most labor-intensive method of overwintering a banana tree, but it is worth the extra effort because you end up with a much bigger, more robust tree the following year.

The increasing popularity of subtropical, jungle-like gardens is being referred to more and more as "exotic gardening" because the range of plant material being used has slowly been extended and become even more imaginative.

I'm not sure I know what is the right thing for you, but it's time you stood up for yourselves and stopped trying to copy gardens from pictures in coffee-table books.

—John Brookes, English garden designer

Key components of a subtropical mild-winter garden are still windmill palms (*Trachycarpus fortunei*), bamboo (various species) and yuccas. To flesh out the composition, hardy perennials and subshrubs that have a bold, tropical look can be added. These include gunnera, bear's breeches, rodgersia, pampas grass, fatsia, red-hot pokers, ligularia, hosta, astilbe, rheum, skunk cabbage, plume poppy and *Peltiphyllum peltatum* (umbrella plant). Other plants that make worthy companions include dahlias, impatiens and exotic bulbous plants, such as the giant Himalayan lily (*Cardiocrinum giganteum*) and various forms of Asiatic lily.

The plant palette now includes all sorts of tender and colorful exotics such as canna lilies, New Zealand flax (*Phormium tenax*), Tasmanian tree fern (*Dicksonia antarctica*), elephant's ears (*Colocasia esculenta*) and kahili ginger (*Hedychium*).

Gardeners with plenty of space have worked in big-leaf magnolia (*Magnolia macrophylla*) and one of the world's oldest trees, *Ginkgo biloba*, which has spectacular yellow foliage in fall. The imaginative garden doesn't stop there. Tender Chinese fan palms, such as *Livistona chinensis*, can be moved outdoors into the garden for summer along with exotic specimens like bird of paradise (*Strelitzia*). The castor bean plant (*Ricinus communis*) and angel's trumpet (*Brugmansia*), both of which are beautiful but poisonous, can also be worked into the overall scheme, along with more commonplace but striking foliage material such as spiderwort (*Tradescantia zebrina*), the purple-flowered cherry-pie plant (*Heliotropium arborescens*), the bright foliage of coleus and the chartreuse leaves of sweet potato (*Ipomoea batatus* 'Margarita'). The secret of exotic gardening is to plant specimens close together and have only the occasional flash of brilliant color for contrast with the lush, green foliage that makes up most of the garden.

None of this is totally new. Gardeners in Victorian England were passionate about subtropical gardening. Their love for palms was only exceeded by their enthusiasm for ferns, but they had an immense appreciation for all kinds of exotic plants. The Victorians were into "zone-denial"—the refusal to accept defined hardiness limits—long before the term was invented by today's gardeners.

Best of Bamboo

Bamboo is a wonderful plant for the garden. It adds an exotic, tropical look, provides a privacy screen and makes a pleasant sound when a breeze rustles through the leaves. What scares most gardeners is bamboo's reputation for being unstoppably invasive. It helps to know before you go shopping for bamboo that there are two main types—clumping and running. If you plant them side by side, the running bamboo will quickly overpower the less vigorous clumper as it starts to colonize the area.

To contain running bamboo, install a 2- to 3-foot (60- to 90-cm) high-density polyethylene plastic barrier around the root system at the time of planting. This has proven more effective than concrete or steel collars. The safest way to grow bamboo, so you enjoy the benefits without the headaches, is to plant it in containers. If you do this, remember to feed your bamboo with a balanced slow-release fertilizer so it doesn't starve; repot it every year or so into a slightly bigger container to accommodate the expanding root system or lift the plant, prune the roots back and repot; and wrap the pot in winter to protect the roots from freezing.

Here are 10 of the best bamboos for the home garden. The majority are extremely hardy. The more tender types, such as golden bamboo, tend to behave more like a herbaceous perennial, dying down in winter and reviving in spring.

- *Fargesia nitida* (blue fountain). This is a hardy clumping bamboo with fine-textured blue-gray leaves. It takes shade and grows to about 8 feet (2.4 m).

- *Phyllostachys aurea* (golden bamboo). Also known as the fishpole bamboo, this is ideal for screening as it grows 20 feet (6 m) and can be cut to the desired height by pruning the foliage. Some garden centers list it as very hardy, but bamboo nurseries report that it often dies back completely in very cold winters and regrows in the spring.

- *Phyllostachys bissetii*. The greenest and hardiest of all the bamboos, this has olive-green canes and big leaves that are a deep emerald color. A mid-size running bamboo, it grows to about 20 feet (6 m) and requires a barrier to stop the roots from invading.

- *Phyllostachys nigra* (black bamboo). This has glossy black stems that add drama to the garden. A running bamboo, it has small leaves and can grow to 25 feet (7.6 m).

- *Phyllostachys nigra* 'Megurochiku'. This has green culms with purplish-black grooves and behaves in colder areas more like a hardy perennial, dying down in winter and reviving in spring. It grows to 30 feet (9 m).

- *Phyllostachys vivax*. This is one of the largest timber bamboos and one of the most attractive because of its straight, large-diameter culms, which have a white band beneath each node. The leaves form a graceful mass and resemble feathers. The stems can soar to more than 30 feet (9 m). It is almost always in short supply. Grow it in full sun to obtain maximum height.

- *Pleioblastus viridistriatus* (dwarf greenstripe bamboo). Stunning! Grows to 3 feet (90 cm) in sun or shade. The new leaves in spring are golden-yellow with green stripes about 7 inches (18 cm) long.

- *Pseudosasa japonica* (Japanese arrow bamboo). A classic in the bamboo family, this has slender, elegant stems and large green leaves. It thrives in sun or shade and is an ideal choice for erosion control. It grows 10 to 12 feet (3 to 3.6 m).

- *Sasa veitichii* (silver-edge bamboo). This has large, dark green leaves with white markings that give them a striking appearance. With the first frost, the leaves turn an attractive tan color at the edges. It is a determined runner, so it is essential to install a deep barrier. It grows to 2 to 4 feet (60 cm to 1.2 m).

- *Semiarundinaria fastuosa*. Also known as the Narihira bamboo, this has a stately presence and is an excellent choice for screening. A running bamboo, it has dark green leaves and grows 20 to 25 feet (6 to 7.5 m). It is not very hardy and needs to be well mulched over winter.

Top Native Plants for a Coastal Garden

Interested in building a West Coast garden entirely out of native plants? This is an idea that has a lot of appeal among gardeners who like to be able to take visitors from other parts of the world around their garden and point to species that are truly native to the region. Here's a simple guide to some of the best native plants for the job.

Broadleaf Evergreens

- *Andromeda polifolia*. A low-spreading evergreen with leathery, lance-shaped to oblong-shaped leaves, this has small, pinkish flowers. It grows 2 1/2 feet (75 cm) high in boggy ground and swamp-like conditions.

- *Arbutus menziesii* (Pacific madrone). Bright red papery bark and white flowers in spring. Requires full sun and excellent drainage. Grows to 30 feet (9 m).
- *Gaultheria shallon* (salal). White to pink flowers in spring followed by purple fruit. Grows to 3 to 4 feet (90 cm to 1.2 m).
- *Mahonia aquifolium* (Oregon grape). Deep, shiny green leaves and yellow flowers in spring followed by bluish-black berries. Grows to 6 feet (1.8 m).
- *Mahonia nervosa* (longleaf Oregon grape). Yellow flowers in spring and glossy, slender leaves that turn red in winter. Grows best in shade. Grows to 2 feet (60 cm).
- *Phyllodoce empetriformis* (pink mountain heather). The most common mountain heather on the coast. It has pink, bell-shaped flowers. Likes exposed, rocky sites. Grows to 15 inches (38 cm) high.
- *Rhododendron macrophyllum* (Pacific rhododendron). Big, leathery foliage and pale pink to rose-purple flowers. Grows to 10 feet (3 m) or more.

Conifers

- *Abies lasiocarpa* (subalpine fir). Conical-shaped tree with bluish, gray-green foliage. Grows to 35 to 45 feet (10.5 to 13.5 m).
- *Chamaecyparis nootkatensis* (yellow cedar). Pyramid shape with bluish-green needles and slightly pendulous habit. Grows to 60 to 90 feet (18 to 27 m).
- *Thuja plicata* (western red cedar). Popular hedging conifer. Prefers cool, moist soil. Grows to 100 feet plus (30 m) if left unpruned.
- *Tsuga heterophylla* (western hemlock). Fast-growing tree with graceful form and dark green foliage. Grows to 120 to 180 feet (37 to 55 m).
- *Tsuga mertensiana* (mountain hemlock). It has dense gray-green foliage and is ideal for growing in the shade. Grows to 50 to 90 feet (15 to 27 m).

Deciduous Trees

- *Acer circinatum* (vine maple). Can be a small shrub or medium-size tree if left unpruned. Brilliant fall color. Grows to 10 to 30 feet (3 to 9 m).
- *Acer macrophyllum* (big-leaf maple). Shade tree with 12-inch (30-cm) leaves. Grows to 30 to 90 feet (9 to 27 m).
- *Alnus rubra* (red alder). Often found on banks of streams and rivers, it is fast growing with smooth, gray bark. Grows to 45 to 50 feet (13.5 to 15 m).

- *Betula papyrifera* (paper birch). Bright white peeling bark and attractive yellow fall foliage. Grows to 30 to 40 feet (9 to 12 m).
- *Cornus nutallii* (Pacific dogwood). Lovely white flowers in spring and dense foliage. Grows to 40 feet (12 m).
- *Quercus garryana* (Garry oak). Large tree with exceptionally graceful form as it matures. Grows 50 to 60 feet (15 to 18 m).
- *Rhamnus purshiana* (cascara tree). Dark, glossy green leaves and greenish-yellow flowers. Grows to 20 to 40 feet (6 to 12 m).

Deciduous Shrubs

- *Amelanchier alnifolia* (Saskatoon berry). Fragrant clusters of white flowers in May followed by black berries. Good fall foliage. Grows to 6 to 10 feet (1.8 to 3 m).
- *Cornus stolonifera* (red osier dogwood). Good shrub for winter interest because of brilliant red stems. White flowers in spring. Grows to 6 to 10 feet (1.8 to 3 m).
- *Lonicera involucrata* (black twinberry). Yellow, tube-shaped flowers are followed by pairs of black berries. Grows to 6 to 8 feet (1.8 to 2.4 m).
- *Myrica gale* (sweet gale). Aromatic wetlands shrub with yellow catkins that appear before the leaves. Grows to 3 to 5 feet (90 cm to 1.5 m).
- *Philadelphus lewisii* (mock orange). Fragrant white flowers in June. Grows to 8 feet (2.4 m).
- *Physocarpus capitatus* (ninebark). This has distinctive three-lobed leaves, loose bark and lots of white flowers in spring. Grows to 8 feet (2.4 m).
- *Ribes sanguineum* (red-flowering currant). One of the most famous native shrubs with red flowers in early spring. Grows to 8 to 10 feet (2.4 to 3 m).
- *Salix hookeriana* (Hooker's willow). Noted for its large catkins. Grows to 20 feet (6 m).
- *Salix scouleriana* (Scouler's willow). A little hardier and grows to 30 feet (9 m).
- *Sambucus racemosa* (red elderberry). Has creamy white flowers and then clusters of red berries. *S. cerulea* (blue elderberry) produces edible blue berries. Both grow to 8 to 10 feet (2.4 to 3 m).
- *Sorbus sitchensis* (Sitka mountain ash). Valued for its clusters of white flowers and red berry-like fruit. Grows to 15 feet (4.5 m).
- *Symphoricarpos albus* (snowberry). Low-growing, upright shrub that tolerates poor soils and has white berries. Grows to 2 feet (60 cm).
- *Vaccinium membranaceum* (black huckleberry). Considered the most delicious of the huckleberries, this also has red-to-purple fall foliage. Grows to 5 feet (1.5 m). Also check out red huckleberry (*V. parviflorum*), which has orange-red edible berries and grows to 12 feet (3.6 m).

Roses

- *Rosa nutkana* (Nootka rose). This has pink flowers and purplish hips. Grows to 3 to 5 feet (90 cm to 1.5 m).
- *Rosa woodsii* (Wood's rose). With pale pink flowers, this is very hardy and fairly shade tolerant. Grows to 3 to 5 feet (90 cm to 1.5 m).

Groundcovers

- *Asarum caudatum* (wild ginger). Heart-shaped green leaves and brownish-purple flowers. Grows to 6 to 10 inches (15 to 25 cm).
- *Cornus canadensis* (creeping dogwood). Also known as bunchberry, this has white, dogwood-like flowers followed by red berries. Grows to 6 to 9 inches (15 to 23 cm).
- *Fragaria chiloensis* (coastal strawberry). This has shiny, deep green leaves with a hard, leathery look to them, and forms a dense groundcover in time. Grows to 6 to 12 inches (15 to 30 cm).
- *Linnaea borealis* (twinflower). Ideal evergreen groundcover for the woodland garden, this has pink, trumpet-shaped flowers. Grows to 6 inches (15 cm) high.

Vines

- *Lonicera ciliosa* (western trumpet honeysuckle). Hummingbirds love the orange-yellow flowers. Grows to 10 to 12 feet (3 to 3.6 m).

Ferns

- *Adiantum pedatum* (maidenhair fern). Popular ornamental fern with graceful fan-shaped leaves with purple-black ribs. Grows to 1 1/2 to 2 feet (45 to 60 cm).
- *Blechnum spicant* (deer fern). Large architectural fern with big fronds. Grows to 3 feet (90 cm).
- *Polystichum munitum* (sword fern). A common sight in woodlands, this has evergreen fronds and is sometimes used in flower arranging. Grows to 3 to 4 feet (90 cm to 1.2 m).

Perennials

- *Anemone occidentalis* (western pasque flower). Flowers range from white to yellow and pink. Grows to 18 inches (45 cm).
- *Balsamorhiza sagittata* (spring sunflower). Produces bright, showy flowers and is able to thrive in poor, dry soils. Grows to 12 to 18 inches (30 to 45 cm).
- *Delphinium menziesii* (Menzie's larkspur). This has blue to purple flowers and is good for naturalizing in meadow-type settings. Grows to 18 inches (45 cm).

- *Dicentra formosa* (Pacific bleeding heart). Heart-shaped pinkish-purple flowers on the familiar lacy foliage. Grows to 18 to 24 inches (45 to 60 cm).
- *Dodecatheon pulchellum* (shooting star). With attractive, cyclamen-like, pink to purple flowers, this deserves more use in home gardens. It thrives in moist meadows and rocky ground. Grows to 18 inches (45 cm).
- *Erythronium oregonum* (white fawn lily). This bears white flowers seen in forest glades all over coastal B.C. It has glossy leaves and is ideal for shade. Grows to 8 to 10 inches (20 to 25 cm).
- *Sisyrinchium angustifolium* (blue-eyed grass). Blue to purple flowers with a tiny yellow center. Grows to 16 inches (40 cm).
- *Trillium ovatum* (western trillium). Lovely white flowers in spring held above three beautifully structural leaves. Grows to 12 inches (30 cm).

Wetland Plants

- *Carex obnupta* (slough sedge). This thrives in marshy areas and looks like an ornamental grass. Grows to 2 feet (60 cm).
- *Juncus effusus* (common rush). Brings a touch of class to boggy ground with its slender decorative stems. Grows to 30 inches (75 cm).
- *Scirpus acutus* (bulrush). A plant that will thrive in a pond as well as on the banks, its stems grow as tall as 5 feet (1.5 m).
- *Typha latifolia* (cattail). Distinguished by its brown, spongy seedhead at the end of erect stalks. Grows to 4 to 6 feet (1.2 to 1.8 m).

The Gardener's Credo: Right Plant, Right Place

The biggest mistake even some experienced gardeners make is putting plants in the wrong place. One of the most important rules of gardening is to get the right plant in the right place. It is amazing how often plants that need full sun and fast-draining soil get plonked in dappled shade in heavy clay soil. Or plants that need plenty of moisture at their feet find themselves gasping for a drink in hot, sandy, porous soil. You'd think it wouldn't happen, especially with the improvement in plant labeling, but it does.

More plants die from misplanting than are killed by insects, diseases or inadequate watering. For example, people still insist on growing sun-lovers like petunias and pelargoniums on cool, shady balconies or shade-lovers like begonias and impatiens on blisteringly hot, west-facing decks and patios. This is partly because we are not getting in touch with our gardens at ground level. We don't take the time to calmly walk our gardens and identify those areas that languish in deep shade most of the day or spots where water drains away very slowly after a moderate rain.

We need to do this exploratory analysis before we go shopping for plants. Instead, most of us race down to the garden center, look around until we see some strikingly beautiful plant (usually something in full bloom) that catches our fancy, then plant it where everyone can see what a superb specimen we've just acquired. The problem is, the plant may hate its new location and immediately embark on a slow descent into disease and death the moment it is planted.

Another problem is planting only according to light requirements. But plants need much more than the right amount of sunlight to become healthy, mature specimens; they also need the right cultural conditions at ground level: acidic or alkaline soil, fast-draining or moisture-retentive soil, and a reasonable mix of essential nutrients—nitrogen, phosphorus and potassium.

The consequence of all this is that plants die, people get put off gardening, and garden centers get blamed unfairly for selling lousy plants. It doesn't have to be that way.

To help your search for the right plant for a specific location this spring, here at a glance are plants for special purposes. There's no room for a lot of detail here, but this guide will give you some idea of your options as you start your search.

Plants for Light Shade

Aquilegia (columbine)
Astilbe (false spirea)
Camellia japonica
Dicentra spectabilis (bleeding heart)
Galium (sweet woodruff)
Geranium (cranesbill)
Hosta (plantain lily)
Hydrangea
Impatiens (busy lizzies)
Kirengeshoma (waxbells)
Pulmonaria (lungwort)
Rhododendron
Viburnum plicatum (Japanese snowball)

Plants for Full Sun

Achillea (yarrow)
Artemisia 'Powis Castle'
Coreopsis (tickseed)
Crocosmia (montbretia)
Delphinium

Gaura lindheimeri
Hemerocallis (daylilies)
Liatris (gayfeather)
Monarda (bee balm)
Pelargonium (annual geranium)
Petunia
Phlox paniculata
Sedum spectabile (stonecrop)
Stachys byzantina (lamb's ears)
Tagetes (marigold)

Plants for Heavy, Clay Soils

Astilbe (false spirea)
Aucuba
Forsythia
Hosta (plantain lily)
Ribes sanguineum (flowering currant)
Skimmia japonica
Stachys macrantha
Viburnum
Weigela

Plants for Moist Areas

Caltha pedatum (marsh marigold)
Gunnera manicata
Hosta (plantain lily)
Iris laevigata
Ligularia
Osmunda regalis (royal fern)
Peltiphyllum peltatum (umbrella plant)
Primula japonica (primrose)
Rheum palmatum (ornamental rhubarb)
Rodgersia pinnata
Zantedeschia aethiopica (calla lily)

Drought-tolerant Plants

Artemisia (wormwood)
Echinops (globe thistle)
Eryngium (sea holly)
Eschscholzia (California poppy)
Lavandula (lavender)
Leucanthemum x *superbum*
Liatris (gayfeather)

Pelargonium (annual geranium)
Rudbeckia (black-eyed susan)
Sedum spectabile (stonecrop)
shasta daisies
Stachys byzantina (lamb's ears)
Yucca

Plants for Tumbling over Walls

Aubrieta (rock cress)
Campanula cochleariifolia (fairy thimbles)
Erica/Calluna (heather)
Euphorbia myrsinites (donkey-tail spurge)
Iberis sempervirens (candytuft)
Phlox subulata
Saponaria (soapwort)

Plants to Espalier against a Wall or Fence

Ceanothus (wild lilac)
Chaenomeles japonica (quince)
Cotoneaster horizontalis
Pyracantha (firethorn)

Plants with Aromatic Foliage

Choisya ternata (Mexican orange blossom)
Geranium macrorrhizum (cranesbill)
Lavandula (lavender)
Melianthus major (peanut butter plant)
Mentha (mint)
Monarda (bee balm)
Santolina (lavender cotton)

Plants with Striking Red Flowers

Astilbe 'Fanal'
Crocosmia 'Lucifer'
Dahlia 'Bishop of Llandaff'
Lychnis chalcedonica (Maltese cross)
Monarda 'Gardenview Scarlet' (bee balm)
Paeonia 'Karl Rosenfeld' (peony)
Papaver orientale (poppy)
Pelargonium (annual geranium)
Rhododendron 'Taurus'
Salvia splendens (sage)

Plants with Outstanding Variegated Foliage

Astrantia major 'Sunningdale Variegated'
Cornus alba 'Elegantissima' (dogwood)
Hosta 'Frances Williams'
Phlox 'Norah Leigh'
Scrophularia 'Variegata'

Plants with Purple Foliage

Anthriscus sylvestris 'Ravenswing'
Cotinus coggygria (smoke bush)
Euphorbia 'Chameleon' (spurge)
Heuchera 'Palace Purple' (coral bells)
Physocarpus opulifolius 'Diabolo'
Salvia officinalis 'Atropurpureum' (sage)

Plants with Blue Flowers

Aconitum (monkshood)
Campanula (bellflower)
Centaura montana (cornflower)
Corydalis flexuosa
Delphinium
Eryngium (sea holly)
Geranium 'Johnson's Blue' (cranesbill)
Helictotrichon sempervirens (blue oat grass)
Meconopsis (poppy)
Nepeta 'Dropmore Blue'
Polemonium (Jacob's ladder)
Salvia 'May Night' (sage)
Scabiosa 'Butterfly Blue' (pincushion flower)

Plants with Yellow Flowers

Achillea (yarrow)
Coreopsis 'Moonbeam' (tickseed)
Corydalis lutea
Helianthus (perennial sunflower)
Hemerocallis 'Stella de Oro' (daylily)
Hypericum (St. John's wort)
Lysimachia punctata (yellow loosestrife)
Oenothera tetragona (evening primrose)
Rudbeckia (black-eyed susan)
Verbascum bombyciferum

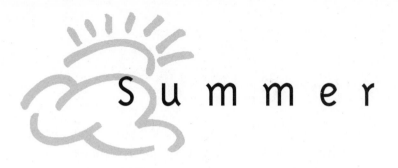

Summer

The Red Wheelbarrow

so much depends
upon

a red wheel
barrow

glazed with rain
water

beside the white
chickens.

—William Carlos Williams

In the Garden

- Sow cucumber, endive, green onions, kohlrabi, rutabaga and cress directly into the soil. Move tomatoes, melon, asparagus, peppers and eggplant to a permanent well-limed location in the garden.

- Prune back wisteria (now two months after flowering) by cutting side shoots back to five or six buds, or about 6 inches (15 cm) from the main branch.

- Feed roses with a well-balanced rose food. Remember roses also like to be well watered without being waterlogged.

- Eliminate weeds. Spend 10 minutes a week snapping off morning glory and horsetail shoots as close to the ground as you can.

- Trim hedges and groundcovers.

- Feed annuals with a half-strength solution of 20-20-20 once a week.

- Water wisely. Lawns will bounce back if allowed to dry out. They need only about an inch (2.5 cm) a week. Containers, hanging baskets and window boxes need almost daily watering.

- Remove excess fruit on peach and apple trees.

- Pinch-prune chrysanthemums to promote bushiness and deadhead roses and flowering bedding plants daily.

- Collect seed from perennials for propagation in seed trays in early fall.

- Cut bouquets of flowers to bring indoors and keep deadheading roses and flowering annuals such as marigolds, impatiens, petunias, snapdragons and pelargoniums.

- Harvest vegetables and pick raspberries and blackberries.

- Take a few pelargonium cuttings and sow wallflower seeds for next spring.

- Snip the finished stems of daylilies.

- Cut back your climbing hydrangea once it has finished flowering.

- Take an objective look at your garden and see if color schemes are clashing and if you need to add midsummer flowering perennials to achieve a natural sequence of blooms and color continuity.

- Patrol the garden, keeping an eye out for bugs, weeds, plants under stress and color clashes.

- Rhodos and azaleas are especially vulnerable in summer to drought. Water regularly and feed with 4-12-8 fertilizer.

- In mild-winter areas, sow lettuce and radish in midsummer for fall use. Sow cabbage, broccoli, spinach and Brussels sprouts for winter-spring use.

- Water newly installed trees and shrubs regularly; they are especially vulnerable to drying out for two or three years after planting.

- Conserve water by spreading a mulch over bare soil once it is thoroughly moist.

- Cut old raspberry canes back to ground level but leave younger canes, which will be slightly green. They will bear next year's fruit.

- Deadhead faded gladioli. This helps corms grow and rebloom next year.

- Pinch out the top bud of tomato plants and use fertilizer with a relatively low nitrogen content. This will direct the plant's energy into ripening fruit instead of growing more leaves.

- Make a note of what perennials you plan to relocate or divide come the cool days of mid-September.

3 Projects for Summer

1. Make a fun "food garden" container. Plant chocolate cosmos (*Cosmos atrosanguineus*) with a cherry-pie plant (*Heliotropium*) and add assorted mints such as apple mint, chocolate mint and pineapple mint. Consider including a pineapple lily (*Eucomis bicolor*), which has a pineapple-shaped flower. The cosmos flowers smell like chocolate, the heliotrope smells like cherry pie and the mints all have delicious aromas.

2. Divide bearded irises. Lift dense clumps. Cut away young, healthy rhizomes and throw away old, diseased pieces. Each division should have a firm rhizome and a fan of healthy, green leaves. Space divisions about 18 inches (45 cm) apart in compost-enriched soil. Water well.

3. This is a great time to increase your plant stock. Take pelargonium, hebe and lavender cuttings. Also, discover how easy it is to root such shrubs as choisya and hardy fuchsia from small tip cuttings. You can also try your hand at layering, which is another way of propagating plants like rhododendron, pieris, daphne, clematis and magnolia. Pick a supple branch low to the ground. Make a slanted cut or slice a sliver of bark from the underside, then bend the branch down into the soil and peg it firmly in place. It will form roots, at which time it can be severed from the parent plant.

In Defense of the Ordinary

"What's the name of that lovely shrub with red and green leaves you see everywhere at the moment? I'd like it for my garden." How refreshing to meet someone who is actually excited about a plant as commonplace as *Photinia fraseri*. I remember the spring that photinia's rich red and green foliage caught my eye for the first time and I thought the same thing: "What a fine plant."

You do indeed see photinia everywhere. It has all sorts of great uses: it can be grown as a neatly clipped hedge; a feature shrub in the mixed border; an espalier against a wall, fence or trellis; or a single-stemmed tree.

In our rush to embrace the new and unusual, the rare and exotic, we often forget or overlook the value of plants like photinia that have served us faithfully for years without faltering. The sad thing is that many of these reliable, tried-and-true plants end up being relegated to the B-league, where only new gardeners get excited about their performance. So, in defense of the ordinary, the unfairly maligned, the unappreciated beauty, the wrongly rejected, here's a plea for plants that often get lost in the shuffle but deserve a little more respect and a lot less criticism.

Isn't it strange how dependability, simplicity and longevity so often get dismissed as boring and predictable? With its sunny, eager-to-please disposition, the plain yellow or orange marigold was for many people the plant that first got them into gardening as children and rewarded them with the success that encouraged them to keep going. Easy to grow from seed, marigolds flower perfectly and inexhaustibly all summer, often in the most hostile locations where they are exposed to extreme heat and drought. They are rejected as a cut flower because of their slightly pungent aroma, but this is mainly concentrated in the foliage. Strip away the leaves and you have a perfectly house-trained flower. Or, of course, you can always grow the signet marigolds (*Tagetes tenuifolia*), such as 'Tangerine Gem', 'Lemon Gem' and 'Red Gem', which have citrus-scented foliage and dainty attractive flowers. But what we often forget about marigolds is that they are not all yellow and orange and not all of them have round, carnation-like flower heads. There is an all-white African marigold called 'Vanilla', and French marigolds now come in an assortment of interesting colors. 'Naughty Marietta', for instance, has big golden flowers with maroon blotches, while 'Red Marietta' has mahogany-red blooms.

What's wrong with deep, full-blooded, red peonies such as 'Karl Rosenfeld', 'America' and 'Dandy Dan'? Yes, 'Sarah Bernhardt' is a lovely apple-blossom pink and there are some excellent whites, such as 'Mother's Choice', 'Leto' and 'White Sands', but haven't we gone overboard in our fascination with coral and peach and soft pinks? Surveys show that men, for whatever reason, are especially fond of red flowers. Perhaps more of them would be gardening if they were shown brilliant red peonies such as 'Red Charm' and 'Felix Supreme' and 'Mikado'.

This defense of striking red flowers also applies to rhododendrons such as 'Vulcan', 'Taurus', 'Temple Bell' and 'Jean Marie de Montague'. Pelargonium, like the poor marigold, also suffers unfairly from rejection. Yet pelargoniums (better known as summer geraniums to most of us) can look remarkable in a row of terracotta pots on a window sill and they also play a reliable role as the central architecture in a hanging basket.

Many of the best gardens in England make unapologetic use of that old-fashioned perennial, lady's mantle, allowing it to seed itself here, there and everywhere. What a pity then that after a few years we seem to get bored and forget how marvelously it serves us at the front of the border or as a groundcover, with its uncanny ability to hold raindrops like diamonds and produce billowing clouds of yellow-green flowers. And thinking of groundcovers, how many of us stop to admire the hard work of periwinkle, lily-of-the-valley, and plain green ivy? All kinds of reliable perennials jump back every spring to fill our gardens with lush foliage and form while we are out racing around nurseries looking for some new and unusual hybrid. So a word of praise and appreciation for hostas, astilbes, daylilies, foxgloves, bleeding hearts, solomon's seal, campanula, hardy geraniums and sedums. Thank you for your utter dependability.

What a pity the two summer-flowering shrubs, potentilla and spirea, are so quickly rejected as boring "gas-station" landscaping. The problem is they are left to fend for themselves in the most exposed, hostile locations in the blistering heat of summer. They understandably end up looking completely tatty and exhausted. Grown where they can enjoy the protection of some light shade in the afternoon, they become very different plants. There's a good assortment of potentillas, including 'Abbotswood' (white), 'Red Robin' (red), 'Pink Princess' (light pink) and 'Primrose Beauty' (golden yellow). 'Goldflame' is a very hardy variety of spirea with bronze leaves that turn a golden yellow as they mature. Other spireas to check out include 'Magic Carpet', 'Anthony Waterer' and 'Little Princess'.

As if it doesn't get walked on enough, grass is under perpetual attack from some quarters nowadays, mainly because it has the nerve to ask for water and a haircut once every couple of weeks. It's really not fair. Grass makes a valuable contribution to our environment—giving off oxygen, cooling the air and quickly soaking up rainwater. But more than this, lawns are great for playing on and very soothing on the eye. They bring a stillness and calm to the garden and they are still one of the most important plants for giving a neighborhood a sense of connectedness and cohesion. We can use ornamental grass to create mow-free lawns and there is no doubt that many yards could use more shrubs and trees and less lawn, but there is still a place for a stretch of plain green grass in the garden.

Don't forget the Tubby the Tuber of garden plants. Along with gladioli, dahlias have suffered some serious shunning over the years, mostly from gardeners who find the colors hard to place or who can't be bothered lifting and storing the tender tubers in fall. But there is no better plant to work hand in hand with asters and ornamental grasses for a much-needed lift of color in late summer. It is so refreshing to find lifetime gardeners who have grown rare and exotic specimens . . . but still insist on finding room for a few dahlias.

Aucuba japonica, through no fault of its own, always causes me to wince because . . . well, it was always planted around outdoor washrooms in parks and gas stations in England. Sorry. Yet aucuba is such a reliable evergreen shrub for brightening up shaded areas with its cream and green variegated foliage. It really deserves more appreciation—from me at any rate. There's a whole bunch of other shrubs that do a similar job and never get thanked for it. So a word of appreciation for the silverleaf dogwood (*Cornus alba* 'Elegantissima'), which has lovely variegated foliage, and *Rhododendron ponticum* with its cream-edged leaves and *Euonymus* 'Gaiety'. Also a quick nod of recognition to the splendid work done by *Viburnum davidii*, which always looks so comfortable tucked under the bellies of larger rhododendrons and structural shrubs like *Pieris japonica*, yet another largely unsung hero of the garden with its wonderful, flame-red new foliage in spring.

The climbing hydrangea with its sprays of white flowers is impressive and we all love the fancy blue lacecaps, but the simple mophead hydrangea could definitely use more appreciation. The white-flowering 'Annabelle' is terrific and plant connoisseurs can rave about the jungle-like elegance of *Hydrangea aspera*, *H. sargentiana* and *H. quercifolia*, but in all of this enthusiasm, let's save a kind word about mopheads like 'Nikko Blue' and 'Merritt's Beauty.'

The Shrubs of Summer

After spring's breathtaking burst of color, it is now up to other shrubs to carry the show into summer. Buddleia, potentilla, hydrangea, hibiscus, viburnum, hypericum, caryopteris and weigela—they all have their role to play in order to complete the garden picture and sustain the sequence of color and flow of foliage and form from June to September.

Buddleia: The Butterfly Magnet

Buddleia davidii (butterfly bush) gets its name not because its flowers or foliage look anything like a butterfly, but because it has the uncanny knack of attracting butterflies. It does this by waving around long, arching stems of sweet-scented cone-shaped flowers. The nervous butterfly apparently feels some security when it lands in the long arms of the buddleia. It will also attract hummingbirds. Grow buddleia anywhere you like, but if you want to make it very happy, plant it in loose, loamy, ordinary garden soil that has good drainage in a spot that gets lots of sun. The only thing buddleia won't tolerate is too much lime.

Buddleia davidii comes in a rich variety of colors. It flowers from midsummer to fall and is also known as the summer lilac. Top names include 'Black Knight' (dark violet-purple), 'Royal Red' (rich red), 'Pink Delight' (bright pink), and 'Harlequin' (variegated leaf). Excellent whites include 'White Cloud', 'Peace', 'White Bouquet' and 'White Profusion'. Hardy to Zone 6, they grow 10 to 15 feet (3 to 4.5 m) in fertile, well-drained soil. There are two dwarf forms, 'Nanho Blue' and 'Nanho Purple', both of which grow to 4 feet (1.2 m).

Buddleia alternifolia is a very decorative form of butterfly bush. It is known as the fountain butterfly bush because it produces a cascade of arching branches covered with tightly knotted mauve flowers, which start to come into bloom in late spring or early summer. With a little effort, it can be nicely pruned to form an attractive small tree in the mixed border. *B. alternifolia* looks particularly handsome when trained in this way.

Heavenly Hydrangeas

Hydrangeas have been called the "queen of flowering shrubs." They are versatile shrubs that fit into almost any kind of garden scheme. They look most natural in woodland settings, where they enjoy the protection of high trees that allow in plenty of dappled sunshine. They thrive in light shade, but they are frequently grown in full sun.

Leave the faded flower heads on your mophead and lacecap hydrangeas over winter and prune the bushes for size and to encourage healthy new stems in mid-spring before the plants start to show signs of vigorous growth. First take out old, unproductive stems along with any branches that are dead or look weak and spindly. Make your cuts as close to the ground as possible. Next, shorten healthy stems back to a pair of healthy buds. New shoots will grow from these buds. Climbing hydrangeas can be pruned back to keep them in check after they have finished flowering.

The popular mopheads, *Hydrangea macrophylla* (also known as *hortensias*), have large, globular flower heads. Top cultivars include 'Nikko Blue', a prolific bloomer that produces turquoise-blue globe-shaped flowers in acid soil and has shell-pink blooms in neutral soil; 'Forever Pink', a dwarf variety growing only 3 feet (90 cm) high and producing pink flowers in May; and 'Merritt's Beauty', noted for its red flowers and robust growth habit. You will also find 'Hamburg' and 'King George', and 'Kluis Superba'. All these grow to about 4 feet (1.2 m).

Lacecap hydrangeas have slightly more decorative flower heads with dense centers skirted by a light garland of single, flat flowers. Look for 'Mariesii Perfecta' and 'Mariesii Variegata'. Those in Zone 6 microclimates or warmer could try growing one of the most outstanding of all lacecaps: *Hydrangea serrata* 'Bluebird'. This has lovely blue flowers that fade to a delicate pink if the soil is allowed to become more alkaline.

Hydrangea 'Annabelle' is one of the most reliable. It is hardy to Zone 3 and produces very large white flower heads from July into October. Hills-of-snow hydrangea (*H. arborescens* 'Grandiflora') is very similar but grows slightly taller, reaching 5 to 10 feet (1.5 to 3 m) and producing large white trusses of flowers from July to September.

The peegee hydrangea (*H. paniculata* 'Grandiflora') grows 8 feet (2.4 m) high and produces masses of large, cascading, creamy white or light pink, cone-shaped flowers from August until frost. It can be trained into a small tree.

> *If you're doing some really dull plant combination like putting silver and pink together—very safe, but yawnsville—stop, and do the most outlandish thing you can possibly think of and you'll jolt yourself out of your status quo.*
>
> —Marco Polo Stefano, director of New York's Wave Hill Garden

The Wonder of Weigela

When you start to design a garden, it's important to think about shrubs not only to give shape and structure, but to go the extra mile and give something a little extra. Weigela is one of the best at doing that. In addition to being a compact, low-maintenance, pest-free shrub that produces sweet-scented clusters of foxglove-like flowers in summer, it also has attractive, lush green foliage and an uncanny knack for attracting hummingbirds. Thriving in full sun or light shade, it prefers rich, fertile, well-drained soil, although it won't sulk if you plant it in average to poor soil. To keep weigela flourishing year after year, enrich the soil with well-rotted manure or compost every second year, and prune the bush regularly to maintain its shape and vigor.

There are a few outstanding cultivars. The best-known member of the weigela family is 'Bristol Ruby'. This grows about 5 or 6 feet (1.5 or 1.8 m) tall, which makes it easy to accommodate in a medium-sized garden. 'Minuet' is a more compact variety that grows less than 3 feet (90 cm) tall and produces light pink flowers against a background of green leaves with a purple tinge.

My favorite is 'Red Prince', which has wonderful, crimson-red, tubular flowers for a six-week period from June to July and blooms sporadically in August. It can be used to create an informal hedge or add color to dull banks and berms. 'Red Prince' can also serve a useful role in the mixed border or shubbery, where its crimson flowers can be enjoyed in June, leaving other plants to hold the stage in May and July. Here are a few other cultivars to check out.

- 'White Knight' and 'Bristol Snowflake' both grow to about 5 feet (1.5 m) and have white flowers in June.

- Pink-flowering weigela include 'Victoria' (dark pink), 'Pink Princess' (light pink) or 'Purpurea' (purple-pink). The foliage of 'Purpurea' has a purple-green tone, while the leaves of 'Victoria' have a definite bronze hue, heightening the color of the pink flowers. They all grow to 4 to 5 feet (1.2 to 1.5 m).

- For something unusual, how about 'Carnaval', which has red, pink and white flowers on the same bush. It grows to 3 or 4 feet (90 cm to 1.2 m) and flowers in June.

- The best of the variegated weigelas is 'Variegata', which has green leaves with deep yellow edges. Like all variegated forms, this thrives best in light shade. It has rose-colored flowers in June and grows 4 feet (1.2 m) high.

The Power of Potentilla

No plant is perfect. Some have great flowers but insignificant foliage. Others have lovely evergreen leaves but flower for a disappointingly short time. Gardeners can be very demanding. It is no joke that you can often hear them at the garden center asking for a plant that blooms perpetually, requires no maintenance, has no disease or pest problems . . . and grows only 2 feet (60 cm) high.

Potentilla is not the perfect shrub, but it comes pretty close. For a start, it has the longest flowering period of all garden shrubs. It is capable of pumping out yellow, orange, red, white or pink blooms (depending on the variety) from early summer through to fall. It thrives in sun or light shade in the poorest of soils, is very drought tolerant and has an amazing immunity to pests and disease. It is also slow growing, putting on less than 12 inches (30 cm) a year, which allows it to keep a nicely rounded shape with minimal pruning.

Potentilla has a number of uses—as a feature, front-of-the-border plant in a perennial or mixed scheme; as part of the foundation planting in a rockery; or planted in a row to form a low-growing, informal hedge. The red cultivars will keep their color if they are protected from hot afternoon sun, which can fade the red flowers to orange. The white- and yellow-flowering varieties also tend to lose their crisp tones in direct sunlight.

Top cultivars available include 'Goldfinger' (golden yellow), 'Pink Princess' (light pink), 'Goldstar' (yellow), 'Primrose Beauty' (pale yellow, silvery gray foliage), 'Tangerine' (orange-yellow), 'Pink Beauty' (clear pink), 'Royal Flush' (rosy-pink) and 'Red Ace' (red). The best of the reds is 'Red Robin'. This has fiery, brick-red flowers that hold their color in full sun instead of turning orange as some red- and pink-flowering types have a tendency to do. The best of the white-flowering cultivars is 'Abbotswood', which also has attractive blue-green foliage. Two other white-flowering types are 'Snowbird' (double white) and 'McKay's White' (creamy white).

Potentilla is a member of the rose family (*Rosaceae*), which includes apples, raspberries and strawberries. It gets its common name, cinquefoil, from its leaves, which are often divided into five lobes or fingers. However, most us call potentilla by its botanical rather than common name.

The many cultivars of *Potentilla fruticosa* are the most widely grown, but here are a few other species to check out for the garden.

- *P. megalantha* (strawberry-leafed cinquefoil) has leaves covered with silvery hairs, as well as cheerful yellow flowers. It grows 6 to 8 inches (15 to 20 cm) tall and forms a low mat at the front of the border.
- *P. nepalensis* 'Miss Willmott'. Named after the infamous British gardener who went about scattering *Erigeron* seeds everywhere, this is a reliable performer, growing to 12 inches (30 cm) and producing crimson-pink flowers in June.
- *P.* x *tonguei* (staghorn cinquefoil) has apricot flowers with red centers in July and August. A good evergreen plant for late-summer color, it grows 12 inches (30 cm) high, making it a useful pick for the front of the border.

Super Spirea

Spirea comes in two forms—those with white flowers and those with rose-pink flowers that are mostly valued for their gold- or lime-colored foliage. You could make room in your garden for one of each. They are all hardy to Zone 4 or better.

- *Spiraea bumalda* 'Goldflame' is one of the most outstanding foliage spireas. It has bronze leaves that turn golden yellow as they mature. The plant then adds a few fireworks to its color show by producing rosy-red flowers that continue from June to fall. It grows only 3 to 4 feet (90 cm to 1.2 m) high.

- *Spiraea japonica* 'Anthony Waterer' is called the dwarf pink spirea. It has bright green leaves and produces rosy-pink flowers from July to September. It grows only 2 or 3 feet (60 to 90 cm) high.

- *Spiraea japonica* 'Lime Mound' has lemon-yellow leaves tinged with pink and produces light pink flowers in summer. This shrub grows only 3 feet (90 cm) high, but it mounds up to 6 feet (1.8 m) wide.

- *Spiraea japonica* 'Little Princess' has mint-green foliage and rose-pink flowers. There is a golden form called 'Golden Princess'.

- *Spiraea japonica* 'Shirobana' is something of a novelty plant. It blooms late in the summer, producing white, pink and red flowers simultaneously from July to September. It grows only 2 or 3 feet (60 to 90 cm) high and has bright green leaves.

- *Spiraea japonica* 'Snowmound' is a short shrub that grows 4 or 5 feet (1.2 to 1.5 m) high and displays masses of white flowers on long, graceful, arching stems in spring.

- *Spiraea thunbergii* 'Fujino Pink' has light pink clusters of flowers in June. It is a small, compact shrub with green leaves that turn bright yellow in autumn.

- *Spiraea* x *vanhouttei*. This is the best of the white-flowering spireas. Its dazzling cascade of snow-white flowers in May gives spring-flowering spirea its common name—bridal wreath. It is a compact, upright deciduous shrub that grows into a fountain shape about 6 feet (1.8 m) high with diamond-shaped, dark green leaves. It is certainly one of the best spring performers.

- Other top performers worth checking out include 'Thor' (white flowers in June, dwarf spirea), 'Goldmound' (pink flowers, bright yellow foliage in July), and 'Garland' (white flowers in June).

Divine Vines

Vines are the aggressive social climbers of the garden: it is simply in their nature to want to scramble to the top and to be head and shoulders above the rest. Some thrust up to heights of greatness using disc-like suction cups or tiny rootlets to attach themselves to rough or smooth surfaces. Others battle their way upward, clinging on for dear life by sending out coiling tendrils, or they skilfully wrap themselves around a post or thread in and out of latticework. Clasping, weaving or twining, the goal is always the same: to cover and smother, to rise up and branch out, to boldly (read rampantly) go where no earth-bound plants have gone before.

Unlike their less endearing human equivalent, however, the garden's social climbers do serve a useful purpose; they make boring spaces beautiful and ugly places more tolerable. With minimal direction, climbers do a first-rate job of covering walls and fences, sweeping over arches and arbors, clambering up pillars and along the top of pergolas. Vines also have the ability to soften the hard edges of a building's facade, disguise unsightly dying trees and leftover stumps, and introduce fragrant flowers and dense foliage to drab, neglected corners of the yard.

A well-designed garden will always make you lift your head. You know something is missing when you visit a garden and everything looks perfect but you find yourself looking down at the ground all the time. Vines on walls and fences, arches and arbors, pergolas and spirals, trellises and obelisks can remedy that. Vines can create that all-important vertical element in the garden.

The Queen of Vines: Your Guide to the Best of Clematis

The most sociable of climbers, clematis is deservedly called the "queen of vines." No garden should be without at least one or two. Some gardeners have planted as many as half a dozen at a time to cover a single trellis or arbor. Choosing the right clematis is the key to success. The selection can be overwhelming. In commercial cultivation at the moment there are at least 50 blue-flowering, 34 pink, 30 purple, 16 two-tone, 34 white, 21 red, and 10 yellow-blooming varieties. Once you've chosen the color you like, the next step is to decide what time of year you want it to flower. You can get clematis that bloom in early spring or summer or fall. Here's a guide to the best of the bunch.

- 'Blue Bird'. One of the macropetala group of clematis which flower from late spring to early summer and require minimal to no pruning. 'Blue Bird' has 2-inch-long (5-cm) lavender-blue flowers and is vigorous enough to cover an area 8 to 10 feet (2.4 to 3 m) wide. Other striking cultivars include 'Ballet Skirt' (white), 'Rosy O'Grady' (light pink), and 'Lagoon' (blue).

- 'Blue Ravine'. There are several fine blue clematis, including 'Will Barron', 'Ramona', 'Sally Cadge', 'Countess of Lovelace' and 'H.F. Young', but 'Blue Ravine', which was developed by the University of B.C. Botanical Garden, is a very popular choice. The flowers are actually a soft violet with darker center veins. It blooms in May, June and a little more in late summer. It grows to 10 to 12 feet (3 to 3.6 m).

- 'Elizabeth'. This has masses of clear pink flowers with a slight vanilla scent from late spring to early summer. It is one of the very popular montana group of clematis which originate in the Himalayas, and grows to 20 to 30 feet (6 to 9 m). These are ideal clematis for growing into trees or for screening eyesores. The only drawback is that they are not appropriate for cold areas (Zone 5 and below) because the stems will be frozen. Other top cultivars of *C. montana* are 'Pink Perfection' (deep pink), 'Rubens' (deep pink), 'Alba' (creamy white) and 'Tetrarose' (rose-pink).

- 'Gypsy Queen'. Among the purples, you can't go wrong with 'Etoile Violette' or 'Jackmanii' or 'The President', but for something a little different, try 'Gypsy Queen', which has deep, plum-purple blooms from July to September and grows to about 12 feet (3.6 m).

- 'Hagley Hybrid'. This is also known as 'Pink Chiffon'. It produces a first flush of shell-pink flowers in June and continues sporadically into late summer. It rarely grows more than 6 or 8 feet (1.8 to 2.4 m) high, which makes it an excellent pick for patios, balconies and small gardens. Another first-rate clematis for a patio garden is 'Niobe', which has ruby-red flowers and grows to 8 feet (2.4 m).

- 'Haku Ookan'. This is one of an exciting collection of Japanese clematis that is now starting to catch the attention of gardeners in mild areas. 'Fuji Musume' is a striking blue-bloomer while 'Haku Ookan' has rich violet-purple flowers. Both of these are excellent picks for growing in small courtyards or on balconies and patios where space is limited. They grow to 6 to 7 feet (1.8 to 2.1 m). If grown in pots they will need to be wrapped for protection in winter.

- 'Helsingborg'. This is a cultivar of *C. alpina*, a species that originates in Europe and northern Asia and is noted for its early flowering in spring. Vigorous and hardy, they thrive in cool, shady, north-facing gardens. 'Helsingborg' has deep purple, bell-shaped flowers. Other popular *C. alpina* cultivars include 'Jacqueline du Pré' (rosy-mauve), and 'Pamela Jackman' (purple-blue). They all grow to 6 to 10 feet (1.8 to 3 m).

- 'Henryi'. There are plenty of white-flowering clematis—'John Huxtable', 'Jackmanii Alba', 'Huldine', 'Snow Queen', 'Duchess of Edinburgh'— but there are few hybrids as dependable as 'Henryi', which produces masses of creamy-white flowers most of the summer and grows to a respectable 14 feet (4.3 m).

- 'Mme. Julia Correvon'. Growing clematis into shrubs is still a popular thing to do, and this vine is one of the most useful for that purpose. Its classy, wine-red blooms also look sensational woven through the stems of climbing roses or over arbors and arches. Once it gets established, will quickly reach 14 feet (4.3 m).

- 'Nelly Moser'. Bicolor clematis are always in demand, especially 'Dr. Rupple', 'Pink Fantasy', 'Bees Jubilee' and 'Mrs. N. Thompson', but the best-seller of them all is still good old 'Nelly Moser', which for more than 100 years now has been beautifying gardens all over the world. It has pastel mauve-pink flowers with a distinctive carmine bar in May and June and again in late summer. It grows to 8 to 10 feet (2.4 to 3.6 m).

- 'Pagoda'. This has as a parent *C. texensis*, a species native to Texas. 'Pagoda' is considered one of the easiest of this group to grow. It has mauve-pink flowers from midsummer to early fall. Other cultivars to look for include 'Etoile Rose', which has delicate nodding cerise-pink blooms with a touch of silver, and 'Gravetye Beauty', which has ruby-red flowers. They all grow to 8 to 12 feet (2.4 to 3.6 m).

- 'Polish Spirit'. This is a cultivar of *C. viticella*, which some gardeners feel has done more to popularize clematis than any other species. 'Polish Spirit' is a relatively new introduction to Canadian gardeners and is catching more attention because of its deep-purple flowers and reliable growth habit, to 10 to 12 feet (3 to 3.6 m). Other top performers include 'Abundance' (rose-pink), 'Little Nell' (creamy white with purple edges), and 'Purpurea Plena Elegans' (double-flowered purple variety believed to date back to the 16th century).

- 'The President'. One of the best purples, this is sometimes mistaken for 'Jackmanii' but the blooms are a little bit bluer, with a red-tipped stamen in the center. Flowers from June to September and grows about 10 to 12 feet (3 to 3.6 m).

- *Clematis tangutica*. This exceptionally vigorous clematis produces lovely, nodding, yellow lantern-like flowers in late summer and early fall. The flowers are followed by silvery seed heads that hang on for quite a few weeks. Popular varieties include 'Gravetye' and 'Golden Harvest'. They grow to 15 to 20 feet (4.5 to 6 m). Similar flowering but slightly less vigorous is *C. orientalis*. Give it plenty of room, and consider training it into a tree for best results.

- 'Ville de Lyon'. One of the best carmine-red clematis, ideal for growing into the purple foliage of a smoke bush (*Cotinus coggygria*) or intermingled among pink-flowering roses such as 'New Dawn'. It grows to 8 to 12 feet (2.4 to 3.6 m) and blooms from June to September.

How to Grow Clematis

Here are some tips from Fred Wein of Clearview Horticultural—one of Canada's top growers—on how to grow the queen of vines successfully.

- Clematis needs a cool, moist, deep root run, plenty of water and regular, balanced feeding. The vine likes its head in the sun, its feet in the shade.

- When planting, dig a hole 18 inches deep and wide (45 by 45 cm). Cover the bottom with a good, rich compost or well-rotted manure. A handful of bonemeal mixed with your soil is always a good idea. Add enough topsoil to cover the compost.

- Place your well-watered clematis in the hole so that about 6 inches (15 cm) of the stem is below the soil line. If you are concerned about this, leave the final filling of the hole until later in the season.

- The stem of the newly planted clematis needs to be securely but carefully attached to a support so that damage to the stem does not occur.

- Planting a small shrub in front will ensure a cool root run for your clematis.

- Slugs, snails and earwigs are common pests that attack clematis, but one of the most puzzling problems is something most gardeners refer to as "clematis wilt." This usually happens when plants are young and stems have been damaged, opening the way for a wide range of fungi, the most common of which is *Asochyta clematidina*.

- If clematis wilt occurs, remove and destroy the affected stems. The fungus will remain in the healthy-looking part of the stem, so it is important that about 1 inch (2.5 cm) of the stem below the infection is also removed. New shoots will soon appear at or below the soil line. Clematis wilt seldom destroys a whole plant.

- If you want to grow clematis into a tree, the trick is to plant it 8 to 10 feet (2.4 to 3 m) away, training the stems along the ground until they reach the trunk. By doing this, you free the vine from having to compete with the tree's roots. It also gets the clematis away from acidic soils directly under the tree.

- Don't be afraid to prune. Early spring-blooming clematis flower on wood produced the previous season. So you don't want to prune this type until after it has flowered in May or June. Most late spring/summer bloomers flower on new growth produced in spring. In early spring these can be pruned back to two strong sets of buds as close to the ground as possible.

Other Top Climbers

Clematis are superb vines, but they are by no means the only climbers useful for growing over arches and arbors, fences and pergolas. Here's a guide to some of the best vines that offer interesting foliage or flowers or both.

Flowers and Foliage

- *Akebia quinata* (chocolate vine). Proof that looks can be deceptive, this has rather delicate foliage but is vigorous enough to twist and twine to 25 feet (7.5 m). It has distinctive leaves, each with five leaflets, and it produces clusters of fragrant, brown-purple (chocolate) flowers in spring. Hardy to Zone 5.

- *Campsis* (trumpet vine). Better known as the trumpet creeper or trumpet honeysuckle, this will thrive in a sunny, sheltered spot in moist, well-drained soil. The eye-catching, red trumpet-shaped flowers are a favorite of hummingbirds. A beautiful cultivar is 'Indian Summer', which has orange-red flowers from July to September. Hardy to Zone 5.

- *Hydrangea petiolaris* (climbing hydrangea). Most useful for covering large walls, since it spreads rapidly and can cover an area 30 by 30 feet (9 by 9 m) with dense, attractive foliage. Happy in sun or shade, it is a self-clinging climber and produces lacecap-type, greeny-white flower heads. Hardy to Zone 5.

- *Lonicera* (honeysuckle). At its best running over bushes or trellises, pergolas or arches, honeysuckle is a solid climber. Look for 'Dropmore Scarlet' or the new UBC introduction, 'Mandarin'. Hardy to Zone 3.

- *Passiflora caerulea* (blue passionflower). Slightly more exotic than clematis or honeysuckle, the blue passionflower is fairly hardy, but needs winter protection. It produces beautifully intricate blooms measuring 3 to 4 inches (7.5 to 10 cm) across. Hardy to Zone 7.

- *Polygonum aubertii* (silver lace vine). A rampant grower, this puts out a white cloud of flowers from August to September. It grows to 25 to 30 feet (7.5 to 9 m). Hardy to Zone 6.

- *Rosa* hybrids (climbing roses). While most climbers would like to bask in a sunny location, climbing roses insist on it, demanding at least six hours of warm sun a day to perform properly. Hardy to Zone 5. (See page 56 for top climbers and ramblers).

- *Wisteria*. At its best, it produces spectacular bunches of fragrant, drooping flowers that add charm to any garden. It performs best in full sun and likes moist but well-drained soil. It is most frequently used to cover pergolas, patios and arbors but looks sensational gracing the front porch of a house. The most popular variety is *W. sinensis*. Hardy to Zone 6.

Foliage Only

- *Actinidia kolomikta*. Why this vine is not more widely used remains a mystery. More graceful and slightly less vigorous than its cousin, the Chinese gooseberry vine (*A. chinensis*), *A. kolomikta* has striking pink-tipped leaves and produces slightly fragrant white flowers in early summer. Hardy to Zone 3.

- *Hedera helix* 'Baltic' (English ivy) or *Aristolochia durior* (Dutchman's pipe) are two possible choices for decorating a large wall or covering an unsightly garage or shed. Hardy to Zone 5.

- *Humulus lupulus* (golden hops vine). This is becoming easier to find at garden centers. It can be used to drape a fence or cover a shed. The leaves turn golden-yellow in full sun. Hardy to Zone 4.

- *Parthenocissus quinquefolia* (Virginia creeper). Its brilliant red leaves turn to orange in fall. Hardy to Zone 2.

- *Parthenocissus tricuspidata* (Boston ivy). Leaves turn a striking red color in fall. Hardy to Zone 2.

- *Vitis* (grape vine). Most useful for providing shade over a patio or arbor in summer, grape vines are grown for their fruit. Some varieties, however, are purely ornamental. Easy to establish and a reliable performer. Hardy to Zone 5.

Stars of Summer

There are certain star-performing plants that have a special place in the summer garden. Daylilies do a remarkable job of providing lush foliage and spectacular flowers, while succulents such as *Echeveria* can look terribly exotic displayed on steps in simple terracotta pots. Other plants like asters, echinacea, chrysanthemums and hardy hibiscus act as late-summer garden helpers. They give the garden a much-needed lift at the end of a blistering season. Here's a tribute to some of the plants that make our summers long and memorable.

Daylilies: One-Day Wonders with Everlasting Charm

Some time ago CBC Radio asked me the hardest question any dedicated gardener gets asked: "If you could pick just one plant—and one plant only—for your garden, what would it be?" Impossible as that is to answer, the plant that immediately sprang to mind was the daylily (*Hemerocallis*). It's hard to decide which of the daylily's outstanding characteristics I value most—the delightful, trumpet-shaped flowers, which now come in an even grander assortment of colors, or the plant's distinctive strap-like foliage, which jumps up from the ground at the first hint of spring to form a long-lasting, cascading mound of attractive, soft-green leaves.

Daylilies are first-rate plants, a must for every garden. The problem is that hybridizers all over the world have gone berserk and registered every new variety that comes out of their greenhouse regardless of its overall quality as a garden plant. Pick up any two books on daylilies and you will have a hard time finding the same cultivars mentioned in each book. This is not so with roses or peonies, maples or rhododendrons. In fact, most other plant families are subject to much more vigorous testing before they get the stamp of approval for promotion.

What all this means is that you are going to have a hard time finding out exactly what daylilies are the best for your garden. You won't find out by talking to the growers—daylily hybridizers are notorious self-promoters. If they write a book, they invariably feature only their own hybrids and completely overlook long-established favorites such as 'Frans Hals' (golden yellow and dark orange), 'Catherine Woodbury' (pale orchid-pink with chartreuse throat) and 'Hyperion' (lemon-yellow). These are now generally dismissed by daylily growers as too common, too boring and too short-blooming. They have been relegated to the league of lazy landscapers who can't be bothered to find more interesting varieties. In reality, however, these old-time varieties are still popular with gardeners, even if newer varieties are longer-blooming and often repeat-bloomers.

Something else has happened to futher complicate the world of daylilies. Many modern daylilies are a product of some very clever and complex genetic wizardry. The new breeds are called tetraploids, which means they have twice as many chromosomes as the regular two-chromosome (diploid) varieties. As a consequence, tetraploid daylilies have bigger, bolder flowers with brighter colors in more imaginative patterns. These "super-plants" have sturdier flower stems (scapes) and more robust foliage, and are generally considered to be more disease and drought tolerant than their popular predecessors. The argument over which daylily is better—tetraploid or diploid—is still a subject of controversy among growers and avid gardeners. One of the most respected authorities on the issue, Bill Munson, author of *Hemerocallis: The Daylily*, says unequivocally: "All these qualities (added vigor, stamina, sun resistance, vibrant colors, healthiness) assure the tetraploid daylily of its rightful place in the world of daylilies." In the 15 years from 1960 to 1975, only 17 tetraploids were registered with the American Hemerocallis Society, but since then several thousand new tetraploid varieties have been reared and registered.

If you go looking for daylilies, here are 10 top hybrids that even the experts seem to agree are reliable, hardy performers.

- 'Chicago Apache'. This is one of a series of hybrids produced by James Marsh of Chicago in the 1970s. There are at least 15 cultivars in the collection, all with Chicago in the name. 'Chicago Apache' has striking, scarlet-red petals with a yellow-green throat. It grows to a little over 2 feet (60 cm).

- 'Dragon's Eye'. This has pastel-pink flowers with a huge, rose-red eye. The blooms start to appear in July and continue through into August. It grows 2 feet (60 cm) tall.

- 'Firestorm'. This has spider-like, coppery-yellow flowers that measure over 7 inches (18 cm) wide. It grows 32 inches (80 cm) high.

- 'Langley Lady'. One of the best of B.C. hybridizer Pam Erikson's series that (true to daylily tradition) are all named after her hometown—Langley, outside of Vancouver. 'Langley Lady' has miniature ruffled pink blooms. It is especially popular with people who garden in small spaces. It grows to about 16 inches (40 cm).

- 'Leprechaun's Lace'. With exceptionally attractive flowers of a distinctive peach-pink hue, this is a hard daylily to get hold of because growers are always selling out the moment people see it. Growing 16 inches (40 cm) high, it is a very productive bloomer and easy to accommodate in small and medium-sized gardens.

- 'Lullaby Baby'. A well-established favorite that makes an impressive sight with its pale pink flowers with attractively ruffled edges. It is one of the best varieties bred by hybridizer Edna Spalding, of Louisiana. It grows to 20 inches (50 cm).

- 'Ptarmigan'. This is one of the near-white daylilies. It grows 20 inches (50 cm) high and flowers from July to August. While needing at least three hours of sun a day, it can be used to brighten up areas under trees. Being very pale, it looks great in dappled shade.

- 'Scarlet Tanager'. This is a midseason bloomer, growing 30 inches (75 cm) high and producing bright red flowers in July. It looks outstanding against the striking blue leaves of big-leafed *Hosta sieboldiana* hybrids.

- 'Siloam Bo Peep'. This is one of the famous Siloam Series—a seemingly endless list of hybrids produced by Pauline Henry and each named after her hometown, Siloam. There's 'Siloam Rose Queen', 'Siloam Red Toy', 'Siloam Little Fairy', 'Siloam Ethel Smith' and dozens more. 'Bo Peep' is considered one of the better ones. It has lilac-pink flowers with a deep purple throat. It grows to 18 inches (45 cm).

- 'Stella de Oro'. The best of the best. This is loved for its short 12- to 18-inch (30- to 45-cm) form and its lightly ruffled orange-gold flowers that bloom from spring to fall. Grow it as an edging plant or in a container— it won't disappoint you with its flower production.

How to Plant and Care for Your Daylilies

The daylily's two major assets, flowers and foliage, play an indispensable decorative role in the summer garden. One of the easiest and most reliable perennials to grow, the daylily gets its botanical name, *Hemerocallis*, from two Greek words—*hemero* for day and *kallos* for beauty. The delicate flowers—more water than substance—last for only a day, two at most, depending how much sun and shade they receive. A major compensation for the shockingly brief life span of such a beautiful flower is that a mature clump of daylilies is perfectly capable of producing dozens of exquisite blooms in a single season.

Daylilies are happiest when planted where they get at least four hours of sun a day. The more sun they get, the more blooms they produce. Dark colors (reds and purples) benefit from afternoon shade to preserve the color. Once you have selected the site for your daylilies, leave them in that spot for at least three years to get the best blooms possible. The plant usually takes the first year to establish itself, the second year to put out a good flush of growth and the third year to produce spectacular blooms.

Divide established clumps every three or four years. Miniatures have a tendency to form clumps faster, while the large tetraploid varieties can be left untouched for four or five years.

Daylilies are drought tolerant but they thrive better with regular watering. An inch or two (2.5 to 5 cm) of water a week will result in larger blooms. In spring, fertilize with compost or well-balanced 10-10-10 fertilizer; a fall feeding of a rose-type fertilizer is also beneficial. Avoid using fertilizer with a high nitrogen content—it promotes too much foliage and fewer flowers.

How to Create a Seamless Sequence of Blooms

To use daylilies to create a sequence of color from late June to September, plant a good selection of early-, mid- and late-season bloomers. Most gardeners are not aware that daylilies fall into these three distinct classifications. It pays to ask if the plant is a repeat-bloomer, for this will give you a second flush later in summer. Here's a list of daylilies that will do the trick, but you can also put together your own collection by asking the right questions and doing a little research at the nursery when you buy.

Early Bloomers (June): 'Stella de Oro' (golden yellow); 'Hallcroft' (pale pink spider-shaped flowers); 'Chicago Violet' (deep purple); 'Evening Bell' (lovely yellow, and fragrant); 'Little Moki' (cream/beige-pink bicolor) and 'Velveteen' (deep soft pink; looks fabulous blooming with astilbes in June).

Midseason Bloomers (July): 'Puddin' (produces hundreds of soft-yellow blooms); the Siloam Series (assorted colors, all wonderful additions to the July garden); 'Purple Peppermint' (miniature lavender-purple); 'Shady Lady' (an older cultivar that has been around seemingly forever, but continues to be a star attraction in July with big, soft-yellow blooms with a wide, deep-maroon eye); 'Canadian Border Patrol' (one of the most exciting of the newer cultivars, this has big, cream flowers, a deep-purple eye and a deep-purple picotee edge); 'Bertie Ferris' (produces hundreds of small, frilled, deep-apricot blooms all July).

Late-season Bloomers (August–September): 'Pardon Me' (a deep burgundy red, with miniature flowers that bloom sometimes into October); 'Flasher' (produces large, hot-orange flowers in July, then reblooms in September); 'Late Cream' (soft cream, with a slight pink flush); 'Annie Golightly' (fire-engine red); 'Late Advancement' (peach-apricot); 'Yellow Lollipop' (miniature yellow, similar to 'Stella de Oro').

Sexy Succulents

It all started one summer when the beautiful blue violas that filled the various pockets of a large strawberry pot started to run out of steam. With no time to pop down to the garden center, I grabbed a basic blue grass (*Festuca glauca*) and a half dozen hens and chicks (*Sempervivum*) and used them to do a complete remake. I stuck blue grass in the top of the pot and slotted the sempervivum into the side pockets. The range of sizes and colors available in sempervivums is impressive. There are mulberry reds, deep purples, silvery blues and apple green with red tips. The result was very satisfying—a complete transformation and yet the strawberry pot looked like it had been planted like that for years. Next, I figured I'd have a go at doing a similar thing using succulents—plants with fleshy leaves that can store water. You'll find all kinds of succulents at the garden center alongside various sizes of cactus.

Echeveria immediately caught my eye as a suitable candidate for my next strawberry-pot project. There is a beautiful blue-leafed form, *Echeveria glauca*, that has a very attractive, flat, rosette shape, while *E. agavoides* has plain green leaves with reddish-brown tips. The only problem I found with echeveria is that although they come in large, substantial-looking 4-inch (10-cm) pots, the plants actually have barely any roots. It is very easy to shake away the potting medium to discover nothing but a few strands of root. Nevertheless, with a little careful manipulation, it is possible to maneuver one or two rosettes of echeveria into each pocket of the strawberry pot to create a handsome display. I filled the top with more blue-leafed echeveria, but you could use one of the tree-forms, perhaps *E. harmsii*, which produces dense clusters of fleshy leaves with red tips on thick branching stems. Or top off the pot with a century plant (*Agave americana*) or a selection of aloes, which are also available in a wide range of colors and forms.

Since all these succulents are tender, requiring a winter temperature of not less than 40°F (4.5°C), I don't combine them with any hardy plant material, such as grasses, heucheras or sempervivums. That way the strawberry pot can sit outside on the patio or balcony in the summer and be brought indoors over winter.

As for the pot full of blue grass and sempervivum, it is hardy enough to be left outside and can serve as a decorative container in a sheltered area close to the house during winter. Sempervivums are hardy to Zone 2 and *Festuca glauca* to Zone 3.

If you don't much care for the idea of packing succulents into a strawberry pot, you could always try your hand at building a succulent

I like pure, clean whites. Some whites are off-white or pinkish. The purity of a white garden is meant to be seen under the lover's moon. That's when all the whites and silvers sparkle.

—Todd Major, director of Park and Tilford Gardens, British Columbia "dish garden." All you need is a terracotta trough or low, bowl-shaped container and some free-draining cactus-potting mix. Using a variety of succulents—echeveria, aloe, crassula, and so on—you can very quickly make a miniature garden landscape that can fit neatly on a window sill or coffee table.

While you're checking out the succulents, look over all the sun-loving, fleshy-leafed stonecrops (*Sedum*), especially the taller border varieties such as the popular 'Autumn Joy' and 'Brilliant', as well as the less-known dark purple cultivars 'Matrona' and 'Mohrchen'. You can also have fun using some of the small-leafed, extremely drought-tolerant, low-growing varieties of stonecrop to fill a strawberry pot or gaps in the rockery or terrace. Especially eye-catching in late summer is *S. ewersii*, with rose-pink flowers, and *S. sieboldii*, with dense clusters of rosy-purple flowers. They both look great along a sunny path or loosely tumbling over a rockery wall or terrace.

One of the most versatile and widely used sedums is the freely spreading *Sedum acre*, which has bright yellow flowers. The silvery-white leaves of *S. spathulifolium* 'Capa Blanco' and the purple-blue foliage of *S. spathulifolium* 'Purpureum' always please the eye. The fun of using these plants is to see what clever combinations you can come up with by mixing foliage textures and colors. Some sedums, such as *S. oreganum*, have tiny leaves that form tight rosettes like a miniature jade plant, while others, such as six-sided stonecrop (*S. sexangulare*), have a soft, dangling spiral of leaves. *S. seiboldii* 'Variegatum' has golden-yellow splotches on blue-green leaves while the Russian stonecrop (*S. kamtschaticum*) has finely scalloped green leaves and bright yellow star-shaped flowers. Strawberry pots are ideal for trying out five or six kinds of dwarf sedum in one small area. Within a year or two, you won't be able to see the pot for all the wonderfully dainty foliage and flowers.

Late-Summer Helpers

My garden always looked bedraggled in August. Then I realized the problem: I had never taken the time to plant a late-summer garden. This is a common oversight among gardeners. We're very conscious of planting for spring and early summer, but we often overlook the need to make use of valuable perennials that can give our gardens that much-needed second wind from August to the end of September. These plants will serve that purpose.

- *Aster* x *frikartii* 'Mönch'. Better known as Michaelmas daisies, asters are available in a wide range of colors from red to pink, light blue to purple-blue. They also range in size from tall, gangly 5-foot (1.5-m) giants to short, compact dwarf specimens that can be grown in a rockery. They are valued for their long blooming period, the cheerfulness of their daisylike flowers, and their appearance when it seems as though the festive fun of summer is finished. They are a welcome late arrival to the party. 'Mönch' has bright lavender-blue flowers with yellow centers. It grows 3 feet (90 cm) tall and about 18 inches (45 cm) wide and flowers from the end of July to October. It is sturdy enough not to require staking, provides excellent cut flowers, and is a useful addition to any perennial border.

- *Aster dumosus.* These bushy dwarf hybrids grow only about 12 to 15 inches (30 to 38 cm) tall and are ideal for the front of the border. Best bet is 'Lady in Blue', which has violet-blue flowers with a yellow center. This is easy to place in the border and it keeps its color long into fall. Other names to look for include 'Audrey' (mauve-blue), 'Diana' (rose-

When a Rose Is Not a Rose

Hibiscus syriacus (rose of Sharon) is not a rose at all, but a shrub form of hibiscus. It gets its name from a vague biblical reference in the Song of Solomon to "a rose of Sharon", which in Hebrew refers to a crocus, not a rose, and certainly not hibiscus. All this, I think, is fun to tell visitors to your garden when they stand admiring the magnificent blooms of your rose of Sharon. What we know for sure about this shrub is that it grows into a substantial bush, 6 to 10 feet (1.8 to 3 m) high, that produces lovely hollyhock-like blooms in a wide variety of colors from August to September. Native to Syria (from which it gets its species name, *syriacus*), rose of Sharon is perhaps most popular of all in France and Italy where it is used extensively in parks and gardens. 'Blue Bird' is one of the best cultivars. It has light blue flowers with a dark center and it has proven itself a reliable performer in many gardens over the years. Other top cultivars include 'Woodbridge' (rose-pink with carmine center), 'Aphrodite' (pink with red center), 'Ardens' (purple), 'Coelestis' (sky blue), 'Lucy' (bright red), 'Blushing Bride' (pink), 'Morningstar' (white), 'Paeoniflorus' (pink), 'Rubis' (red), 'Single White' (white), 'Tricolor' (red, white and blue) and 'Red Heart' (large white flowers with intensely red centers).

To flower perfectly, *Hibiscus syriacus* needs plenty of sun and a long, hot summer. Plant it in ordinary but well-drained soil in the warmest, most protected site in your garden. 'Blue Bird' can be used as an accent plant in the shrub border or trained into a tree form and used to create privacy or block out eyesores. You can also grow hibiscus in containers, but regardless of where you grow it, it will need to be protected from cool breezes and chilly night temperatures. Be patient. This shrub is slow to get established and takes a couple of years before it gets into full swing and starts blooming profusely. A lot of gardeners think their hibiscus is dead because it is so slow to leaf out in spring. Relax. It is not dead, just sleeping.

Hardy to Zone 5, it needs winter protection in cooler areas. Prune back the bush for size and shape and to encourage bushy growth. Cut back to two buds on the previous season's growth. Most important with hibiscus—keep the soil moist, but not soaking wet, especially in hot, dry summers. Also keep an eye out for aphids and mealy bugs. Potentilla, hydrangea, English roses, buddleia, euonymus and spirea are all excellent partners for your rose of Sharon. If you include it in a border with bush forms of magnolia, French lilac and burning bush (*Euonymus alata*), you get a complete sequence of color from May to October. Throw in some red or yellow twig dogwoods and you'll extend the colorful picture into the winter months.

pink), 'Little Pink Beauty' (bright pink), 'Violet Carpet' (violet-blue), 'Nesthaskchen' (clear pink), 'White Opal' (white) and 'Jenny' (red).

- *Aster novae-angliae* (New England aster). This is a taller species, growing to 5 feet (1.5 m). It can become gangly and benefits from being pinch-pruned at the tips in early July to make it bushier. Good names to look for include 'Andenken an Alma Pötschke' (deep pink), 'September Ruby' (dark red), 'Mrs. S.T. Wright' (lilac), 'Lye End Beauty' (deep pink) and 'Harrington's Pink' (light pink).

- *Aster novi-belgii* (New York aster). These grow 3 to 4 feet (90 to 120 cm) tall and are the hybrids of a species native to New York State. Top cultivars include 'Alert' (crimson), 'Coombe Rosemary' (violet-purple), 'Royal Ruby' (deep red), 'Coombe Margaret' (reddish-pink), 'Ada Ballard' (mauve-blue) and 'Chequers' (purple-violet).

- *Echinacea purpurea* (purple coneflower). This is a drought-tolerant, easy-to-grow herbaceous perennial that gets its name from the Greek word for "hedgehog"—a good description of the bristly cone at the center of the daisy-shaped flower. Before planting, dig plenty of well-rotted compost and manure into the soil: echinacea has a good appetite and does not thrive well in poorly nourished soils. Plant in a location that gets full sun and in soil that is moist, but well-drained. 'Magnus', which grows only 30 inches (75 cm) high and has a very compact habit, was named 1999 perennial of the year by the American Perennial Plant Association. If you like white echinacea, try 'White Swan', which has a black-gold cone at the center and pure white flower petals. Remove flower heads regularly in order to prolong flowering and prevent the stems of taller varieties from flopping over. Grow echinacea with liatris, crocosmia, eryngium, gaura, monarda, echinops, shasta daisies, daylilies, and various ornamental grasses and end-of-summer flowering plants like aster and rudbeckia. Echinacea is purported to have many health-giving qualities. Herbalists say it stimulates the immune system and has antibacterial and antiviral properties.

- Chrysanthemums. These show up in garden centers in September, simply labeled "garden mums." They are mostly varieties of cushion- and spray-type chrysanthemum and they come in a good selection of colors from yellow and gold to white and pink, deep rust and burgundy. The cushion types are low-mounding plants 18 to 24 inches (45 to 60 cm) tall, which produce a myriad of small flowers. The spray types are more upright, 2 to 3 feet (60 to 90 cm) tall, with open sprays of blooms. Both kinds provide a fresh injection of color for pots and containers, as well as flower beds, from early September to mid-

October or until the first hard frost. There are too many named cultivars to list here and new varieties are being introduced every year. If you want to incorporate them into your garden in May along with other bedding plants, pick up young seedlings at your local chrysanthemum society's plant sale in spring, when dozens of varieties are offered at a very reasonable price.

The late chrysanthemums, or "specialty mums", are a category to themselves. These bloom very late in the year, from the end of October into December. Growing these greenhouse varieties is considered the ultimate test of a gardener's skill, as it requires patience and great care to bring them to perfection in fall. Charms, spiders and cascades are three of the most attractive groups of late-flowering chrysanthemums, but the most popular among hobbyists are the large, one-bloom-per-stem, globe-shaped varieties. These come in three basic forms—intermediate (petals are a mixture of incurved and reflexed); incurved (petals turn toward the center to form a tight ball); and reflexed (petals curve out and down from the center).

The lengthy process of growing these large, decorative chrysanthemums starts around Christmas when enthusiasts give their overwintered plants a little water and a shot of nitrogen to perk them up. In January, they lift and pot up cuttings that have started to appear around the base of the old plants.

In May, plants are moved outdoors. The goal is to grow two or three large, 6-inch (15-cm) blooms per plant, so stems are pinch-pruned in order to concentrate energy into four main stems. In June, plants are pruned back to three flower stems. Each one will produce one single, giant bloom. From June to August, side shoots are continually pinched away. By the end of October, enthusiasts go looking for the best of the blooms to exhibit at fall flower shows.

Garden Design

You can sit in your sun chair and read for only so long. Most gardeners end up itching to do something other than laze around contemplating the beauty of their handiwork. The lazy days of summer are the time we think how lovely it would be to have the cooling presence of a pond or water garden. July and August are great months to check out water lilies and other water plants. And if you're keen on establishing (or improving) your white garden, the summer months are the ones to go looking for new and interesting plants that offer the desired shades of silver and ivory.

Brilliant White

Does an all-white garden sound boring? It doesn't have to be. Done properly, it can offer an ethereal beauty and simple elegance not found in the joyful jumble of a cottage garden scheme or the happy riot of color in a herbaceous border.

All-white schemes are certainly among the classics of garden design. "White is the ultimate inspirational garden, full of elegance and delicacy, yet leaving much to the imagination," according to Elvin MacDonald, author of *The Color Garden*. "All-white speaks of passion and romance . . . on a moonlit stroll, the whites show the way, some hovering in the air like night angels." The world's most popular all-white garden is undoubtedly the one designed in the 1930s by Vita Sackville-West and Harold Nicholson at Sissinghurst Castle in England. It attracts thousands of visitors from all over the world every year, many bearing pen and notebook to jot down clever planting ideas.

An all-white scheme sounds simple enough, but it is no easy thing to get right. There is much more to it than assembling a random collection of plants with white flowers or silver foliage. The acid test is how well an all-white scheme performs from season to season. It takes thoughtful planning and skilful planting to get plants to flower in a natural sequence, while at the same time making sure the garden has structural definition throughout the year.

Top British garden photographer Andrew Lawson says all-white schemes should be planted so they peak every three or four weeks. Plants that flower continuously, such as *Viola cornuta* and *Centranthus alba*, can be reinforced, he says, by those that are repeat-flowering, like roses, and annuals such as snapdragons and nicotiana. "Think about combining the tightly clustered flowers on delphinium spires with the loose sprays of crambe and gypsophila," he says. "Imagine softening the blobby flower heads of viburnums and azaleas with the more scattered flowers of dogwoods or *Magnolia stellata*.

Here are some suggestion for a white scheme.

Trees

Prunus serrulata 'Mt. Fuji' (Oriental cherry)
Prunus subhirtella 'Alba' (flowering cherry)

Groundcovers

Artemisia 'Silver Brocade' (wormwood)
Cerastium tomentosum (snow in summer)
Convallaria majalis (lily-of-the-valley)
Galium odoratum (sweet woodruff)
Lamium maculatum album (spotted dead nettle)
Stachys byzantina (lamb's ears)

Vines

Clematis armandii
Clematis 'Duchess of Edinburgh'
Clematis 'Gillian Blades'
Clematis henryi
Clematis 'Mme. Le Coultre'
Hydrangea petiolaris (climbing hydrangea)
Jasminum officinale (jasmine)
Wisteria sinensis 'Alba' (Chinese wisteria)

Shrubs

Buddleia davidii 'White Bouquet' (butterfly bush)
Choisya ternata (Mexican orange blossom)
Deutzia crenata 'Nikko'
Deutzia gracilis
Erica carnea 'Springwood White' (heather)
Hydrangea arborescens 'Grandiflora' (hills of snow hydrangea)
Hydrangea paniculata
Lavandula angustifolia 'Alba' (lavender)
Lonicera 'Winter Beauty' (honeysuckle)
Philadelphus 'Belle Etoile' (mock orange)
Potentilla 'White Queen'
Spiraea 'Snowmound'
Viburnum plicatum 'Mariesii'
Viburnum 'Summer Snowflake'

Roses

'Blanc Double de Coubert'
'Iceberg'

'Margaret Merril'
'Mme. Alfred Carrière'
'Mme. Hardy'
'Rambling Rector'
'Wedding Day'
'White Dawn'

Bulbs

Agapanthus praecox alba
Anemone blanda
Erythronium 'White Splendour' (dog's tooth violet)
Galanthus (snowdrops)
Galtonia candicans (summer hyacinth)
Leucojum (snowflake)
Lilium candidum (madonna lily)
Lilium 'Casa Blanca' (lily)
Narcissus
Tulipa 'White Trumpeter'
Zantedeschia (calla lily)

Perennials

Anemone japonica 'Honorine Jobert'
Anthemis punctata cupaniana
Aruncus (goat's beard)
Aster ericoides (heath aster)
Astrantia major (masterwort)
Bergenia 'Bressingham White'
Boltonia asteroides 'Snowbank'
Campanula carpatica 'White Clips' (bellflower)
Campanula persicifolia 'Alba' (bellflower)
Cimicifuga 'White Pearl' (bugbane)
Dicentra 'Langtrees' (bleeding heart)
Dicentra spectabilis 'Alba' (bleeding heart)
Dictamnus albus (gas plant)
Digitalis (foxglove)
Erigeron 'Sommerneuschnee' (fleabane)
Galega officinalis 'Alba'
Geranium clarkei 'Kashmir White'
Geranium pratense 'Album'
Geranium renardii
Geranium sanguineum 'Album'
Geranium sylvaticum 'Album'

Gypsophila paniculata 'Bristol Fairy' (baby's breath)
Helleborus x *sternii*
Hosta 'Francee'
Hosta 'Royal Standard'
Iris setosa 'Alba'
Macleaya cordata (plume poppy)
Paeonia 'Snow Princess' (peony)
Phlox divaricata 'Dirigo Ice'
Phlox paniculata 'Fujiyama'
Physostegia virginiana 'Summer Snow' (obedient plant)
Pulmonaria officinalis 'Sissinghurst White' (lungwort)
Salvia 'Snow Hill' (sage)
Sidalcea candida (mallow)
Stachys byzantina 'Cotton Ball' (lamb's ears)
Viola cornuta 'Alba' (violet)

Annuals

Alyssum
Antirrhinum (snapdragon)
Argyranthemum (marguerite daisy)
Impatiens 'Carnival White'
Lavatera 'Mont Blanc' (annual mallow)
Lobelia
Nicotiana (flowering tobacco)
Petunia

The Midas Touch: Bold Use of Plants with Golden Foliage

Forget about having a green thumb. Do you have the Midas touch—the power to turn dull, uninteresting areas of your garden into treasure troves of beautiful golden foliage? It's easier than it sounds. All you need are a few of the latest and best golden foliage plants to do the trick. The transformation can be quite magical.

You probably won't want to mass too many golden foliage plants together. The effect could be jarring. But when warm-yellow foliage is intelligently placed to contrast or complement the soft grays of artemisias, blues of lavenders, whites of hardy geraniums, or subtle burgundy shades of gorgeous foliage plants such as *Euphorbia* 'Chameleon', the impact can be quite brilliant.

- For starters, how about *Hydrangea serrata* 'Golden Sunlight', a relatively new introduction from Europe? Extremely resistant to sunburn, the foliage starts out a striking golden color in spring and slowly softens to a very pleasant, mellow chartreuse by summer. The lacecap flowers have dark pink petals with blush-pink, almost white, edges. 'Golden Sunlight' is hardy to Zone 6, and grows to about 4 feet (1.2 m), making it easy to place in modest-sized gardens.

- To brighten a shady corner, there's the new golden-leafed bleeding heart (*Dicentra* 'Gold Heart'). This is in short supply, so you'll have to hunt around for it. Once you get one, you'll be pleased at how magically it can bring light and warmth to areas hidden in the shadows.

- Gold-leafed shrubs such as *Euonymus fortunei* 'Emerald 'n' Gold' or *Euonymus japonica* 'Aureo-marginata' can be used with dwarf conifers with golden foliage, like *Thuja orientalis* 'Aurea Nana' or the *Taxus baccata* 'Fastigiata Aurea' (golden Irish yew) to sustain the Midas theme.

- For something special, how about the beautiful, but relatively unknown, golden grass *(Milium effusum* 'Aureum')? It only grows 12 to 16 inches (30 to 40 cm) high and thrives best in cool, moist shade, ideally beside a pond or brook. And while you're poking around in the grass section of the garden centers, check out the all-gold dwarf form of sweet flag grass (*Acorus* 'Minimus Aureus') and the popular variegated golden foliage of *Hakonechloa macra* 'Aureola', ideal for growing in containers but equally lovely, once established, as a cascading feature plant in light shade.

- Back on the sunny side, *Spiraea* 'Goldflame' is aptly named for its very rich golden-yellow foliage, which will stay fresh and lively, given a little light shade from the searing afternoon sun of summer.

- On the ground, *Genista pilosa* 'Vancouver Gold' is a fast-spreading evergreen shrub that will carpet the edges of paths or sunny banks with thousands of tiny golden-yellow flowers. For attractive, soft golden-yellow foliage, creeping jenny (*Lysimachia nummuralia* 'Aurea') makes a smashing groundcover. All it requires is reasonably moist soil and light shade protection in order to avoid scorching. If soil conditions are right, this popular plant for trailing in hanging baskets will even thrive in deep shade. The golden-yellow leaves of *Lamium maculatum* 'Aureum' also make a bright groundcover, but this plant is not happy if it is exposed to direct sun.

- If you're looking for the special golden look in a new tree for your garden, you can do no better than pick the lovely *Robinia pseudoacacia* 'Frisia.' Flourishing best in plenty of sun in well-drained, even dryish, soil, 'Frisia' has exquisite golden-green foliage that always benefits from being placed (where possible) against a darker green backdrop of conifers.

- Two other well-behaved golden-leafed deciduous shrubs for gardens where space is limited are *Sambucus racemosa* 'Plumosa Aurea', which has finely cut yellow leaves, and the golden mock orange (*Philadelphus coronarius* 'Aureus'), which has leaves that start out golden-yellow and slowly turn more green-yellow in midsummer, about the time the white flowers begin to appear with their heavenly orange-blossom scent.

- Herbaceous perennials also have a majestic role to play in the Midas scheme of things. The king of the golden hostas is 'Sum and Substance', which has enormous golden-chartreuse leaves. Too big for small borders? More manageable to place are 'Sun Power', 'Golden Sunburst', 'Golden Tiara' or 'Piedmont Gold'. Other perennials that will add flashes of golden foliage texture to your garden could include *Campanula* 'Dickson Gold', which is ideal for a rock garden, growing only 6 inches (15 cm) high; *Gaura lindheimeri* 'Corrie's Gold', a new variety with blotchy, creamy-yellow leaves; *Geranium* 'Ann Folkard', which has chartreuse-yellow foliage; and the very useful golden creeping thyme (*Thymus* 'Gold Edge').

Silver Sensations

Gertrude Jekyll, the famous English garden designer (better known to some as Aunt Bumps, Mother of All Bulbs) was one of the first, if not the first, to make a big design statement using plants with silvery-gray foliage. Because of its color neutrality, Jekyll thought gray foliage added brilliance to the perennial border and she made emphatic use of plants like stachys, santolina, artemisia, senecio and lychnis. Here's a guide to some of the best silver-gray foliage plants.

- *Anaphalis margaritacea* (pearly everlasting). This plant has attractive gray foliage with a wooly feel to it; its clusters of white flowers are a bonus. It grows to 1 to 3 feet (30 to 90 cm), thrives in full sun and makes a good companion for roses and sun-loving ornamental grasses and sedums.

- *Artemisia* 'Powis Castle'. A beautiful cross between *A. absinthium* and *A. arborescens*, 'Powis Castle' produces a bushy, upright clump of finely divided silvery leaves. It grows to 1 foot (30 cm) high by 2 1/2 feet (75 cm) wide. Also check out 'Silver Mound', a popular rock garden plant that produces a compact mound of feathery silver-gray leaves. It also performs well in containers. Grows 2 1/2 to 3 feet (75 to 90 cm) high and wide.

- *Ballota pseudodictamnus*. This is easy to care for, has no pests and few diseases, and is evergreen if planted in a protected spot in milder areas. It grows about 2 feet (60 cm) tall and spreads a little wider. The small, oval-shaped, gray-green leaves look like tiny bowls and are arranged in pairs up the silver stems. In a clump, they have a highly patterned, very decorative look. Ballota will tolerate poor soil but don't make it suffer too much.

- *Lychnis coronaria* (rose campion). It has felty, gray foliage and long stems bearing bright magenta-rose flowers. Great for cutting, it grows 3 to 4 feet (90 cm to 1.2 m) and blooms in July and August. There is a white version, 'Alba', and a soft pink and white cultivar, 'Angel Blush'.

- *Phlomis fruticosa* (Jerusalem sage). This has wooly gray-green foliage and isolated clusters of yellow banana-like flowers. It grows to 3 to 4 feet (90 cm to 1.2 m) and thrives in full sun.

- *Salvia argentea* (cabbage-leaf salvia). This plant's large, furry, silver leaves grow in a compact, flat, cabbage shape. It seems to do best off the ground, although some gardeners have had success growing it in the perennial border. It looks exceptionally good when grown in a terracotta pot.

- *Senecio*. There are a few excellent silver foliage plants in this genus. The best known is dusty miller (*Senecio maritimus*/*Senecio cineraria*), which has felty silver-gray leaves and is mostly grown as an annual, although in mild areas it can survive the chill of winter. *Senecio greyi* 'Sunshine' is a silver-leafed shrub that grows about 3 feet (90 cm) high and has bright butter-yellow flowers in spring. It thrives in well-drained soil and looks good at the foot of shrubs like purple smoke bush and mock orange. It is tender in all but Zones 7 and 8.

- *Stachys byzantina* (lamb's ears). One of the most-used silver-foliage plants in the gardens, this makes a great groundcover in a sunny location, an excellent decorative edging plant for paths, or a fine feature plant in the herbaceous border. The soft, silver-gray leaves look and feel rather like the ears of lambs. In mid-June the plant sends up solid silver spikes, which by early July produce tiny lilac-purple flowers. Top cultivars are 'Silver Carpet', which grows to only 6 to 8 inches (15 to 20 cm); 'Primrose Heron', which grows to 12 to

When people suggest that growing annual flowers is an expensive proposition, I often compare the amount spent on dinner at a good restaurant to the cost of planting a garden with bedding plants. Both are pleasurable experiences. A nice meal, however, lasts only a single evening, while a garden is full of fragrance, color and beauty for several months and can be enjoyed by family, friends and passersby alike; both are about the same price.

—Lois Hole, Alberta garden center owner and author

18 inches (30 to 45 cm) and has pale, yellow-green, felty leaves; and 'Countess Helene Von Stein', which grows to 12 to 18 inches (30 to 45 cm).

- *Thymus vulgaris* 'Argenteus' (silver thyme). This small, bushy, low-growing herb with silver-edged green leaves tumbles over containers easily and produces lilac flowers during summer. One of the best varieties for cooking.

- *Verbascum bombyciferum* (mullein). This herbaceous perennial grows to 5 feet (1.5 m) tall in full sun and produces bright yellow flowers in July, but its most appealing exotic characteristic is its soft, silver-gray foliage. It is a real show-stopper that will have all your visitors oohing and aahing over its theatrical impact.

Your Guide to Water Gardening

There is always room in a garden, no matter how small, for a water feature and a few water plants. It doesn't matter if you live in an apartment with a balcony or a townhouse with a tiny patio, you can still have at least a ceramic pot or half-barrel with a few well-chosen water plants and a small fountain or bubbler. The look and sound of a water feature is immensely relaxing. Water features are easy to install, take little time to maintain, and can make a world of difference to the atmosphere of your outdoor living space.

You can now buy easy-to-assemble pond kits that come complete with everything you need—pump, rubber liner, filter, fountain, plants—to create the look you want. Some suppliers even throw in Japanese trapdoor snails to gobble up any algae that might form. Oval-shaped ponds are very popular, but simple rectangular ponds have a special charm and elegance, to my mind.

10 Tips for Building a Pond

Best tip: Do your research. Before you even dig a hole, join a club or go on a pond tour and see how others have done it. Or call in a professional and have them build your pond for you or give you the benefit of their years of experience.

1. **Decide if you want a fish pond or a plants-only water garden.** It is important to make up your mind on this right at the beginning. If you are going to have fish, you will need to build a pond that is deep enough to deter raccoons and herons. Raccoons can be a major headache, but they won't enter ponds with steep sides that go straight down more than 2 feet (60 cm). A heron likes to stand in water and wiggle its toes to attract fish. If it can't stand in the pond because the

water is too deep, it can't catch fish. Some people weave complex webs of fish line over their pond to deter herons, but this can be unsightly and often defeats the whole purpose of having a pond in the first place.

2. **Get your pond in the right location.** It is a common mistake to build the pond too far from the house. Make sure you locate it where you can get maximum enjoyment with minimal effort. Usually this means placing it where you can see it from your kitchen or living room window. If you're making a free-form pond of your own design, use a hose to outline the shape, then mark the line with spray paint.

3. **Don't locate your pond in too much shade.** If you intend to have water lilies, you'll need sun to get the plants to bloom properly. It is a mistake to build a water-lily garden in a shaded area on the north side of the house.

4. **Don't make your pond too small.** The most common complaint of people who have just installed a pond is that it isn't big enough. If you have plenty of room, consider a pond that is at least 11 by 16 feet (3.3 by 5 m). This allows plenty of room for water lilies and other water plants as well as plants for decoration on the sides. You can get complete pond kits in this and bigger sizes.

5. **Choose a rubber liner rather than concrete.** Water freezes in winter and unless you've done a good reinforcement job, you'll find the walls of concrete ponds often crack. Rubber (EDPM) liner is the most popular choice of pond builders. It is flexible, easy to install, less expensive than concrete, and allows you to make changes and last-minute adjustments.

6. **Install a proper filter system.** Green water is the result of not having an adequate filter system. Discoloration is caused by fish, plant fertilizer and decaying plant material. It is a serious oversight not to incorporate an efficient filtration system.

7. **Make sure your pond is on the level.** Check the levels when you build your pond or you may end up with one end higher than the other.

8. **Consider including a waterfall in the design.** A waterfall adds interest and a sense of excitement. It also helps keep the water clean and brings the relaxing sound of running water to the garden.

9. **Avoid pots that leak.** Don't use ordinary nursery potting soil for submerged plants. The soil will get into the pond and the fertilizer will end up polluting the water.

10. **Choose fish carefully.** Once you have established a family of fish, introduce new fish slowly. Quarantine them and watch them closely for a couple of weeks to make sure they are disease free.

Water Lilies: The Quintessential Water Plant

You don't need a lot of plants for a water garden, but you will certainly want some water lilies (*Nymphaea*). They are, after all, the quintessential pond plant. Most need five or six hours of sun to bloom properly, though the lily pad has charm with or without flowers. Water lilies are not cheap. Expect to pay $30 to $40 for one plant. And there are thousands from which to choose.

There are tropical and hardy water lilies, so be sure you know which kind you are buying. Tropical lilies should be treated as annuals that bloom for a single season. Hardy water lilies will bounce back every year and go through the winter safely.

Water lilies can be separated into three basic sizes—large, medium and small—according to how far the leaves spread. Always ask about the "spread" when you buy: lilies are listed as small, 1 to 6 feet (30 cm to 1.8 m); medium, 6 to 12 feet (1.8 to 3.6 m); or large, 12 feet (3.6 m) and up. The more water surface you have, the bigger the lily you can place. In a small pond you probably don't need more than a couple. In a tub, barrel or small pond, you definitely need only one. Look for miniature plants, which spread only a few feet and don't require deep water.

Water lilies will flower reliably, provided they are planted in rich soil in warm, shallow water and get at least five hours of direct sunlight. The more sun they get, the more flowers they produce. They are heavy feeders and need to be well fertilized before being plonked in the water. To do this without polluting the water, use heavy clay to sandwich slow-release fertilizer in the soil in the pot. Use fertilizer tablets (10-26-10) at a rate of one per gallon (4 L) per month. You can increase your stock through division in the fall.

Dead and decaying leaves should be removed to prevent any buildup of rotting vegetation in the water. Water lilies thrive best when they don't have to compete too vigorously with other plants. Oxygenating plants will do a great job of keeping the water clean and free of algae, but you should also change the water in small tubs and troughs regularly. A fountain or spouting ornament also helps oxygenate the water.

Here are some top hardy water lilies.

- 'Attraction'. One of the largest of the hardy, free-flowering red water lilies. The inner petals are deep garnet with a glowing orange stamen. Makes one of the best cut flowers. Suitable for a medium to large pond.

- 'Charlene Strawn'. This sweetly scented water lily has rich yellow inner petals with soft yellow outer petals. A very prolific bloomer. Specks and mottles dot the abundant leaves. Leaf spread is 3 to 5 feet (90 cm to 1.5 m), making it suitable for a medium to large pond. Blooms are held high above the water.

- 'Firecrest'. The clear lavender-pink blooms are held above the water with sepals hanging down. Stamens are orange with red anthers, creating a fiery effect. New leaves are a deep purple maturing to green. A good lily for a medium-sized to large pond. If it's given plenty of room, you will be rewarded with the most frequent blooming.

- 'Masaniello'. A full, very free-flowering, bicolored water lily. The inner petals are strawberry-pink with outer petals fading to pale pink. The stamens are golden-orange with golden-yellow anthers. This lovely lily is valued for its ability to bloom in light shade. An excellent plant for any size pool.

- 'Mrs. C.W. Thomas'. The soft, shell-pink blooms are held high above the bronzy-green leaves. A beautiful, free-flowering and vigorous cultivar which will do well in a large container or medium to large pond.

- 'Odorata'. A smaller-growing lily with fragrant, white or pale pink, star-shaped blossoms. Mahogany-colored flower stalks are surrounded by soft green leaves. The cup-shaped flowers are held above the water. A very reliable lily for tubs or medium-sized ponds.

- 'Sioux'. This long-established hybrid is still one of the best available. The flower color deepens from yellow-orange to orange-red over three days.

- 'Splendida'. This beautiful, large, deep reddish-pink flower will provide an even deeper color in rich soil. The fragrance is delightful, especially on the second day. Best suited to a medium or large pond.

- 'Virginalis'. Considered to be one of the best all-around hardy white lilies, this is very free flowering, with a noticeably full fragrance in new blooms. New leaves are purple or bronze and mature to green. Suitable for any size pond.

Top Water Plants

You need more than water lilies to give your pond or water feature a lush, tropical look. A variety of reliable shallow water and marginal plants—rushes, irises, reeds—will give your pond a natural look. As well as using hardy fare like pickerel weed, irises and hornwort, try to find room on the banks for tender plants, such as cannas and bird of paradise (*Strelitzia*). As

long as you are prepared to overwinter some of the more tender plants—
and many can be overwintered as indoor plants—you can create very
interesting displays. For gardeners with a new pond to plant, here's a
water-plant starter list.

- **Arrowheads** (*Sagittaria*). These are now regarded as prerequisite pond
  plants, along with hard-flowering marginals such as marsh marigold
  (*Caltha palustris*) and the sky-blue flowers of water forget-me-nots
  (*Myosotis palustris*). Hardy to Zone 5.

- *Cannas.* Spectacular water canna lilies are now available, some of
  which can soar to 6 feet (1.8 m) high. Look for 'Bengal Tiger'
  (variegated foliage and orange flower), 'Black Knight' (purple with
  bright red flowers), and the Longwood Hybrids (pink, red and yellow).
  The cannas are all tender and need to be brought into a frost-free place
  over winter.

- **Dwarf cattail** (*Typha minima*). The narrow leaves, 12 to 18 inches
  (30 to 45 cm), and the small, round, chocolate-brown seed heads are
  what make this plant so popular. Hardy.

- **Egyptian papyrus** (*Cyperus papyrus*) will give you a lovely spray of
  green foliage atop 4-foot (1.2-m) stems. Tropical.

- **European brookline** (*Veronica beccabunga*). A shallow-water plant,
  ideal for disguising the pond perimeter. The stems, growing from the
  slightly submerged pot, will scramble up and over the pond edge. The
  small blue flowers with white centers are a bonus. Hardy.

- **Hornwort** (*Ceratophyllum demersum*). A valuable oxygenating plant. Its
  submerged foliage helps to clarify the water. Hardy.

- *Iris laevigata* 'Variegata'. Native to Japan and eastern Siberia, this thrives
  in a water depth up to 4 inches (10 cm) above the pot. It has pale
  lavender-blue flowers with attractive, cream and white, striped foliage.
  Other aquatic irises with bold sword-like leaves include the yellow flag
  iris (*Iris pseudacorus*), which has a bright yellow flower at the top of a
  stem that can reach 4 or 5 feet (1.2 to 1.5 m) high, and the more
  manageable blue flag iris (*I. versicolor*), which grows only 3 feet
  (90 cm) high. Variegated iris (*I. pseudacorus* 'Variegata') is another good
  choice. Hardy.

- **Parrot feather** (*Myriophyllum aquaticum*). Another water clarifier with
  attractive foliage that helps to disguise the perimeter of a pond. Hardy.

- **Pickerel weed** (*Pontederia cordata*). The glossy, deep green leaves
  resemble bird of paradise foliage. It grows 18 to 24 inches (45 to
  60 cm) high and produces soft blue flower spikes. Hardy.

- **Rushes and reeds.** Zebra rush (*Scirpus* 'Zebrinus') is a wonderful decorative specimen. Also consider blue rush (*Juncus glaucus*), goldrush reed (*Phragmites australis*) and flowering rush (*Butomus umbellatus*). All are hardy to Zone 6.

- **'Black Magic' taro** (*Colocasia esculenta* 'Black Magic'). A fine marginal water plant, this cultivar has spectacular, charcoal-black leaves. It needs to be overwintered as a houseplant. Tropical.

- **Water hyacinth** (*Eichornia crassipes*). Widely used to prevent algae blooms, this floating plant has thick succulent-like leaves and attractive, lilac-colored flowers that only last one day. Two other first-rate floating plants are fairy moss (*Azolla filiculoides*) and water lettuce (*Pistia stratiotes*). Tropical.

- **Water violet** (*Hottonia palustris*) and Canadian pondweed (*Elodea canadensis*) are excellent oxygenating plants. Nature's water purifiers, they float on the surface or sink under the water and help to keep a pond free of algae. Both are hardy.

- **Yellow snowflake** (*Nymphoides geminata*). It gets its common name from the fringed yellow blooms. It is valued for the interesting, snakeskin-like brown mottling on the green, waterlily-type leaves. Hardy.

Some people say they only grow native plants, but there is nothing wonderful in that. Gardening is a work of art. You can imitate nature, but you have to remember that you are in control, nature isn't.

—Penelope Hobhouse, British gardening writer and lecturer

Garden Maintenance

Keeping your garden looking healthy and attractive means you can't neglect it—not even during the long, lazy days of summer. Lawns need to be maintained and perennial borders must be kept trimmed or they very quickly turn into chaotic jungles of yellowing foliage and brown seed heads. The secret is to engage in good gardening practices. This is the key to a healthy garden and healthiness is the first prerequisite of a beautiful garden.

Good Garden Practices: Keep Your Garden Healthy Year Round

The one sure way to keep your garden pest and disease free is to maintain a high standard of garden hygiene and general maintenance. Good design and a creative mix of flowers and foliage are important, but the best thing you can do to make your garden look terrific is to concentrate on plant healthiness. This means carefully thinking about what professional landscapers call "good garden practices"—basic maintenance chores that give a garden a fighting chance against pests and diseases. Here are some tips.

- **Have a regular maintenance schedule.** One of the biggest mistakes many gardeners make is irregular watering, fertilizing and cutting. Healthy gardens are always maintained on a regular schedule.

- **Water wisely.** Water lawn areas deeply once a week and flower beds as needs dictate. If you see a plant under stress, water it right away.

- **Don't waste money on cheap, fast-acting fertilizers.** Quality, slow-release fertilizer is the only kind you should use. Liquid fertilizers are best used to give plants a quick green-up, but for long-term health use a balanced, slow-release type such as 6-8-6.

- **Mulch with well-aged mushroom manure.** Steer and horse manure are good but tend to have more undigested weed seed, which can become a nuisance. When mulching in spring, always carefully side-dress around actively growing plants to avoid shock or burning.

- **An organic mulch will draw nitrogen from the soil.** This can result in starving plants of the nitrogen they need. You can compensate for this by using a balanced fertilizer as a supplement.

- **Use a rotary spreader to fertilize your lawn.** A rotary spreader gives you a more even finish. With drop spreaders, you invariably end up with striping, no matter how careful you are.

- **Use herbicides and insecticides appropriately.** Practice what landscape professionals call "integrated pest management," which means going from the least toxic to increasingly toxic measures to control unwanted pests. You can solve a slug problem very simply by going around the garden every night with a flashlight for a couple of weeks and picking the slugs off plants. A strong jet of water will knock aphids off plants. Once on the ground, they won't be able to climb back. There are a lot of things you can do before using chemicals, and some chemicals are less harmful than others. Some persistent weeds can be eradicated by using a dab-on weed killer rather than a spray. Some herbicides become inert the moment they touch the soil so there is no danger of it leaching into the water system.

- **Clean up litter to eliminate root weevils and sowbugs.** Sowbugs like to live under old pieces of wood, and root weevils—the little pests that chomp holes in rhododendron leaves—live in leaf litter. If you clean up the leaf litter and make sure old pieces of wood are not left lying around, you won't have to worry about sowbugs and weevils.

- **Don't look on moss killer as a long-term solution.** However, it may be the most appropriate way to temporarily eliminate moss until you have the time and money to install better drainage, upgrade soil and improve light conditions.

- **Beware of gardeners bearing gifts.** Watch that you aren't given a whole bunch of weedy plants that will take over your garden. Often friendly gardeners are only too pleased to give away plants that have colonized their own gardens and become a nightmare.

- **Always play it safe in the garden.** Use a tarp to drag plants, and when moving heavy items, call for help. Wear protective goggles and good gloves when working among shrubs.

- **Consider hiring a professional for some chores.** You can have a landscaper come in to prune trees, shear hedges and fertilize lawns, leaving more time for jobs you like to do.

> *In many ways, gardening is very similar to ceramics—an amazingly complex medium where the final result is based on understanding, experience and an alchemistic collaboration with the deities, the potter with the God of Fire, the gardener with Mother Nature.*
>
> —Robin Hopper, Victoria, British Columbia gardener and potter

10 Ways to Love a Lawn

Not everyone loves a lawn. In fact, it is vaguely fashionable nowadays not to love a lawn. There are three main reasons for this: it is a waste of space that could be better used to grow vegetables, shrubs or trees; it is a waste of time and energy because of all the endless fertilizing and mowing and liming and hole-poking; it is a waste of vast amounts of water that could be better used for drinking or showering or washing vegetables and important things like that.

So before we get into the point of this story—10 ways to make your lawn green and sensational this summer—we ought to hear a few words from those who love, value and appreciate grass for its calm, green, swardy charms. The late English poet and dramatist Gordon Bottomley felt passionately about grass: "When you destroy a blade of grass / You poison England at her roots / Remember no man's foot can pass / Where evermore no green life shoots." Poet Rupert Brooke felt much the same: "Breathless, we flung us on the windy hill / Laughed in the sun, and kissed the lovely grass."

Not only do lawns beautify our neighborhoods and give children a place to play, they also keep us cool in summer, reduce pollution, absorb sound and control erosion. The temperature over a lawn will be 10 to 14 degrees cooler than over concrete. A lawn also acts like a sponge, catching airborne dust, pollen and spores. Runoff water from lawns is less polluted than rainwater that runs across asphalt and concrete. Lawns smother noise as effectively as a heavy carpet on a felt pad. Along with ornamental plants, they reduce undesirable noise levels by 20 to 30 percent. In addition, grass holds soil in place and can prevent steep banks from crumbling away.

Here are 10 ways you can make your lawn green and sensational.

1. **Always aerate.** This is the most important and kindest thing you can do for any lawn, especially one battling for survival in hard, compact, clay soils. Compacted soil can literally choke the life out of grass. To aerate, poke holes a few inches (8 cm) deep every 6 inches (15 cm) or so into the lawn or pull out 2- or 3-inch (5- to 7.5-cm) plugs of grass. Either way, the idea is to get more oxygen and nutrients to the roots. Some experts say if you aerate, you can forget about fertilizing.

2. **Lime every year.** Lime sweetens the soil and reduces acidity that builds up from all the rain we get. The idea is to get the soil to a moderate pH of 6 to 6.5. Fine, powdered lime is better than agricultural lime because it breaks down into the soil faster. While it is best to lime in fall, you can also spread the stuff around in spring.

3. **Never mow grass shorter than one-third its height.** This is especially true in shady, moss-prone areas where the grass needs as much length as possible to drink in light and stay healthy. Raise the level of your mower one notch every month as you go through the year. Start out in the spring with the mower low to the ground and

Between a Rock and a Hard Place

Digging comes naturally to me. I can do it all day, non-stop, almost machine-like. People who come by my garden are sometimes amazed at how many spades full of dirt I have been able to turn in a day. I reckon it's really all genetic predisposition. When I'm spading away in the garden, I feel a definite connection to my ancestors—generation after generation of sod-turners from Derbyshire. When there was no work for them clod-thumping in potato and turnip fields, they found employment shoveling coal from the belly of the earth in north Nottinghamshire collieries.

This is how the rhythmic motion of spade down, spade in, spade out was perfected in genes passed down from my forefathers. Bull-necked and ox-shouldered, the Whysalls probably shoveled whole hillsides from one part of England to the other without pausing for a tea break.

In my garden one spring there was no time for indulging in the more cerebral side of gardening, scheming out new plant combinations, redesigning and upgrading flower beds, contemplating what new cultivar to add, what species to take away. It was weeks and weeks of brutal trench warfare as I dug deep to terrace a slope, install a French drainage system, and create new levels of lawns and deeper perennial borders.

It was day after day of patiently shifting and sifting soil and sods, sand and rocks. One of my most respected gardening pals claims the English hate rocks and insist on burying them given every opportunity. He says it has something to do with the fact that they associated rocks and stones with sinister, evil, witch spirits.

So when I told him I had just spent days wrestling with two giant boulders, he said it was completely in character. The rocks, two brutes with hideous bulk, stood in the way of my new, soil-less, perfectly level lawn. I bought a sledge hammer but each blow did more damage to me than to the rocks. I struck them hard and square but the shock waves shot straight back up the shaft of the hammer and into my body. Undeterred, I visited a tool rental place, but they told me it would be futile to try jack-hammering the rocks.

As snow fell one freaky spring Saturday morning, I stood alone in the garden. Just me and two giant rocks of ages. Two immovable objects. Thoughts of Druids and Stonehenge sprang to mind. Pulley and levers. Ropes and rollers. Using two heavy timbers, I managed to raise the rocks, ever so slightly, but enough to give room to dig underneath. Then I released the supports and allowed the monster stones to sink deeper into the earth, well below the surface.

My friend thinks I have made a big mistake. I should have raised the rocks and made a display of them. But perhaps the need for a lawn is also genetically inherited, and, anyway, being an Englishman, a rock poking out of the lawn is just not my cup of tea.

Hours spent digging and wrestling with rocks reminded me how immensely physical gardening can be. Once the basic digging was done, I had yards and yards of sand and soil to wheelbarrow into place. At the end of the day, when my hands continued to involuntarily form the grip of a wheelbarrow handle and the ache in my back muscles refused to be consoled by a soft couch and a cold beer, I comforted myself with the knowledge that gardening is working with nature on many levels. This just happened to be one of the more tedious ones.

slowly raise it up as summer arrives. This allows the grass to develop a better root system, which in turn helps it cope better during the hot days of summer. It is not short grass that makes a lawn look nice, but the uniformity of the cut.

4. **Consider not bagging clippings.** There are mulch mowers on the market that cut grass so finely you can leave the cuttings to compost back into the lawn. One study found time spent mowing a lawn decreases by 38 percent, or from 93 to 58 minutes, when clippings are left to decompose naturally back into the lawn. A good mulching mower will cut a blade of grass five or six times before it is allowed to fall back into the lawn. The downside: if clippings are too large and bulky they mess up the lawn, and if it rains the moist atmosphere created between clippings and lawn can be a perfect breeding ground for pests and diseases.

5. **Fertilize twice a year.** The numbers on a bag of fertilizer represent the percentage of nitrogen (N), phosphorus (P) and potassium (K) in the total mix. Lawns need more nitrogen than potassium and more potassium than phosphorus, according to the U.S. Lawn Institute, so a ratio of 3-1-2 is recommended. Do not fertilize your lawn during the heat of summer. Use a fertilizer with a high nitrogen number in spring, once the grass has started to grow. This will produce a lush green lawn. In the fall, use a fertilizer with a low nitrogen number and high potassium number. This will feed the roots and increase the healthiness and winter hardiness of the lawn.

6. **Water deeply and less frequently.** Make sure the whole lawn is well-watered. Too much water is wasted on sprinkling lawns for no useful purpose. Water carries nutrients down to the roots and drier spells send roots deeper, looking for moisture.

7. **Don't keep fighting moss.** A lawn full of moss has one or all of these problems: poor drainage, inadequate light or acidic soil. The answer is to change everything. Amend and aerate the soil. Add a layer of sand to improve drainage. Improve the light by carefully pruning limbs off shade trees or shrubs. Lime generously. Then reseed or returf the area with a quality seed mix. Or, don't change a thing and go out and buy some plants that like damp, shady conditions. (But that's another story.)

8. **Renovate your lawn by raking.** This gets rid of all the dead and dying old grass and overseeding to grow new grass. Any lawn 10 years old and more is a likely candidate for overseeding. There are some perennial ryegrass seed mixes that have been specially developed for overseeding.

9. **Weed out weeds.** Toss tender, young leaves of dandelions in a salad or cook them as greens. Weeds are actually a lawn's cry for help. If it is healthy, there is no room for weeds to grow. They literally get squeezed out of existence. So don't resort to chemicals to solve your weed problem—improve the growing conditions for your lawn and the grass will take care of the weeds for you.

10. **Call in a pro.** If you are not having success, call in a professional landscaper who will take out the old lawn, lay a whole new soil foundation for you and get you to the point where all you need to worry about is maintenance. Landscape professionals have the equipment, the knowledge and the time. You will be amazed at what they can do with the most tired, worn-out lawn. This could be your best option.

So What's Bugging You?

Insects are the gardener's biggest bugbear. You work hard all year to raise a fine crop of vegetables or a handsome bed of flowers and then along comes the insect mob to work its vandalism. There is no way to stop them getting into the garden, but there is a lot you can do to discourage or eliminate them. They can spoil all your efforts in the garden and they do it with nose-thumbing impunity in many yards simply because some gardeners haven't a clue what the culprits look like.

So here's a basic guide to the most prevalent bugs and plant predators in the garden. Once you know what is doing the damage, you can decide how to deal with the problem. We are not saying here exactly how you should deal with them all—you may wish to squish them with your fingers, walk them to a neighbor's yard, use an environmentally friendly insecticidal soap, or resort to more deadly chemical warfare, if the problem is way out of hand. But knowing the enemy is half the battle.

- **Slugs.** Okay, it's not a bug, but it's the No. 1 pest in most gardens. Everyone knows the vast damage they can wreak, especially on hostas and ligularias, is diabolical. In our naivete, we have tried to thwart them with egg shells, diatomaceous earth and saloons serving free beer. The English laugh when they hear our confidence in these methods. Gardeners here exterminate or exile slugs in a variety of creative ways: drowning them in hot water, stabbing them through the heart, slicing them in two, throwing them into the neighbor's yard. Some gardeners even use slug-bait, not to kill the slimy mollusks, but to lure them into the neighbor's yard by carefully planting the bait on the border. One of the most compassionate methods is to collect them in a pail, walk them a few hundred yards down the road to a wasteground or woodland and release them, the idea being that a

10-minute walk for you is a week's walk for the slugs. Cynical gardeners laugh at this idea too—slugs can move faster than foxes when they have to, they say.

- **Aphids.** This is a term that also includes greenfly, blackfly and assorted sap-suckers. They have soft, pear-shaped bodies, live in colonies and can be green or yellow, black or brown. They can all spread viral diseases and create honeydew, which sticks to leaves and causes sooty mold to develop. Ants often can be seen bullying them around—ants milk aphids for the sweet honeydew. Best control method: pick them off and squish them or use a jet of water to knock them to the ground where they are unable to climb up again.

- **Weevils.** The snout-nosed root weevil feeds on the edges of leaves— clematis, cotoneaster, camellia, azalea and rhododendrons are especially prone—leaving a distinctly chomped appearance. Nocturnal creatures, weevils hide during the day, making them tricky to catch. One method is to collect them at night by shaking them from the plant onto newspaper; or you can place a short plank under the plant and collect weevils hiding there. They will also hide in folded pieces of

An Ode to Slugs: In Defense of the Much-maligned Mollusk

In his timeless tale of Archy, a cockroach with the soul of a *vers libre* poet, Don Marquis tells how an angleworm once tried, without success, to talk a robin out of eating him. "I am sorry but a bird has to live," said the robin, gulping down the worm, and as the hapless wriggler is slowly digested, his outlook changes, his individuality melts away and he exclaims exultantly, "Yes, a robin must live." Yes, indeed, a robin must live, but what about the lowly garden slug, that slime-slithering, belly-footed mollusk. Universally despised and rejected for its unlovely form and insatiable appetite for all that is good in a garden, the grotesque and gluttonous gastropod is without doubt one of the most terrorized and violated of earth-born creatures. Squished under boot, speared with cold steel, salted and left to squirm in agony, the detested slug has been poisoned, sliced, crushed, tossed over fences and walls, tricked over lacerating substances or lured into deadly traps. If its presence is spotted in a vegetable patch or flower bed, it can expect a violent attack of merciless force to be unleashed. At best, it may merely be hurled at a vicious velocity into a neighbor's yard; at worst, it faces an ignoble but swift execution.

While its illustrious cousins, the periwinkle, conch and helix (escargot) enjoy a degree of fame for surrendering their lives to the great god of gastronomy, the pathetic, persecuted slug inspires only disgust and dies a murderous death without dignity. Even the gentlest, most compassionate of horticulturists seem unable to speak a kind word in defense of the slinky stomach-walker.

"Call me sick but it gives me great pleasure picking the slimy little devils off plants and squishing them underfoot," says Marjorie Harris, author of the popular book, *The Canadian Gardener.* "It must be incredibly cruel to throw them in a dish of salt to dry out. They writhe and, anthropomorphically I imagine, scream in sluggy agony. Not that I am sentimental about slugs but it's faster to grind them under your heel anyway."

burlap. If this doesn't work, you may have to resort to a chemical control.

- **Whiteflies.** These tiny, white insects look like a cross between an aphid and a moth. They feed on the underside of leaves, sucking the plant's juices, and fly off in clouds when disturbed. Adults are easy to kill but young whiteflies have thick skins and appear invulnerable to insecticides. The bane of greenhouse growers, they apparently love the color yellow and therefore can be easily captured on a piece of yellow cardboard smeared with grease.

- **Froghoppers or spittle bugs.** These are little green creatures that live inside frothy "spit" that often disfigures plants, although it doesn't harm them. To dislodge them, you can squeeze them with finger and thumb or you can use insecticide.

- **Carrot flies.** This is a serious pest in all vegetable gardens. The maggot of the fly attacks the roots of carrots, celery, parsnips and even parsley. The foliage turns yellow and collapses. There are some varieties of carrot that now claim to be carrot-fly resistant. The best prevention is

---

While garden centers sell metaldehyde-based Slug Death by the boxful, Marjorie gleefully offers an assortment of imaginative lethal strategies for eliminating slugs, from sprinkling them with ginger or putting down razor-like barriers of sand, ashes, lime and salt to impaling them on a needle-sharp spike.

In England, it was recently discovered that the most satisfactory way of dispersing metaldehyde bait is to sandwich it between two layers of brown paper tape. The tape can be buried in the ground, wrapped around the trunks of trees and shrubs or coiled around the crowns of herbaceous plants. The dullard gastropod nibbles the bait after scraping away some of the tape surface, but birds and other animals are unaffected. The great advantage is that the active ingredient isn't washed away when it rains.

Perhaps the kindest execution for old, lumbering belly-foot is the irresistible invitation for a night out at the local slug saloon, where the beer is free and the company simply sub-slime. Slugs are natural party animals, they love to drink, but beer has fatal consequences for them. After swilling back a jug or two, the slug slithers off to die, likely with a smile on its face.

But there is love and romance in this world, even for the slug. Ann Lovejoy, Seattle's garden guru, describes the courtship and mating ritual of slugs this way. "Apparently as they merge, a clear and crystalline droplet forms, dangling on a long thread and spreading slowly into a scalloped, pulsating sac. As the embrace is complete, the bag of living water is drawn up and re-absorbed. The process is lengthy, lovely and moving, almost lyrical. Perhaps we ought to reconsider, making room in our hearts for these little creatures, defenseless and guileless."

So to downtrodden gastropods everywhere, we say: happy slime trails to you . . . until we meet again.

to rotate crops regularly. Sow seeds as early as possible and harvest as soon as possible. Wood ashes sprinkled around plants have also proven effective.

- **Cutworms.** This isn't a worm at all but a caterpillar that lives in the soil. It loves to chomp on the stems of young plants. They usually keel over once bitten through, which is one way of diagnosing the problem. One preventive measure is to put a protective collar around plants—paper, tin cans, and milk cartons can all be used.

- **Earwigs.** Known as hornie gollachs in Scotland, they spoil flowers and ruin foliage. They are particularly fond of chrysanthemums and dahlias. They hide during daylight, which usually renders spraying ineffective. The best method of dealing with them is to capture them in flower pots loosely stuffed with papers and upturned on the top of 3-foot (90-cm) canes or sticks.

- **Leafhoppers.** Another bug that likes to hide under leaves, it causes foliage to turn a mottled yellow. Small and slender, it sucks the sap from a plant and jumps to safety when the leaf it is feeding on is examined. Leafhoppers start to appear in mid-May. They love sun, so you might try giving the plant a little shade.

- **Spider mites.** These tiny mites look like specks of pepper on white paper. They show up on flowers, shrubs, vegetables and trees in midsummer. They can turn leaves a sickly yellow, eventually causing the leaves to die and fall. They are most active during hot, dry weather. You can kill them with garlic spray or insecticidal soap.

Not all the bugs in your yard are bad. There are some good bugs worth encouraging.

- **Ladybird beetles.** Also called ladybugs, they dine on aphids—hundreds of them a day.

- **Lacewings.** Sometimes referred to as "aphid lions," they are voracious feeders on aphids and their eggs. They are attracted by nectar-rich flowers and plants that produce a lot of pollen.

Dangers in the Garden

Gardening can be a dangerous business. Slipping and falling is one of the biggest dangers to gardeners. Wet wooden steps can be lethal, and while hunting for slugs at night with a flashlight is a good idea, it is important to be aware that you can take quite a nasty tumble if you happen to slip on one of the slimy creatures in the dark.

Many garden injuries are caused by mechanical equipment, notably lawn mowers and weed-cutters. The danger with electric mowers is obvious. The cord can be run over and cut, which is why it is so important to make sure it is plugged into a socket with a ground-fault interrupter—if the cord gets cut the power immediately shuts off.

Long pruning poles can also pose a risk. Sometimes people use them to reach branches that are dangerously close to power lines. There have also been cases where the handle has snapped back unexpectedly and hit the operator in the face. But the biggest danger in using pole-pruners is that gardeners tend to underestimate the size and weight of branches being cut. From the ground, a tree branch often looks a lot lighter than it actually is. Once cut, it can fall on the pruner with considerable impact. Here are some other dangers to be aware of in the garden.

- **Pointed branches.** It is easy to get poked in the face or eye by a branch when pruning or working away in a shrubbery. If you get jabbed once, consider pruning away the branch so it can't do worse damage the next time you are working in that area.

- **Prickly plants.** Rose and blackberry canes can scratch and slice your hands, but the other danger they pose is that they can suddenly whip back and hit you in the face, or worse, the eye. It's worth wearing shop-glasses when working with brambles and thorny stems and canes.

- **Lifting and moving plants.** Back injuries are very common among gardeners. Professionals know it is far safer and easier to drag plants on a tarp from one place to another than to lift and carry them. Another alternative to carrying a sizable plant by hand is to turn a wheelbarrow on its side, drag or push the plant in, then right the wheelbarrow and wheel the plant to its new location. Whatever lifting you have to do, always ask for help. It's true that many hands make light work.

- **Rakes and hoes.** Despite all the times it has been featured in comedies and cartoons, gardeners are still stepping on rakes and being smacked in the face. A worse danger is slipping, falling on an upturned rake and ending up impaled on the prongs.

- **Chemicals.** If you use chemicals to kill bugs and weeds, remember they can also poison you. Herbicides and pesticides are designed to kill things. Make sure you read and follow the directions on the label to the letter. You can damage vital organs—your liver, eyes and brain cells—by breathing in the stuff. Never spray when there is a breeze.

- **Water.** Ponds and water features are increasingly popular, but they pose a danger to young children, and wet rocks around a pond can be very slippery. If children are regular visitors to the garden, ponds need to be fenced. A person can fall and drown in even 6 inches (15 cm) of water.

Safety Tips

- Warm up your muscles before starting work. Do some simple stretching exercises to limber up at the beginning of your day in the garden.

- Change jobs frequently. After weeding for half an hour or so, go and do some pruning or deadheading, a job that requires you to stand rather than squat.

- Avoid stretching above your head. Take the time to get a stepladder and make the job easier on your body.

- Instead of filling your wheelbarrow or watering can to the brim, make two trips. This will give your back a break and make the task much more enjoyable.

- Don't try to do too much in one day. It is easy to get caught up in the enthusiasm of the project and be tempted to do far too much. Set yourself a reasonable goal at the outset and show some discipline when it is time to quit. At the end of the day, reward yourself with a warm bath.

# Fall

Tree at My Window

Tree at my window, window tree,
My sash is lowered when night comes on;
But let there never be curtain drawn
Between you and me.

Vague dream-head lifted out of the ground,
And thing next most diffuse to cloud,
Not all your light tongues talking aloud
Could be profound.

But, tree, I have seen you taken and tossed,
And if you have seen me when I slept,
You have seen me when I was taken and swept
And all but lost.

That day she put our heads together,
Fate had her imagination about her,
Your head so much concerned with outer,
Mine with inner, weather.

—Robert Frost

In the Garden

- Continue deadheading annuals, taking cuttings, and tidying up perennial borders as plants finish flowering.

- Divide perennials and buy new ones. You'll find excellent buys at garden centers this month, especially if you know your plants and don't need to see them in flower.

- Rake up fallen leaves. Healthy ones are best left as a natural mulch around shrubs. Others can be shredded with the lawn mower and added to the compost.

- Apply aluminum sulphate to the base of hydrangeas if you want bright blue blooms in spring. Add dolomite lime to make them pink.

- Check out ornamental grasses. They're are at their best this month and you can decide what to buy next spring.

- Early fall is a good time to plant new peonies or divide and replace old clumps. Don't plant deeper than 2 inches (5 cm) below the surface.

- Plant spring bulbs. Wait until the ground temperature drops below 60°F (16°C) at planting depth.

- Check for insects and disease before bringing indoor plants inside for winter.

- Transplant evergreens and perennials so they have time to develop new roots before winter.

- Give hedges a final trimming before winter and mulch trees and shrubs.

- Lawns can be fertilized with a low-nitrogen, high-potassium fertilizer.

- Early fall is a good time to reseed and renovate an uneven lawn or install a new one using turf or seed.

- Move tender plants—datura, tibouchina, lantana, fuchsias, pelargoniums—into a frost-free environment to overwinter.

- In mild-winter areas, replant window boxes and planter boxes with winter pansies. They will flower through to spring with only a pause during the coldest weeks of winter.

- Plant a new boxwood or cedar hedge.

- Cut down the seed heads of perennial plants or leave them until early spring to provide visual interest and attract birds over winter.

- Sow green manure crops of fall rye, winter wheat or crimson clover in empty spaces.

- Plant new trees or shrubs, or move existing trees and shrubs to a new location.

- Lift and store dahlias before or immediately after frost has blackened the foliage.

- Prune hybrid tea and floribunda roses back to about 2 feet (60 cm). Pick up all leaves with black spot and put them in the garbage. In colder areas, roses will need winter protection.

- Add dolomite lime to vegetable beds, lawns, established roses, lilacs and clematis.

- Have a soil test done this month. It will give you time to decide what needs to be done in time for spring.

3 Projects for Fall

1. **Plant a new tree.** Think carefully about its size at maturity when making your selection. Dig the hole at least 6 to 12 inches (15 to 30 cm) wider than the rootball. Check for good drainage by filling the hole with water and seeing how long it takes to empty. Ideally, the hole should empty completely in 10 to 15 minutes. If water is still sitting in the hole after an hour, you will need to improve the drainage or find a new planting site. Mix bonemeal into the soil at the bottom of the hole. Lift the tree by the whole rootball, not by the trunk. Don't plant too deeply; the top of the rootball should be level with the ground. Water well, especially through summer. (For more detailed information on trees and tree planting, see page 158.)

2. Plant allium (ornamental onion) bulbs, for a great show of color next spring. (See page 149.) Purple-flowering 'Purple Sensation', *Allium christophii* and *A. sphaerocephalon* are great performers. Also check out yellow-flowering *A. moly* and purple-flowering 'Globemaster'. For something different, ask for *A. siculum*, which has pinkish pagoda-shaped flowers, or 'Mount Everest', which has white flowers.

3. Put together a winter container to brighten your entrance, balcony or patio (see page 198). Use winter pansies and dusty miller along with foliage plants like *Skimmia japonica*, nandina, heuchera, purple sage and black mondo grass, as well as berried plants such as wintergreen (*Gaultheria procumbens*) and Japanese holly (*Ilex crenata*).

The Bard's Yard

It is perhaps predictable that after spending a summer studying *Hamlet* and *King Lear*, it crossed my mind that it would be neat to build a Bard's Garden—a border or island bed full of the flowers known and loved by Shakespeare and featured in his plays and sonnets. What plants do you need to re-create the Bard's Yard? Bee balm or not bee balm? That is the question. Actually, it's not that difficult because we now know a lot about what flowers Shakespeare was referring to.

The Bard's Yard, for example, would have some very familiar fare like monkshood (*Aconitum napellus*), blue granny-bonnet columbines (*Aquilegia vulgaris*), wild pansies (*Viola tricolor*), pinks (*Dianthus*), honeysuckle (*Lonicera periclymenum*) and marsh marigolds (*Caltha palustris*). In *Henry V*, Shakespeare compared the poisonous monkshood, also known as wolfsbane, to "rash gunpowder," and he called the wild pansy by its common Warwickshire name, love-in-idleness, in *The Taming of the Shrew*. The fragrance of honeysuckle caught Shakespeare's attention (he referred to it in both *Much Ado About Nothing* and *A Midsummer Night's Dream*) and he knew the habits of the marsh marigold, which he called "winking mary-buds" and observed that it "goes to bed wi' the sun, / And with him rises, weeping."

Here are a few other plants you'd need to build a Shakespearean garden.

- **Cowslip** (*Primula vulgaris*). Shakespeare used common yellow English primrose to describe the size of fairies. Ariel in *The Tempest*, for instance, was small enough to be able to rest in the tiny bell of a cowslip. ("In cowslip's bell I lie. There I couch when owls do cry.") You will find cowslips growing in England in pastures and hedgerows. They are hardy to −20°F (−29°C), like moist, fertile soil in partial shade and grow to about 6 inches (15 cm) high.

- **Ragged robin or crowflower** (*Lychnis flos-cuculi*). In *Hamlet*, Ophelia's "fantastic garlands" contained ragged robin, a hardy perennial with delicate, bright-pink petals that resemble a cluster of bird's feet. It thrives well enough in moist soil throughout Europe and almost qualifies as a bog or damp meadow plant in some parts.

- **Lady's smock** (*Cardamine pratensis*). This is also known as the "cuckoo flower" because it blooms around the time when the first cuckoo is heard in spring. In *Love's Labour's Lost*, spring sings a song about "when daisies pied and violets blue / And lady-smocks all silver white / And cuckoo-buds of yellow hue / Do paint the meadows with delight . . ." Lady's smock grows about a foot (30 cm) high and likes a sunny, well-drained position in the garden.

- **Long purples** (*Arum maculatum*). This is also known as cuckoo-pint and is not the most desirable form of arum for your garden. The plant has arrow-shaped leaves, tinged with purple, but it was the erect flower spike (the spadix) that caught Shakespeare's imagination when in *Hamlet* he referred to "long purples" as the flower "liberal shepherds give a grosser name / But our cold maids do dead men's fingers call them." The Italian arum (*A. italicum* 'Pictum') is one of the best varieties for the home garden.

- **Sweet briar, or eglantine** (*Rosa eglanteria*). With leaves that smell of green apples when touched, this vigorous shrub/climbing rose produces dainty pink flowers in clusters in late spring. Shakespeare used the sweet smell of briar's leaves to describe the heavenly scent of Imogen's breath in *Cymbeline*.

- **Harebell.** Shakespeare compares the blue of these wispy, bell-shaped flowers to the color of Imogen's veins in *Cymbeline*—"thou shall not lack the flower that's like thy face, pale primrose, nor the azur'd harebells, like thy veins." Some think the flower was actually the bluebell of Scotland (*Campanula rotundiflora*), which has gray-green leaves and bright blue, 1-inch (2.5-cm) flowers. Others think the harebell could be the English bluebell or wild hyacinth (*Scilla nutans*, also known as *Hyacinthoides non-scripta*).

- **Oxslip** (*Primula elatior*). Oberon, in *A Midsummer Night's Dream*, says: "I know a bank where the wild thyme blows,/ where oxslips and the nodding violet grows." The oxslip produces a simple, beautiful loose cluster of yellow flowers at the top of a short single stem. This primula is very common in woods in eastern England, around Cambridge and into Norfolk.

- **Sweet violet** (*Viola odorata*). Shakespeare refers to the pansy, which he knew better as "love-in-idleness" or "heartsease," at least 18 times in various works, but scholars believe he singled out the sweet violet for special attention, perhaps because of his love for deeply scented flowers and the color blue.

You can fail in the garden. It's okay. To fail in the garden is to learn. That's one of the reasons we like to garden— because we know we can relax and have fun and not worry that we are being marked on our performance.

—Mark Cullen, president of Weall and Cullen Garden Centres in Ontario

- **Roses.** "What's in a name? That which we call a rose, by any other name would smell as sweet." Shakespeare mentions roses in his plays and poems more than any other flower, but they would have all been the oldest of old-garden varieties—*Rosa gallica* (red rose of Lancaster), *Rosa alba* (white rose of York), the richly scented damask roses, as well as musk and cabbage roses.

- **Herbs.** No Bard's Yard would be complete without herbs. Shakespeare referred to lavender, mint, marjoram, chamomile, garlic, parsley and thyme.

- **Johnny Jump-up.** And for fun, it would not be amiss to add johnny jump-up, which has the longest common flower name in the English language: meet-her-in-the-entry-kiss-her-in-the-buttery. It is also known under many other names including kitty-come, kit-run-about, three-faces-under-a-hood, come-and-cuddle-me, pink-of-my-Joan, kiss-me, tickle-my-fancy, kiss-me-ere-I-rise and jump-up-and-kiss-me.

Plan for Spring

You want a beautiful spring garden? Then you need to get busy planting bulbs in fall to make it all happen. Those spectacular spring gardens full of tulips, daffodils and hyacinths don't just appear out of nowhere—they are patiently planted, row by row, by gardeners who know how to think ahead by planning and planting months in advance.

Your Great Bulb Planting Guide

The ideal time to plant spring- and early summer-flowering bulbs is from mid-September to late October, as soon as the ground temperature drops below 60°F (16°C) at planting depth, and before the first hard frost. Plant bulbs as soon after you buy them as possible. They should be planted three times as deep as they are high: 8 inches (20 cm) for tulips, hyacinths and daffodils; 4 inches (10 cm) for scilla, muscari, anemone and snowdrops. Plant them with the points facing up and make sure the bulbs don't touch.

"Naturalizing" is a term used to describe bulbs that will multiply and become part of the natural garden landscape. Ideal for this purpose are scilla, snowdrops, anemone, crocus, aconite, muscari, puschkinia and chionodoxa.

Bulbs can be planted all over the garden: in full sun or light shade, in borders, on terraces, along fences, in rockeries, and under shrubs and trees. Being tiny storehouses of nutrients, bulbs don't need extra fertilizer to flower the first year. However, adding slow-release bulb food, such as 9-9-6, or well-rotted cow manure is a good idea when planting bulbs you want to naturalize.

To thwart squirrels, use chicken wire about 3 inches (7.5 cm) below ground level to cover the planting site. Also consider mixing in a few alliums and fritillaria. The pungent smell of these bulbs can deter squirrels from noshing on your tulips. For the best effect, plant tulips and daffodils in generous clumps of 10, 20 or more. Mix colors for fun and artistic expression.

Good drainage is essential. Like roses, bulbs hate sitting in soggy soil. Poor drainage is the main reason bulbs fail to perform properly and flower on time. It is, however, also important to water bulbs immediately after you have planted them.

Well-drained, sandy or loamy soil is the best for bulbs to grow in. The ideal site is under deciduous trees and shrubs where they can enjoy full sun in spring and dappled shade once the trees and shrubs have leafed out for summer. The worst site? Heavy, poorly drained, clay soil that never sees the sun.

After blooming, deadhead (pinch off the faded flower head) and work a dose of slow-release fertilizer into the soil as the leaves start to die back. Allow the leaves to die back naturally. During this phase the bulb replenishes the essential nutrients it needs to flower again next year.

To put together a sequence of blooms that will stretch from the first days of spring to the beginning of summer, plant a collection of the best early, midseason and late-season bloomers. These are now very clearly labeled at garden centers. These lists will get you started.

Early-Blooming Bulbs

- *Chionodoxa* (glory of the snow). There's the standard blue form with white centers as well as 'Pink Giant', which has soft pink flowers. Grows to 6 inches (15 cm).

- *Crocus.* The colorful species crocuses (also known as "bunch-flowering crocus") bloom a little earlier than the more familiar hybrids and have smaller, more abundant flowers, which emerge before the foliage. Look for 'Lady Killer' (purple opening to white), 'Gypsy Girl' (yellow with a burgundy stripe), 'Ruby Giant' (satiny violet), 'Zwanenburg Bronze' (yellow and bronze petals) and 'Violet Queen' (lavender flowers with a bright yellow eye). They all grow about 3 inches (7.5 cm) high and are great for naturalizing.

- *Eranthis hyemalis* (winter aconite). These have bright yellow flowers and grow only 4 inches (10 cm) high.

- *Galanthus* (snowdrops). The traditional harbinger of spring, these grow 4 inches (10 cm) high and look best in dense clumps.

- *Hyacinth.* Colors range from bright mauve to pure white to light pink to porcelain blue. They are also very fragrant. Highly recommended are 'Woodstock' (dark reddish-violet), 'Delft Blue' (light blue), 'Gypsy Queen' (tangerine orange), 'Blue Jacket' (dark blue) and 'Splendid Cornelia' (lavender). They all grow to 10 inches (25 cm).

- *Iris reticulata* has lovely blue flowers and grows 6 inches (15 cm) high. The variety 'Harmony' is a softer, light blue. *I. danfordiae* is a popular yellow dwarf iris.

- *Muscari* (grape hyacinth). You'll find two kinds of grape hyacinth available at most garden centers—*M. armeniacum* and *M. latifolium*. Both are terrific, but *M. latifolium* (the giant grape hyacinth) has eye-catching, two-tone blue spikes and bigger leaves. It grows to 12 inches (30 cm), twice as tall as *M. armeniacum*. Both kinds combine well with pale blue squills.

- *Narcissus.* There are at least a dozen early-flowering daffodils and narcissus. Some of the best are 'Fortissimo' (yellow petals and orange trumpet), 'Gigantic Star' (bright yellow), 'Mount Hood' (pure white), 'Ice Follies' (creamy white) and 'Dutch Master' (yellow). They all grow to between 16 and 18 inches (40 and 45 cm).

- *Puschkinia libanotica* (striped squill). These pale blue, bell-shaped flowers grow to about 6 inches (15 cm) and make excellent partners for grape hyacinth.

- *Scilla* (bluebells). The Siberian bluebell (*S. siberica*) is the earliest of the bluebells to flower, but the later-blooming Spanish bluebell (*S. campanulata*) is also worth planting. They grow to 5 inches (12.5 cm).

- *Tulipa* (tulips). There's a wide variety of outstanding early-flowering tulips. The strikingly colorful Kaufmanniana types, sometimes called "waterlily tulips," are among the earliest to bloom. 'Ancilla' is yellow with red markings, 'Fashion' is carmine-red with an orange center, and 'Scarlet Baby' is bright red with a yellow center. Multi-petaled "double" tulips like 'Peach Blossom' (dark rose with white) and 'Monte Carlo' are a good pick. Among the classic vase-shape varieties, 'Christmas Marvel' is a great red, 'Christmas Dream' is a lovely clear pink and 'Diana' is a pure white. They all grow to 12 to 16 inches (30 to 40 cm). Also check out the short-stemmed Greigii tulips, notably 'Red Riding Hood' (bright red) and 'Pinocchio' (red with white edge).

Mid-season Bloomers

- *Erythronium* 'Pagoda' (dog-tooth violet). The nodding, sulfur-yellow, lantern-like flowers look superb under deciduous trees and shrubs.

- *Fritillaria persica* (Persian fritillaria). The maroon-purple, bell-shaped flowers are displayed on 30-inch (75-cm) stems. Also consider *F. meleagris* (checkered fritillaria), which has purple and white checkered flowers and grows to 8 inches (20 cm).

- *Narcissus.* The desirable peony-like narcissi are especially beautiful in the mid-spring garden. Great performers are 'Tahiti' (yellow with orange center), 'Ice King' (white), and 'Flower Drift' (white with orange-yellow center). For the rock garden, there's 'Thalia' (creamy white'), 'Little Witch' (pale lemon) and two favorites, 'Jack Snipes' (white with yellow trumpet) and 'Jetfire' (yellow with orange cup).

- *Ornithogalum umbellatum* (star of Bethlehem). This has attractive, silvery white flowers and grows to 6 inches (15 cm).

- *Tulipa* (tulips). There's no shortage of choice for mid-spring, with two key groups from which to choose: the Triumphs, offering many bicolors on 18- to 20-inch (45- to 50-cm) stems, and the Darwins, with extra-large flowers in bold, single colors. Top Triumphs include 'Anna Jose' (rose with cream edge), 'Attila' (lavender) and 'Dreaming Maid' (soft purple). Top Darwins include 'Oxford' (scarlet), 'Daydream' (apricot orange) and 'Pink Impression' (deep pink).

Late-season Bloomers

- *Allium* (ornamental onions). You can't plant enough of these, in my opinion. *A. christophii* is a magical work of botany. Also known as the star of Persia, it slowly opens in May into a giant, 8-inch (20-cm) globe made up of hundreds of tiny, star-shaped florets with a shiny, metallic, high-tech glint to them. Superb cut flower. Plant plenty of 'Purple Sensation', which grows to 3 feet (90 cm), and 'Globemaster', which grows to 40 inches (1 m).

- *Camassia leichtlinii*. This will give you tall, 4-foot (1.2-m) spikes of beautiful, china-blue, star-shaped flowers, displayed in clusters in late May or early June. Camassias grow happily in the perennial border and tolerate moist soil.

- *Fritillaria imperialis* (crown imperial). They're a little stinky up close, but from a distance, fritillaria look majestic with their regal crowns of exotic leaves and colorful, nodding, bell-shaped flowers. 'Lutea' has yellow flowers, while 'Rubra' has orange-red flowers. The blooms appear at the top of sturdy 3-foot (90-cm) stems.

- *Leucojum aestivum* (snowflake). This produces dainty, cup-shaped white flowers with a distinctive green spot. Snowflakes grow 16 inches (40 cm) high, tolerate moist soil, and look best planted in dense clumps. Flowering in April and May, they combine beautifully with other late-spring bloomers such as *Scilla campanulata alba*, and the star of Bethlehem (*Ornithogalum umbellatum*). They can also be teamed up with simple grape hyacinths to create a seamless continuity of bloom.

- *Narcissus*. 'Cheerfulness' flowers in late spring, producing white blooms with a yellow center. 'Yellow Cheerfulness' is another late-bloomer. They grow 16 to 18 inches (40 to 45 cm) high.

- *Tulipa* (tulips). The most exotic tulips of all—fringed, parrot, lily-flowered, and exotic Darwins—come into bloom in late spring. There are also some fine, green-streaked tulips, notably 'Greenland' and 'Spring Green'. Great parrot tulips are 'Blue Parrot' (velvet blue) and 'Fantasy' (salmon pink). Top lily-flowered tulips are 'West Point' (bright yellow), 'Mona Lisa' (lemon-yellow) and 'Elegant Lady' (creamy yellow). Star fringe tulips include 'Blue Heron' (violet-purple) and 'Burgundy Lace' (wine-red). And outstanding Darwins are 'Blue

Aimable' (velvet blue), 'Queen of the Night' (darkest black), and 'Black Diamond' (black). These all grow between 16 and 24 inches (40 to 60 cm).

- *Zantedeschia aethiopica* (calla lily). For an exotic, tropical touch, this hardy calla produces sculptural, creamy-white flowers (technically spathes). Native to South Africa, it grows 20 inches (50 cm) high. You can buy this variety in full flower in pots in spring, but the bulbs are more readily available in fall. Also known as the common calla, it will flourish in full sun or light shade in most types of soil. It likes to be well watered and will thrive very nicely beside ponds and in moderately boggy sites. It is hardy to Zone 5.

Beautiful Bulb Combos

Partnership planting—that's one of the hottest trends in the planting of spring-flowering bulbs. It's a simple idea that can produce very sophisticated results. Take two great bulbs that bloom around the same time in spring and plant them together to create a colorful partnership. You can simply combine early-flowering red tulips with giant white crocus. Or put together a classic combination of fragrant creamy white and yellow 'Cheerfulness' daffodils. Both schemes will give you a floral display to lift your spirits in spring.

- One of my favorite combos is a two-tone blue scheme comprising porcelain-blue striped squills (*Puschkinia libanotica*) with the deeper blue of grape hyacinths (*Muscari armeniacum*). A mix of white and blue grape hyacinths looks just as effective. For a warmer contrast of colors, mix dwarf yellow daffodils such as 'Tete-a-Tete', 'Jetfire' or 'Jack Snipes' with the delicate blue flowers of *Iris reticulata* or Siberian bluebells (*Scilla siberica*).

- Tulips offer an inexhaustible range of combinations. You can do yellow and white, pink and purple, or a soft pastel mix with tones of lavender and rose. The satiny red blooms of 'Christmas Marvel' or the rose-pink flowers of 'Christmas Dream' stand out beautifully when surrounded by a dense planting of blue grape hyacinths. Other classic combos include 'Ancilla' tulips (yellow center ringed by red) with blue chionodoxa; 'Apricot Beauty' tulips with the classically elegant 'Delft Blue' hyacinths; and early-blooming 'Giant White' crocus with red 'Showwinner' tulips. For dramatic impact, you can't beat a combination of 'Queen of the Night' or 'Black Diamond', the two blackest of tulips, with exotic red lily, fringed or parrot-style tulips such as 'Burgundy Lace' (wine-red) or 'Texas Fire' (sun-scorched red). Equally theatrical is a solitary white 'Maureen' tulip in the center of a clump of red or black tulips. Other outstanding white tulips for adding contrast are 'Ivory Floradale', 'Mount Tacoma', 'City of Vancouver' and 'White Trumpeter'.

- Daffodils and tulips also make great partners. Try a mix of cream-white 'Thalia' daffodils with cherry-pink 'Christmas Marvel' tulips. For a scheme with a vibrant orange accent, there's what bulb suppliers call the "Dutch sunrise duet"—orange Emperor tulips with 'Fortissimo' daffodils, which have a glowing orange trumpet edged with red and sunny yellow outer petals.

- Using bulbs to provide color and cover for slowly emerging perennials in spring is one of gardening's best camouflage tricks. Timing is all-important. You want the bulb flowers to fade away just as the perennials rise up to take over. Erythroniums and bluebells make excellent partners around clumps of hostas, astilbes and lady's mantle, while grape hyacinths can add contrast and texture to spidery clumps of black mondo grass.

  Purple and yellow crocus work well as groundcover bulbs and *Anemone blanda* and late-flowering lily-shaped tulips such as 'Elegant Lady' (soft yellow, edged with lavender-pink) or sophisticated, green-streaked 'Spring Green' offer a good sequence of color.

  Winter pansies and spring bulbs also make a good team. In mild-weather gardens, the bulbs can be planted in a pot, then overplanted with pansies for winter color. The pansies will bloom through to late spring; the bulbs will push up through the pansies in early spring. With white pansies, mix 'Delft Blue', 'Lady Derby' or 'Pink Surprise' hyacinths, or 'Apricot Beauty' tulips. With purple or blue pansies, throw in some 'Yellow Cheerfulness' or 'Touch of Lemon' daffodils. With rose pansies, consider the yellow-flowered 'West Point' lily-type or 'Pink Surprise' hyacinths. Yellow pansies mix happily with 'Blue Blazer' or 'Blue Giant' hyacinths or the cupped, creamy white petals of 'Ice Follies' daffodils. Forget-me-nots and violets are also good companions for spring bulbs, which can be planted to push up through groundcovers such as ivy and sweet woodruff.

Triple-Decker Planting

Gardening enthusiasts who live in apartments and townhouses don't have to be left out of the fun of planting bulbs in the fall. To create a natural sequence of spring-flowering bulbs on a balcony, patio or deck, all you need is a sturdy, well-drained container—something that can stand outside all winter and won't crack in freezing weather—and a few well-chosen bulbs. In very cold areas, the containers will need to be wrapped for protection.

Using a half-barrel or large pot, here's how to create a triple-decker planting.

- Put 30 single late tulips, such as 'Big Smile' (yellow), 'Avignon' (red) or 'Esther' (silvery pink) on the bottom level; 20 hyacinths on the middle level; and 25 to 30 narcissus on the top level. This will give you a succession of color. Be as creative as you like with the color contrasts.

- For a stunning, all-yellow scheme in a long narrow balcony container, use 30 double early tulips ('Monte Carlo') on the bottom, 50 crocus ('Romance') on the second level and 50 winter aconites (*Eranthis hyemalis*) on the top.

The Allure of Alliums

Every October I dutifully go into the garden to plant tulips and daffodils, snowdrops and crocuses. It feels like the right thing to do. And, of course, it is. Planting daffs and tulips in fall for spring is what I was taught to do by older, more knowledgeable gardeners when I started gardening.

But every year when spring rolls around, I always kick myself for being such a slave to tradition and for not planting more of the bulbs that always give me so much more pleasure than daffodils and tulips—ornamental onions, better known in gardening circles as alliums.

Don't get me wrong. I love the cheerful sight of all the popular harbingers of spring—snowdrops, bluebells, hyacinths and so on—but for me there is nothing more exciting than seeing the parade of ornamental onions that starts in late spring and continues into the heart of summer.

Everyone who comes to my garden in May immediately falls in love with *Allium christophii*, also known as star of Persia. If there is one allium to start with as a new gardener, this is it. The flower head is a gigantic 10-inch (25-cm) sphere composed of hundreds of tiny, silvery-purple, star-shaped florets which almost have a metalic sheen to them. The purple sphere looks, to my eye, rather like a space station. Sometimes in the garden it does appear to hover magically above other plants. Others have described it as a huge Christmas tree bauble.

We had our house painted this spring and the painter had a hard time staying on his ladder after seeing the star of Persia for the first time. I caught him on more than one occasion with his face only inches from the surface of the flower head as he studied the delicate engineering that

Container Tips

- Don't skimp on the number of bulbs you put in a pot. You want it to look full without being crowded. A 6-inch (15-cm) pot can accommodate 3 hyacinths, 6 tulips, 5 daffodils or 12 crocuses.
- Avoid planting one bulb directly over another.
- When planting a variety of bulbs in a container, remember that the bigger the bulb, the deeper it should be planted.
- Big bulbs go on the bottom, little bulbs at the top. Bulbs should not touch one another or the side of the container.
- Water the containers daily, but make sure the bulbs have good drainage. More bulbs are lost because they are left to rot in wet, boggy soil than are lost to pests and disease.
- Where winter temperatures regularly dip below freezing, protect bulbs in containers. Move small pots into an unheated garage or frost-free greenhouse, or wrap a blanket or burlap around pots too heavy to move.

connected each of the flower's starry florets to form a perfect globe about 14 inches (36 cm) off the ground.

Allium christophii combines beautifully in the perennial border with the dark purple foliage of *Euphorbia* 'Chameleon' and offers a striking contrast against the purple-black foliage of *Cimicifuga* 'Brunette'. It also mixes well with aubrieta, dianthus and low-growing phlox and it can be grown very successfully in a pot.

As lovely as *Allium christophii* is, it is still rather a novelty plant. Much more practical and generally more useful in the overall garden scheme is *A. aflatunense*, also called the cricket ball allium because that's just what the purple, spherical flower heads look like. Others have described it as the drumstick allium. Either way, it is exquisite and well worth having in your garden. This is the variety that I can never seem to plant enough of. Rosemary Verey, the grand dame of English horticulture, was the first to see how well masses of *A. aflatunense* fit under the drooping golden-yellow blossoms of laburnum trees in late May. Her inspired use of this allium at Barnsley House in Gloucestershire has made a star out of the humble ornamental onion.

Allium aflatunense grows about 3 feet (90 cm) high, blooms in early June, and combines effortlessly with roses and a wide variety of perennials.

Specialty Tulips

If you've become bored planting the same old tulips every October, here are some more unusual and exciting kinds to try for a change of pace.

- **Fringe and parrot tulips.** You don't have to stay with the traditional vase-shaped tulip; there are all sorts of exciting alternatives. Fringe and parrot tulips have ruffled or feather-like petals. Excellent parrot tulips are 'Estella Rijnveld' (red and white), 'Orange Favorite' (apricot-orange), 'Blue Parrot' (dark lavender) and 'Flaming Parrot' (lemon-yellow and flame-red). Top fringe tulips are 'Blue Heron' (lavender-blue), 'Burgundy Lace' (wine-red) and 'Fringed Elegance' (primrose-yellow with bronze center).

- **Emperor tulips.** The tallest and largest-flowered of all early-flowering tulips, these are designed for impact. Top varieties include 'Pink Emperor' (rosy pink with yellow center), 'Red Emperor' (lipstick-red), 'Albion Star' (creamy yellow with gold, red and black center) and 'Sweetheart' (lemon-yellow with white edge).

- **Darwin Hybrids.** These are the best mid-season tulips, with large flowers, bright colors and strong stems. Star performers are 'Ollioules' (rose/pink/white blend), 'Golden Oxford' (yellow), 'Red Matador' (carmine-red), 'Big Chief' (rosy pink) and 'Striped Apeldoorn' (yellow and red).

- **Lily-flowering tulips.** Handsome, graceful flowers with pointed, lily-shaped, reflexed petals, these always add style to the spring garden. Check out 'West Point' (golden yellow), 'Mariette' (deep rose), 'White Triumphator' (pure white) and 'Aladdin' (scarlet with golden edge).

- **Species tulips.** Excellent for naturalizing in the perennial border, these are growing in popularity. 'Lilac Wonder' has eye-popping pale lavender petals and a sun-yellow center. Also recommended are *Tulipa saxatilis* (similar to 'Lilac Wonder' but taller) and *T. tarda* (yellow edged with white, fragrant).

'Purple Sensation' is a reliable and easy-to-find variety, while 'Mount Everest' is a similar performer that has charming white flower heads and grows a little taller. All of these alliums are especially eye-catching when planted to pop up among perennials, especially the pink bottlebrush spikes of *Persicaria bistorta* 'Superba' (knotweed) or the elegant flowers of hardy geraniums such as *Geranium endressii* 'Wargrave Pink' or 'Phoebe Noble'.

When *Allium aflatunense* has finished flowering, the gobular flower heads turn green and eventually produce tiny, black seeds. Many gardeners like to leave the faded flower stalks in the garden to add architectural interest. Andrew Lawson, one of Britain's top garden photographers, actually saves the stalks and then reintroduces the dried flower heads into the garden in winter for visual interest.

If you like *Allium aflatunense* but would like to have a drumstick allium that packs more of a visual punch, there's 'Globemaster'. This produces 8-inch (20-cm) purple flower heads at the top of sturdy 40-inch (1 m) stems. Put half a dozen bulbs together in the center of your herbaceous border and you'll have a sensational centerpiece that will last from June to July.

Not all ornamental onions are great towering specimens. *Allium karataviense* is a dwarf variety that produces light purple-pink globes only 8 inches (20 cm) high from May to June, which makes it perfect for growing in the rockery or at the front of the border or in containers.

Allium moly (also known as the lily leek) is another diminutive ornamental onion that grows only 12 inches (30 cm) high and is much loved for its bright clusters of buttercup-yellow flowers in early spring. You may hear that it can be invasive, but while it does multiply quickly it rarely becomes a problem. Plant the lily leek under shrubs at the base of hedges and at the front of a well-drained border in a sunny spot that gets some afternoon shade.

In our hurry to pick up exotic forms of allium, there's always the risk that we'll end up overlooking two of the most valuable—*Allium schoenoprasum* (chives) and *A. sphaerocephalum* (round-headed leek). These are always a welcome sight in the garden. Clumps of chives burst into bloom with lilac-pink flowers on soft, green, edible stems from May to June, while the round-headed leek produces delightfully dainty reddish-purple drumsticks on 25-inch (63-cm) stems in July. The secret is to remember to plant them close together in generous clumps in fall to get a great show in spring and summer.

If purple bores you, there are blue- and pink-flowering alliums to consider. *Allium caeruleum* (also called *A. azureum*) brings the sky to the ground with its gorgeous light blue flowers on 2-foot (60-cm) stems; *A. oreophilum* (also called *A. ostrowskianum*) has bright carmine flowers; *A. rosenbachianum* 'Album' has distinctive white flowers atop 2-foot

(60-cm) stems; and *A. neapolitanum* (Naples garlic) has fragrant white flowers and grows about 12 inches (30 cm) high.

For something totally different (and a little freaky looking), there's *Allium schubertii*, which looks likes a creature from space with its ball of purple starry tentacles at the top of an 18-inch (45-cm) stalk. Plant it in groups to create a small bush-like effect. It also combines very impressively with the creamy-white stripes of ribbon grass (*Phalaris arundinacea* 'Picta').

Another unusual type is *Allium bulgaricum*, which produces hanging clusters of tiny, pink and green, pagoda-shaped flowers at the top of 3- or 4-foot (90-cm to 1.2-m) stems. This looks best when planted in numbers rather than as a solitary specimen.

You might also find a place in your perennial border for the Welsh onion (*Allium fistulosum*). This is generally grown in vegetable patches, but a clump of Welsh onion with its thick stems and yellowish-white, ball-shaped flower heads can also look very attractive in a flower border in June. *A. tuberosum* (garlic chives) has white flower heads in late summer. It grows to 1 to 2 feet (30 to 60 cm).

Peony Perfection

Sometimes you have to walk by faith as a gardener. This means doing something that does not give you an immediate reward, but that you trust will produce a very desirable result in the long run. This philosophy is particularly applicable to peonies. All our natural gardening instincts seem to tell us to shop for and plant peonies in the spring. That's when most garden centers stock them. That's when we see them in bloom and think how nice it would be to have them in our own garden. But, in reality, the best time to buy and plant peonies is from late August through to October. The soil is still warm and this allows the plants to get nicely settled in so they get a great start in spring. To do this with any enthusiasm requires a degree of faith in the process—a trust that what you plant now will produce an exciting and abundant show of flowers next spring.

Peonies are a long-lasting, hard-working garden plant. Once the flowers are done you have wonderful lush foliage, which stays a pleasant, restful shade of green all summer long. The fact that most people don't know peonies by their name is not unusual. Garden centers often don't bother to name them, preferring to slap simple color labels on them instead. This is a dishonor peonies share with daylilies, which are also extremely useful in the garden landscape and universally loved, but which are rarely referred to by their proper and complete botanical name. Here are some tips on selecting, growing, dividing and caring for peonies.

- You can extend the peony blooming period by as much as three weeks by planting early varieties that start flowering in spring. Outstanding early-flowering types include 'Red Charm' (rich red), 'America' (scarlet), 'Paula Fay' (shocking pink with a golden center), 'Coral Sunset' (coral with overtones of rose-pink), and 'Coral 'n' Gold' (large, coral, cup-shaped petals form a bowl around a center of golden stamens).

- Japanese or anemone-form peonies represent an entire group on their own. They have large, graceful blooms formed from a row of single petals surrounding a dense tuft-like center. The most famous is 'Bowl of Beauty', which has fuchsia-rose flowers with a pale lemon-yellow center. Other outstanding varieties in this class include 'Leto' (pure white), 'Kukenu-Jishia' (light pink), 'White Sands' (white with a yellow center and noted for its fragrance) and 'Largo' (vivid rose-pink with a golden-yellow center).

- Double peonies constitute a third category. These flower about the same time as Japanese peonies, from mid-May into June, and have tightly packed, multi-petaled, chrysanthemum-like flowers or cup-shaped blooms, like roses that are wide open. Famous doubles include the fragrant 'Sarah Bernhardt', which has apple-blossom pink flowers, and 'Karl Rosenfeld', with very rich deep-red blooms. Other excellent performers include 'Mother's Choice' (sensational pure white) and 'Mons Jules Elie' (large chyrsanthemum-like blooms of deep silvery pink).

- *Paeonia tenuifolia* (fernleaf peony) is unlike any other peony. It has elegant, finely cut, fernlike leaves and produces dark crimson flowers in May. They are more difficult to propagate than the other types and therefore tend to be less available and more expensive.

- Tree peonies are true shrubs with a permanent woody framework. Growing up to 6 feet (1.8 m) tall, they flower in spring and come in a wide range of colors, from snowy white through delicate pink to rich maroon. All exhibit classic peony fragrance. There are hundreds of varieties from which to choose. Many are descended from *Paeonia suffruticosa* and have wonderfully poetic Japanese names that translate into titles such as 'Honeydew from Heaven' or 'Coiled Dragon in the Mist Grasping a Purple Pearl'. Also very popular is *P. lutea*, which has single, vivid yellow flowers and attractive foliage. It grows to 6 feet (1.8 m).

- Grow peonies in full sun in fertile, well-drained soil with a mixture of other perennials and flowering shrubs. They combine quite happily with other plant material in the perennial border. Once flowering is over, they form a great backdrop with their soft, shapely leaves.

- Before planting your new peony, think carefully about where you are placing it. Once it is in the ground, it does not like to be disturbed. Plant in late September, then leave it alone to establish itself. This could take more than one season. Don't be alarmed if flowers are scarce the first year after planting.

- Peonies hold themselves up perfectly well while they are developing in early spring, but once they start to flower, especially if they get hit by heavy rain, the stems can topple sideways and the bush will begin to look ragged and unkempt. Stake the emerging stems to give the bush the support it will need later on when it reaches its peak blooming period.

- Ants can seem like a problem. They can often be found running all over the plant, especially over unopened flower buds. Some gardeners say this actually stimulates the buds to open more rapidly. The consensus of opinion, however, is that ants do neither harm nor good; they just busy themselves and disappear.

- Since peonies vanish completely back into the ground over winter, the space they occupied can look barren in early spring. Surround the peony crown with various spring-flowering bulbs. Bluebells (*Scilla*), dog's-tooth violet (*Erythronium*), grape hyacinth (*Muscari*), crocus, glory-of-the-snow (*Chionodoxa*) and dwarf narcissus are all good choices. They will provide color and cover while the pink-red peony shoots are slowly rising. Once the leaves have formed, the peony will need some supporting neighbors. Try campanulas, centaurea, euphorbia, aquilegia, salvia, lupins, foxgloves, shrub roses, lychnis and alliums.

- Old clumps can be lifted and divided in September. Wait until the foliage has begun to yellow, then cut and remove the stems at ground level and lift the entire clump. Let the clump sit in the sun for a few hours before dividing. This causes the brittle roots and buds to become more rubbery and less likely to break. Shake or wash off the soil and then, with a sharp spade or knife, slice the old crown so that each division has three to five pink buds, or eyes. Make sure the buds are pointing up and are replanted no deeper than 2 inches (5 cm) below the surface. If you plant too deeply—say 5 or 6 inches (12.5 to 15 cm) deep—you're not going to get many blooms. This is the most common complaint from gardeners who have planted new peonies.

Classical Grasses

Grasses are at their best in late summer and early fall. This is the time to check them out, make notes about which ones you like and look around your garden and decide where they will look best. Plant your ornamental grasses when they are at their peak through to early fall. If you miss this opportunity, you will have to rely on your notes and your memory when you go looking for them at the garden center in spring. Often, they do not start to appear on the shelves at garden centers until the middle of summer.

There are ornamental grasses for all situations. Big, beautiful miscanthus grasses for creating screens and special features. Blue and bronze grasses for injecting color. Short, evergreen grasses for filling crevices between stepping stones or for creating mowless lawns.

What makes the tall decorative grasses so special is not just their color and architectural shape but the way they can catch the barest breeze and bring sound and movement to the garden. The gentle swaying of the rose-red plumes of purple fountain grass (*Pennisetum setaceum* 'Rubrum') or the rustle of the distinctive blades of the white-striped Japanese silver grass (*Miscanthus sinensis* 'Cosmopolitan') can bring a whole new dimension to the beauty of a late-summer garden.

Here's a guide to the best grasses for the home garden.

- *Acorus gramineus* 'Pusillus'. A dwarf green Japanese sweet flag, this is ideal for filling gaps between paving stones as it tolerates light foot traffic. Grows to 3 or 4 inches (7.5 to 10 cm). Hardy to Zone 4.

- *Carex buchananii*. It may look dead, but the rich, coppery-bronze color of this stiff, upright grass makes it the perfect foil for the blue of *Festuca glauca* or dwarf conifers. There is a pale-green form called 'Viridis'. Grows to 18 to 24 inches (45 to 60 cm). Hardy to Zone 6.

- *Carex* 'Ice Dance'. Among the two-tone grasses, this is one of the best newcomers. It has outstanding white-green foliage and grows to 8 inches (20 cm). Hardy to Zone 6.

- *Carex comans* 'Bronze'. The mophead sedge never fails to please the eye with its particularly fine chocolate-brown foliage. 'Frost Curls' is very similar in habit, but has pale-green blades and is more compact. Grows to 8 inches (20 cm). Hardy to Zone 6.

- *Carex flagellifera* (weeping New Zealand sedge). This is similar to *C. comans* 'Bronze' but has a softer, paler bronze color. Grows to 8 inches (20 cm). Hardy to Zone 6.

- *Chasmanthium latifolium*. A great grass for light shade areas, this has blue-green, bamboo-like foliage and produces thin stems topped by oat-like flower heads. Grows to 30 to 36 inches (75 to 90 cm). Hardy to Zone 5.

- *Festuca cinerea* 'Elijah Blue'. The bluest of the blue grasses, this will brighten up any border and is very happy growing in a container. Divide every two or three years. Grows 8 to 10 inches (20 to 25 cm). Hardy to Zone 3.

- *Hakonechloa macra* 'Aureola'. Everyone falls in love with this grass when they see it for the first time. The bright yellow leaves are streaked with green and have a somewhat bamboo-like texture. Wonderful container plant for light shade. Grows to 18 to 24 inches (45 to 60 cm). Hardy to Zone 5.

- *Helictotrichon sempervirens* (blue oat grass). Many grasses deserve a place in the garden, but few are as attractive, versatile or easy to grow as this one. It has a fabulous upright form, intense silvery blue blades, and long, arching stalks that slowly turn to straw by the end of summer. In mild areas it stays evergreen, which brings much-valued color to the garden in winter. It needs room to be seen at its best. Growing at least 2 feet high (60 cm), it sends up pale blue flower stalks another 2 feet (60 cm) and forms a round mound at least 2 feet (60 cm) wide. Use this grass as an accent plant or plant it in groups for dramatic effect. Perfect for the sunny perennial border, its color contrasts well with silver-leafed plants such as *Artemisia* 'Silver Mound' or dark-leafed plants like *Heuchera* 'Plum Pudding' and *Cimicifuga* 'Brunette'. Grow blue oat grass in fertile, well-drained, average soil in a sunny location. Hardy to Zone 3.

- *Imperata cylindrica* 'Red Baron' (Japanese blood grass). The leaves are blood-red at the top, green at the bottom. It prefers full sun or light shade and well-drained soil. A striking decorative feature, it is immensely popular as an accent plant in sunny, well-drained, well-protected sites. Grows to 18 inches (45 cm). Hardy to Zone 5.

- *Leymus condensatus* 'Canyon Prince'. This has very broad powder-blue blades and looks exceptional grown on banks next to a pond or in a container. Grows to 2 to 3 feet (60 to 90 cm). Hardy to Zone 4.

- *Miscanthus floridulus*. If you're looking for a big, bold grass to create a screen or give bulk and height to the back of your perennial border, this will do the trick. You need plenty of space for this giant silver grass, which has no difficulty reaching 10 to 12 feet (3 to 3.6 m). In a large garden, this is an excellent feature plant. Hardy to Zone 4.

- *Miscanthus sinensis* 'Gracillimus' (maiden grass). Very structural, this forms a graceful stand, 4 to 6 feet high (1.2 to 1.8 m), that looks as good in a container as it does in a formal border planting. It has a slightly arching habit and its elegant, deep-green blades have a thin white stripe down the center. There are several outstanding forms of *M. sinensis*. 'Malepartus' is popular for the sparkle of its delicate purple-pink inflorescence. The foliage turns bronze in autumn. Grows to 5 to 6 feet (1.5 to 1.8 m). 'Yaku Jima' is appreciated for having all the qualities of 'Gracillimus', only in a more containable dwarf form, making it a good choice for small gardens. Grows to 3 to 4 feet (90 cm to 1.2 m). 'Zebrinus' and 'Strictus' both have long green blades with horizontal zebra-like bands of yellow. Of the two, 'Strictus' is generally easier to work with, being more erect and less floppy than 'Zebrinus'. Both grow to 5 to 7 feet (1.5 to 2.1 m). 'Cosmopolitan' has wide, cascading blades with striking white and green stripes. It looks exceptional placed next to a bank of yellow *Rudbeckia* 'Goldsturm' or the salmon-pink flower heads of *Sedum* 'Autumn Joy'. 'Cosmopolitan' grows to 6 to 8 feet (1.8 to 2.4 m). All are hardy to Zone 5.

- *Panicum virgatum* 'Prairie Sky'. Very pretty, upright blue switch grass which is going to become very popular as more people see it. There is a similar variety called 'Heavy Metal' but 'Prairie Sky' is thought to be the more attractive, being bushier and slightly more arching. Both grow to 3 to 4 feet (90 cm to 1.2 m). Hardy to Zone 3.

- *Pennisetum alopecuroides* 'Hameln'. The best of the fountain grasses, 'Hameln' looks exceptional grown as an accent plant or in rows at the front of a border. Grows to 24 to 30 inches (60 to 75 cm). Makes a good companion for *Hemerocallis* 'Stella de Oro' and *Sedum* 'Autumn Joy'. Hardy to Zone 5.

- *Pennisetum setaceum* 'Rubrum'. This purple fountain grass is unbeatable for adding exotic purple-burgundy color to the garden in midsummer. The graceful foxtail plumes are very elegant and manage to catch even the barest wisp of a breeze. Grows to 3 to 4 feet (90 cm to 1.2 m). Hardy to Zone 9.

- *Phalaris arundinacea* 'Picta' (common ribbon grass). Possibly the most widely used variegated grass, 'Picta' is starting to lose popularity to 'Feesey', which is much less invasive and has brighter, whiter variegated foliage. Both grow to 2 to 3 feet (60 to 90 cm). Hardy to Zone 2.

- *Sesleria autumnalis*. A short, evergreen, clumping grass that can take the place of junipers or cotoneaster when mass-planting sunny or semi-shaded areas. Grows to 8 to 18 inches (20 to 45 cm). Hardy to Zone 4.

- *Stipa gigantea*. The beauty of this grass is that it has just a small clump of foliage, which makes it ideal for growing in a pot. The clump grows to 18 to 24 inches (45 to 60 cm) but the airy, graceful flower plumes can reach 6 or 7 feet (1.8 to 2.1 m) in late summer. Hardy to Zone 6.

Your Guide to Great Trees

Fall is the perfect time to plant or move a tree. The ground is still warm, the soil is still workable, and there is an excellent selection of trees available. Here's a guide to the best of the deciduous trees. Note the hardiness zone rating.

Spectacular Big Trees

- *Acer platanoides* 'Emerald Queen' (Emerald Queen maple). Fast-growing to 60 feet (18 m) or more with an oval-shaped crown, this is considered one of the best varieties of Norway maple. Hardy to Zone 4.

- *Acer saccharinum* 'Legacy'. One of the best sugar maples, this beautiful big shade tree has a graceful oval shape and lush green foliage that turns orange-red in fall. It grows to 50 feet (15 m) at maturity. Hardy to Zone 5.

- *Acer saccharum laciniatum* 'Weri' (cutleaf silver maple). Rapid grower with spreading crown and dramatically dissected leaves. Grows 45 to 50 feet (14 to 15 m). Hardy to Zone 4.

- *Aesculus* x *carnea* 'Briotii' (red horse chestnut). This has superb fan-like leaves and large rose-crimson flowers in May. The flowers attract hummingbirds. Grows 45 to 50 feet (14 to 15 m). Hardy to Zone 5.

- *Ailanthus altissima* (tree of heaven). Fast growing to 60 feet (18 m), this tree's leaves start out bronze-purple and turn dark green. Good choice for difficult sites. Hardy to Zone 5.

- *Davidii involucrata* (handkerchief or dove tree). The white flowers in spring resemble white paper tissues scattered among the branches. The leaves are serrated and heart-shaped. Grows 50 to 60 feet (15 to 18 m). Hardy to Zone 6.

- *Fraxinus pennsylvanica* 'Patmore'. The most popular of the ash shade trees, it has a graceful, oval form and medium green leaves. It grows 50 feet (15 m) high. Hardy to Zone 3.

- *Magnolia grandiflora* (evergreen southern magnolia). The magnificent, lemon-scented, white bowl-flowers are irresistible. Grows to 50 feet (15 m). Hardy to Zone 7.

- *Paulownia tomentosa* (empress tree). This has big, heart-shaped, catalpa-like leaves and vanilla-scented purple flowers that resemble foxgloves. Grows to 50 feet (15 m). Hardy to Zone 5.

- *Populus* (poplar). Most used in country properties where a tall screen or windbreak of trees is needed. But it is amazing how often poplars get misguidedly planted in the city on small lots. Short-lived, their roots can be invasive and the branches brittle. Grows to 60 feet (18 m). Hardy to Zone 2.

- *Quercus palustris* (pin oak). The perfect pick for moist sites, pin oak, also known as swamp oak, has a stately pyramidal form, drooping lower branches and bright scarlet foliage in fall. It will grow to 50 feet (15 m). Hardy to Zone 5.

- *Quercus rubra* (red oak). This fast-growing oak develops a beautiful round canopy that turns brilliant scarlet in fall. It will grow to 70 feet (21 m). Hardy to Zone 4.

- *Tilia americana* (American linden). A tree for a large country estate, it is fast-growing, reaching 60 feet (18 m) or more and has a reputation for being intolerant of air pollution. There is, however, a more manageable variety called 'Raymond' that grows to only 40 feet (12 m). Hardy to Zone 3.

Medium-sized Trees

- *Acer campestre* 'Queen Elizabeth' (hedging maple). This is an excellent tree to use for a screen of pleached trees. If you want to obscure a view that is 15 to 20 feet (4.5 to 6 m) above the ground, but you are not keen on a super-high hedge and you also want space underneath for other plants, this an idea to consider. Lime and hornbeam trees have been used for this purpose but *Acer campestre* is a good alternative. Hardy to Zone 5.

- *Acer davidii* (snake-bark maple). This has green and white "snake" bark and glossy green leaves that turn yellow in fall. Grows to 35 feet (10.5 m). Hardy to Zone 5.

- *Acer platanoides* 'Crimson King' (Crimson King maple). An excellent shade tree, this is the most vigorous of the red-leafed Norway maples. It has a very pleasant oval shape, which slowly turns into a more rounded form as the tree matures. However, a whole street full of 'Crimson King' can be overwhelming and too somber in summer. Grows to 35 to 40 feet (10.5 to 12 m). Hardy to Zone 4.

- *Cercidiphyllum japonicum* (katsura). Beautiful, small, heart-shaped leaves reported to give off a toffee-like aroma on warm days. Brilliant gold-pink or amber-red fall color. Grows to 35 to 40 feet (10.5 to 12 m). Hardy to Zone 5.

- *Cladrastis lutea* (American yellowwood). Round-headed tree with fragrant white flowers and yellow fall color. Grows to 35 feet (10.5 m). Hardy to Zone 4.

- *Gleditsia* 'Sunburst'. If you need a large deciduous tree that will bathe your house in dappled shade in summer and add color and charm to your neighborhood, this will do the trick. Its golden-yellow new leaves look exceptional against a darker background of deep-green or purple-leafed trees. The golden leaves turn medium green by midsummer. Grows to 40 feet (12 m). Hardy to Zone 4.

Marvelous Magnolias

- *Magnolia* x *soulangiana* (saucer magnolia). The saucer magnolia is one of the most reliable of all magnolias. It flowers for four weeks in spring with creamy white, goblet-shaped blooms, flushed with purplish-pink. It can be grown as a bush in the mixed border or as a specimen tree. Popular cultivars are 'Alexandrina', 'Coates', and 'Rustica Rubra'. Grows to 30 feet (9 m). Hardy to Zone 5.

- *Magnolia stellata* (star magnolia). This has a profusion of pure white, multi-petaled flowers in early spring. It grows to 10 feet (3 m) and is most commonly grown as a small shrub in gardens where space is limited. Look for 'Royal Star'. Hardy to Zone 4.

- *Magnolia* x *loebneri* 'Leonard Messel' has masses of 12-petaled purple-pink flowers in early May and attractive green foliage all summer, turning yellow in fall. It is generally grown as a multi-stemmed tree or large shrub, reaching 15 to 20 feet (4.5 to 6 m) after 20 years. Also consider *M.* x *loebneri* 'Merrill', which has a growth habit similar to *M. stellata* but is slightly more vigorous and has larger, 15-petaled white flowers in May. Hardy to Zone 5.

- *Magnolia denudata* 'White Yulan' (Yulan magnolia). This small, rounded tree has very fragrant, white, cup-shaped flowers in May and striking foliage in fall. The buds need some protection from late frost. Grows 25 to 35 feet (7.5 to 10.5 m). Hardy to Zone 6.

- *Magnolia sieboldii*. Loved by plant connoisseurs because of its classy, white, fragrant, cup-shaped blooms, it also has delicately colored green leaves. You can grow it as a tree or a shrub, but since it has a spread of 15 feet (4.5 m) high and wide, you need space in your garden to accommodate it properly. The fragrance of the flowers has been described as being like a flavorsome bouquet of pineapple-orange lilies. Hardy to Zone 4.

- Other magnolias with bright white, star-like flowers include the Kobus magnolia (*Magnolia kobus*), which produces more substantial flowers, although they have been described as "dirty white" compared to the blooms of the more familiar *M. stellata*, and the graceful anise magnolia (*M. salicifolia*). *M. kobus* grows to 45 feet (13.5 m). Hardy to Zone 6. The cultivar 'Wada's Memory', which is hardy to Zone 6 and grows to 30 feet (9 m), has a high rating for the whiteness and abundance of its blooms.

- Yellow-flowering magnolias are increasingly popular. People often snap them up the moment they see them in bloom. There are two excellent cultivars—'Butterflies' and 'Elizabeth'. But 'Yellow Bird' is a new variety that is gaining a lot of praise. Its claim to fame is that it starts to flower at an earlier age than the other yellows and the soft yellow blooms appear just as the tree gets its leaves. They all grow to about 35 feet (10.5 m) and are hardy to Zone 5.

Other excellent varieties include 'Shademaster', vase-shaped and an excellent pick if you want light shade. It grows to 40 feet (12 m). 'Skyline' is a slightly taller tree, more pyramidal and symmetrical than 'Shademaster', reaching almost 50 feet (15 m). 'Ruby Lace' is a round-headed graceful tree, with ruby-red foliage in spring that turns bronze-green with a red tinge in fall. It grows to 40 feet (12 m).

- *Magnolia grandiflora* 'Little Gem'. This has all the attractive characteristics of the standard *Magnolia grandiflora*, only it is a dwarf form that grows to 30 feet (9 m) in 20 years. It also has fragrant white flowers that bloom in early summer and again in late summer.

- *Parrotia persica* (Persian ironwood). Available as a single or multi-stemmed tree, its leaves are reddish-purple when they first appear, changing to dark green for summer. The fall color is a spectacular mixture of yellow, orange and scarlet. Grows 30 to 40 feet (9 to 12 m). Hardy to Zone 4.

- *Quercus robur* 'Fastigiata' (oak). An extremely popular oak, this form of English oak has an attractive columnar shape and deep green leaves that turn copper in fall. It grows 35 to 40 feet (10.5 to 12 m). Hardy to Zone 5.

- *Tilia cordata* (linden). The cultivar 'Greenspire' grows to 30 to 40 feet (9 to 12 m), remains beautifully compact, and has a nice straight trunk. Another first-rate little-leaf linden is 'Glenleven', which grows faster and is slightly taller and less dense than 'Greenspire'. Hardy to Zone 3.

Special Trees for Small Gardens

- *Acer griseum* (paperbark maple). When the soft light of the setting sun strikes the peeling, cinnamon-colored bark of this special tree, the sight can be quite mesmerizing. The red fall foliage is also very attractive. Grows 23 to 30 feet (7 to 9 m) at maturity. Hardy to Zone 4.

- *Acer pseudoplatanus* 'Brilliantissimum' (sycamore maple). Not an easy tree to find, but a lovely, slow-growing specimen that is used a lot in British gardens. It has an extremely graceful form, slowly rounding at the top as it matures into a full, lollipop shape. Outstanding, shrimp-pink new foliage in spring easily compares to the cherry blossom for elegance and charm. Once the leaves have unfolded, they turn a pale green. New leaves continue to appear through the summer and they decorate the tree with bright patches of pinkish-green. The effect is very subtle and attractive. Grows 15 feet (4.5 m) tall. Hardy to Zone 6.

- *Albizia julibrissin* (silk tree). An exotic, tropical-looking creature with tiny, feather-like leaves, the silk, or mimosa, tree produces masses of fabulous, pink pompom-shaped flowers in midsummer. Although slightly tender, it will tolerate wind, partial shade and poor, well-drained soil. It can be fast-growing, and it blooms profusely. Grows 20 to 35 feet (6 to 10.5 m). Hardy to Zone 6.

- *Elaeagnus angustifolia* (Russian olive). The beauty of the Russian olive is that you can grow it either as a tree or a shrub without forfeiting its graceful, silver-gray, willow-like foliage. The leaves look splendid

Magnificent Maples

- *Acer ginnala* 'Flame' (Flame Amur maple). A large, multi-stemmed shrub or small tree, this has brilliant, flame-red leaves in October. Grows to 15 feet (4.5 m). Hardy to Zone 5.
- *Acer negundo* 'Flamingo' is another outstanding tree for the small- or medium-sized garden. Its new leaves have a flamingo-pink edge to them. The color is even more pronounced in cooler areas where the tree's hardiness rating gets pushed to the limit. It grows about 15 to 20 feet (4.5 to 6 m). Hardy to Zone 6.
- *Acer palmatum* 'Bloodgood'. One of the most popular feature trees for the home garden, 'Bloodgood' has bright, crimson-red foliage and attractive blackish-red bark. It is an outstanding tree because the leaves retain their striking blood-red color all summer, and then turn a spectacular fiery red in fall. With the graceful shape of its branches (a characteristic common to all *palmatum* maples), 'Bloodgood' also provides a delightful contrast for trees and shrubs with green leaves. Grows to 20 feet (6 m). Hardy to Zone 5.
- *Acer palmatum dissectum* 'Crimson Queen'. Distinguished by its finely cut, almost feathery, reddish-purple leaves that cascade over twisted and contorted branches, this tree forms an extremely graceful and compact, mostly weeping, shape. 'Crimson Queen' is acclaimed for its crimson-red foliage that holds its color throughout the summer. It stays quite small, rarely growing more than 5 feet (1.5 m) tall. Hardy to Zone 6.

- Other popular cultivars of *Acer palmatum dissectum* to look for include 'Atropurpureum', 'Garnet', 'Inaba-shidare' and 'Red Dragon'. 'Atropurpureum' is noted for the summer color of its leaves, which can range from orange-red to dark crimson. Grows to 5 to 7 feet (1.5 to 2.1 m). 'Garnet' has exceptional crimson-red fall color, and eventually forms a beautiful mound of weeping branches. It gets its name from the rich color of its summer foliage. Grows to 8 feet (2.4 m). Zone 5. 'Inaba-shidare' means "leaves of rice paper," which should signify how delicate and graceful the deep purple-red foliage is on this tree. Grows to 7 feet (2.1 m). Zone 5. 'Red Dragon' is a relatively new introduction from New Zealand, touted by some nurseries as the best of the red laceleafs. Grows to 5 feet (1.5 m). Hardy to Zone 5.
- *Acer palmatum* 'Osakazuki' (green Japanese maple). Bright green foliage turns crimson in fall. Grows to 20 feet (6 m). Hardy to Zone 5.
- *Acer rubrum* 'Armstrong' (Armstrong maple). Fast-grower, yellow-orange in fall. Grows to 45 feet (13.5 m). Also consider 'October Glory' (brilliant red to orange) and 'Morgan' (deep red). 'Red Sunset' has dark, glossy green leaves that turn a spectacular deep orange-red in fall. It grows to 45 feet (13.5 m), which makes it a very useful shade tree. Hardy to Zone 4.
- *Acer truncatum* 'Norwegian Sunset' (Norwegian Sunset maple). Symmetrical tree with orange-red color in fall. Grows to 35 feet (10.5 m). Hardy to Zone 4.

moving in a breeze and they contrast beautifully with the dark foliage of other trees and shrubs. It grows to 15 feet (4.5 m). Hardy to Zone 2.

- *Halesia carolina* (silverbell tree). It produces snowdrop-like, bell-shaped flowers in late spring. It thrives in acid soil and should be planted in a place where you can look up into the blooms. It combines well with rhododendrons. Grows to 30 feet (9 m). Hardy to Zone 5.

- *Koelreuteria paniculata* (goldenrain tree). Popular with professional garden designers, this has clusters of golden flowers resembling small paper lanterns in summer, which form a golden carpet when they fall to the ground. It really should be grown more than it is. Grows 25 to 30 feet (7.5 to 9 m). Hardy to Zone 5.

- *Laburnum* x *watereri* 'Vossii' (goldenchain tree). A tree that for many people is a symbol of the spring garden. It is the ideal companion for a dense underplanting of purple-flowering ornamental onion bulbs. Unfortunately, it's not hardy enough for colder zones. Grows to 20 feet (6 m). Hardy to Zone 6.

- *Magnolia* 'Little Girl Series'. Developed specifically for their ability to tolerate cold winters, these magnolias ('Betty', 'Randy', 'Ricki' and 'Susan') are also very short, growing only 6 to 8 feet (1.8 to 2.4 m) high, which makes them especially useful in small gardens and courtyards. Flowers are varying shades of purple. Hardy to Zone 5.

- *Oxydendrum arboreum* (sourwood tree). If I fail to nurse my silk tree through to adolescence, I'm going to try one of these. A small, slow-growing tree, it comes into its own in midsummer when branches fill up with clusters of fragrant, lily-of-the-valley-type white flowers. A natural partner for rhododendrons and azaleas, the sourwood tree has glossy, reddish leaves in spring and attractive fall color. Grows to 25 feet (7.5 m). Hardy to Zone 5.

- *Pyrus salicifolia* 'Pendula' (willow-leafed pear). With high-contrast, silvery-gray leaves and weeping willow-like branches, this small, mounding tree has become increasingly popular over the last few years. Grows to 25 feet (7.5 m). Hardy to Zone 5.

- *Sorbus aucuparia* (European mountain ash). It has white flowers in spring and large clusters of red berries in fall. Grows 25 feet (7.5 m) high. Hardy to Zone 2.

- *Sorbus aucuparia* 'Fastigiata'. This column-shaped European mountain ash has attractive dark green leaves and large orange berries in fall. It can be planted where space is limited, fairly close to the house, without becoming a problem. Grows to 30 feet (9 m). Hardy to Zone 2.

- *Sorbus aucuparia* 'Rossica' (Russian mountain ash). It has a very attractive pyramidal shape, produces clusters of large red berries in fall and grows to 35 feet (10.5 m) tall. Hardy to Zone 2.

- *Stewartia pseudocamellia* (Japanese stewartia). Wonderful white camellia-like flowers in June. The leaves turn a brilliant scarlet in fall. Grows to 30 feet (9 m). Hardy to Zone 6.

- *Styrax japonica* (Japanese snowbell tree). A lovely tree with graceful form and a flush of white flowers in June. Some prefer *S. obassia*, which is slightly more fragrant and later-blooming but is less readily available. Grows to 25 feet (7.5 m). Hardy to Zone 5.

Dogwoods to Die For

- *Cornus alternifolia* (pagoda dogwood). This gets its name from the pagoda-like structure of its horizontally tiered branches. It has fragrant, yellowish-white flowers from May to June. Grows to 20 feet (6 m). Hardy to Zone 4.

- *Cornus controversa* 'Variegata'. This is a much-coveted tree because of its rarity, its green-white variegated foliage and the graceful, tiered branching habit that maintains a pyramidal shape. It also produces masses of white blooms. It is best seen with the setting sun behind it, which brings out the magic of the two-toned foliage. A relatively fast grower, it reaches about 30 feet (9 m) at maturity. Hardy to Zone 6.

- *Cornus florida* 'Rubra' (red-flowering dogwood). This is a very popular small tree that produces light pink flowers. 'Cherokee Chief' has the deepest red flowers, bright red foliage in May and burgundy foliage in fall. Other top varieties are 'Florida Sweetwater Red' and 'Cherokee Princess'. They all grow to about 20 feet (6 m). Hardy to Zone 5.

- *Cornus kousa* (Chinese dogwood). This is actually a native of Japan, not China. It flowers in June, about a month after most other dogwoods, and is loved for its creamy white flowers that are larger than those of other dogwoods. It grows as wide as it does tall, reaching 18 feet (5.5 m) after about 10 years. A red-flowering variety called 'Satomi' has crimson-purple foliage in fall and grows to 18 feet (5.5 m) at maturity. Hardy to Zone 5.

- *Cornus mas* (Cornelian cherry). A small tree or multi-stemmed bush with yellow flowers on bare branches in April and bright, cherry-red fruits in fall. It grows to about 20 to 25 feet (6 to 7.5 m). Hardy to Zone 4.

- *Cornus nuttallii* 'Eddie's White Wonder' (white-flowering Pacific dogwood). A cross between the eastern dogwood (*C. florida*) and the native western dogwood (*C. nuttallii*), this has semi-weeping branches and produces masses of long-lasting white flowers up to 5 inches (12.5 cm) across. It has exceptional fall foliage color. Grows to 20 feet (6 m). Hardy to Zone 4.

Trees for Color or Form

Purple-leafed Trees

- *Acer palmatum* 'Atropurpureum' (red Japanese maple). Reddish-purple leaves, spectacular fall color. 'Bloodgood' is similar but leaves do not fade in summer. Both grow to 20 feet (6 m). Hardy to Zone 5.

- *Cercis canadensis* 'Forest Pansy'. This has rose-purple flowers and heart-shaped leaves that open to reddish-purple. Grows to 30 feet (9 m). Hardy to Zone 5.

- *Prunus cistena* (purple-leaf sand cherry). Dainty tree with charming plum-colored foliage and light pink flowers in May. Grows 6 to 10 feet (1.8 to 3 m) high. Hardy to Zone 7.

- *Prunus pissardii* 'Nigra' (purple-leaf plum). This has dark purple leaves and pink flowers in May. Grows to 15 to 18 feet (4.5 to 5.5 m). Hardy to Zone 6.

Trees with Golden Foliage

- *Acer shirasawanum* 'Aureum' (golden fullmoon maple). This has beautiful, tightly clustered, yellow-green leaves that can light up a corner of the garden. It grows to about 20 feet (6 m). Hardy to Zone 6.

- *Catalpa bignonioides* 'Aurea' (golden Indian bean tree). Loved for its large, heart-shaped, golden leaves. Grows to 35 feet (10.5 m). Hardy to Zone 5.

- *Ginkgo biloba* (maidenhair tree). One of the plant world's great survivors, it is estimated this tree has been around for at least 160 million years! Imagine that it once shared the Earth with dinosaurs and you realize why it is so respected by horticulturists. I include it here because of the sensational golden-yellow color of its butterfly-shaped leaves in fall. Completely pest and disease resistant, it is a wonderful character tree with an elegant pyramidal shape. Hardy to Zone 4, it grows to 35 to 40 feet (10.5 to 12 m). Make sure you plant the male tree, as the female produces messy, stinky fruit.

- *Robinia pseudoacacia* 'Frisia'. An exceptionally beautiful and graceful medium-sized deciduous tree, this is suitable for small- and medium-sized gardens. Perhaps even more than *Gleditsia* 'Sunburst', its yellow-green leaves look sensational when seen against the backdrop of dark brooding conifers. This is a tree to lust after if you don't have one. Some people love it so much, they have planted two. 'Frisia' takes at least 10 years to reach 25 feet (7.5 m), and another 20 years to attain its full height, usually not more than 40 feet (12 m). Hardy to Zone 5.

Weeping Trees

- *Betula* 'Youngii' (Young's weeping birch). A graceful tree with a mushroom-shaped canopy, it is ideal for courtyard gardens or for growing next to a small pond. Grows to 40 feet (12 m). Hardy to Zone 2.

- *Cercidiphyllum japonicum pendula* (weeping katsura). This has blue-green leaves and the same wonderful fall color as the upright version. Some people see cascading water in the weeping leaves. Grows 15 to 20 feet. (4.5 to 6 m). Hardy to Zone 5.

- *Salix babylonica aurea* (weeping willow). Large, weeping tree with distinctive yellow branches. Thrives very nicely alongside lakes and streams. Grows to 45 to 50 feet (13.5 to 15 m). Hardy to Zone 3.

Column-shaped Trees

- *Acer platanoides* 'Columnare' (columnar maple). Tall, column-shaped maple with yellow fall foliage. Grows to 50 feet (15 m). Hardy to Zone 4.

- *Acer platanoides* 'Crimson Sentry' (Crimson Sentry maple). Ideal for narrow streets and small gardens, it grows to 30 feet (9 m). Hardy to Zone 4.

Planting a Tree: Your Step-by-Step Guide

1. **Move the tree gently.** Never lift it by its trunk; this can damage the roots at the center. Lift the tree by its rootball. If it is too heavy to lift, place it on a tarp and drag it or enlist the help of a few volunteers. The rootball contains tender live roots that should never be disturbed; always keep it moist while the tree is waiting to be planted.

2. **Dig the right-sized hole.** The traditional instructions are that the hole should be twice as wide and one and a half times as deep as the rootball. But there is a risk of planting the tree too deeply. It is better, especially in a wet climate, to plant shallower rather than deeper. A tree or shrub planted deeper than the previous soil level will suffocate and die within one or two growing seasons.

3. **Check the drainage.** Trees are more often killed or damaged by having their roots drowned by poor drainage than by drying out. Test the drainage of the site before planting. Fill the hole with water and see how long it takes to drain. If it stands more than 15 minutes, drainage is a problem. You can fix it by creating a raised bed, installing a drainage pipe or ditch or adding sand and organic material.

4. **Plant and backfill.** Put the tree in the hole, making sure it is high enough, and that the trunk is vertical. View it from various directions to make sure. Amend the soil you have lifted from the hole with peat moss and well-rotted compost and add some fertilizer high in phosphorus (the middle number of the three on a bag of fertilizer) to promote healthy root development.

5. **Water thoroughly.** And remember to water regularly during the growing season for the first year.

- *Prunus serrulata* 'Amanogawa'. Perfectly erect tree with fragrant pink flowers in mid-spring. Ideal for small yards. Grows to 25 feet (7.5 m). Hardy to Zone 5.

Trees for the Boulevard

- *Acer platanoides* 'Deborah'. Brilliant red-purple new foliage in spring slowly fades to dark green and turns bronze-purple in fall. Grows to 50 feet (15 m). Hardy to Zone 4.

- *Acer rubrum* 'Red Sunset' (Red Sunset maple). Very popular with landscapers, this is used in many urban planting schemes. It has medium green leaves that turn deep orange-red in fall. Grows to 45 feet (13.5 m). Hardy to Zone 4.

- *Liquidambar styraciflua* (sweet gum). A popular street tree, this has maple-like foliage that turns wine-red in fall. It grows to 40 to 50 feet (12 to 15 m). Hardy to Zone 5.

- *Prunus serrulata* 'Kwanzan'. Popular because of its pleasing vase-shape, bronzy-red new foliage, profusion of deep-pink flowers in spring, and orange-red fall color. Grows to 25 feet (7.5 m). Hardy to Zone 5.

Trees with Winter Interest

- *Acer griseum* (paperbark maple). See Special Trees for Small Gardens, page 161.

- *Betula jacquemontii* (white-barked Himalayan birch). Tall, narrow tree with marvelous, snowy-white, peeling bark. More resistant to leaf miner than other white-barked birches, it is also available in clumps of two and three. Grows to 35 feet (10.5 m). Hardy to Zone 5.

- *Sorbus aucuparia* 'Cardinal Royal' (European mountain ash). Vigorous grower with dark-green foliage and clusters of bright-red berries in September. Grows to 30 feet (9 m). Also check out *Sorbus* 'Joseph Rock', which has yellow berries. Hardy to Zone 2.

Houseplants

Bring the garden indoors and use plants to create a healthier and more relaxing home environment. Orchids, palms and ferns are ideal candidates for creating a tropical indoor garden. If you also make use of beautiful flowering bulbs, such as amaryllis and hyacinths, you can have a fragrant paradise even in late fall and into the dark days of winter.

How to Keep Your Houseplants Happy

If you are planning to create an entire indoor landscape out of house-plants, here are a few tips about how to create the perfect environment.

- **Check the lighting.** This is one of the most important aspects of growing plants indoors. The right plant material in the right lighting will last longer and look healthier. In too much or too little light, plants become stressed and prone to disease and attack from spider mites, mealy bugs, aphids and scale insects.

- **Check for access.** Are there windows that will need to be cleaned? Is there a doorway that will be blocked by plants? Keeping entrances clear and making sure windows are accessible is important for both convenience and safety.

- **Pay attention to scale.** Planters and pots need to be an appropriate size for the location and ought to complement the architectural style of the building or interior. Using plants is still one of the most inexpensive ways of decorating a new home.

- **Clean your plants regularly.** The No. 1 problem with most houseplants is that they are covered with dust. Light cannot get through to the surface of the leaves and the plant ends up getting stressed and attracting spider mites. Spend as much time cleaning houseplants as you do watering. Hand-wash each leaf, front and back. It takes time, but your plants will be much healthier.

- **Water properly.** People give their houseplants a cupful every Monday whether they need it or not. That's not a good idea. First, use a chop-stick or other wooden probe to check the soil's moisture level. Feeling the top 2 inches (5 cm) of soil with your fingers isn't good enough.

- **Don't buy cheap plants.** Cheap plants are usually non-acclimatized specimens just off the truck from Florida. Tropical plants need to spend time reacclimatizing in a greenhouse before they are put on sale. Most garden centers know this, but some discount outlets don't. Telltale signs are exceptionally glossy leaves and very bushy plants.

- **Think combinations.** Don't put a plant in a corner by itself; try to create a combination of textural contrasts.

- **Feed your plants.** Don't forget that plants need to eat. A weekly application of liquid fertilizer will make a major difference. Avoid slow-release fertilizers, which put too much salt into the soil. In a container, this can be fatal to houseplants.

Workhorse Houseplants

Here are 10 plants that will create an attractive interior-scape and also do an excellent job of removing chemical toxins from the air in your home.

- Areca palm (*Chrysalidocarpus lutescens*). This is also known as the yellow or butterfly palm. Happy to be indoors, it helps to keep the air moist and removes chemical toxins.

- Lady palm (*Rhapis excelsa*). This large, popular palm has a hairy main trunk and arching stems. It is exceptionally resistant to insects and easy to grow and look after.

- Bamboo palm (*Chamaedorea seifrizii*). With graceful fans and rich green color, this puts moisture into the air during winter months. The slender canes make it one of the more attractive houseplants.

- *Dracaena* 'Janet Craig'. A great plant to have in a home office, this is very effective at removing trichloroethylene, the chemical released by photocopiers, printers and duplicating machines.

- Fig (*Ficus alii*). This rates higher than the common weeping fig (*Ficus benjamina*) because it is less temperamental, although it will also drop its leaves when moved to a different location. Part of the reason for this is that the leaves are held on brittle stems and when they realign themselves to the new light source, they can snap off. The secret is to keep the same orientation to the light.

- Boston fern (*Nephrolepis exaltata*). It must have frequent misting and watering to prevent the leaves from browning, but the Boston fern is one of the best for removing chemical vapors and adding humidity.

- Peace lily (*Spathiphyllum*). An outstanding foliage plant that produces white spathes. It is useful for cleaning the air of alcohol, formaldehyde and benzene fumes. (See p. 172)

- Golden pothos (*Epipremnum aureum*). A vine with glossy green, heart-shaped leaves with gold or cream variegation. It won't lose its color in a dark spot, and is very good at removing pollutants from the air. (See also p. 172)

- Rubber plant (*Ficus robusta*). A favorite of Victorians, it is still immensely popular today. Apparently, it is especially good at removing traces of formaldehyde from the atmosphere.

- Spider plant (*Chlorophytum comosum*). Also known as the airplane plant because of its habit of flying new plants at the end of long arching stems, the spider plant got international attention in 1984 when NASA first released information about how well it swallowed up indoor air pollution. The baby plants can be left on the stems or cut and potted to form new colonies. (See also p. 171)

How to Make a Bathroom Jungle

With a few well-chosen plants, you can transform your basic utilitarian bathroom into an exotic, jungle-like environment—a place to relax in a hot bath on a dreary winter's night and imagine you're on vacation in the tropics. Most bathrooms have low light and relatively high humidity—perfect conditions for a wide variety of lush-leafed tropical plants.

Plants, especially ferns with their relaxed feathery foliage, and peace lilies with their large, heart-shaped leaves, are ideal for softening the hard, glossy surfaces of tiled walls and porcelain sinks, chrome and glass. But homeowners are looking for more than an exotic look, they're turning their bathrooms into a personal retreat, a restful refuge for body and soul,

The Exotic World of Orchids

If orchids are a complete mystery to you, here's a starter guide to the 10 most popular kinds.

1. *Cattleya*. Named by members of the American Orchid Society as their favorite orchid, these are native to the jungles of Central and South America. Considered the queen of orchids, *Cattleya* have large lush flowers in various colors and are relatively easy to grow.

2. *Dendrobium*. The name means "living on trees," but these grow in a wide variety of places throughout Asia as well as Australia and New Zealand. One of the largest groups within the orchid family, they come in a wide range of colors and flower forms.

3. *Cymbidium*. One of the best-known orchids, often sold by florists and garden centers, these thrive in breezy, moderate climates. The waxy flowers come in a spectrum of colors.

4. *Phalaenopsis*. Better known as the "moth orchid" or "phal," these are found in the damp forests of India, the Philippines and northern Australia. They produce arching sprays with 3 to 14 blooms in a variety of colors, including pink, white, yellow and mauve.

5. *Paphiopedilum*. More commonly known as "lady slipper orchids," these are valued for their rich colors and unusual shape. They are available in green with white; almost entirely burgundy; and a mixture of green, white and burgundy. They thrive in low to medium light. Leaves bleach if the plant gets too much light.

6. *Oncidium*. These orchids are also known as "dancing ladies" because their flowers resemble ball gowns. A complicated genus because of all the mixed parentage, oncidiums are available in yellow with red, burgundy or brown markings. Some varieties are fragrant. They thrive in daytime room temperatures of 66° to 80°F (19° to 27°C) and night temperatures of

where they can escape the pressures of the world and find total relaxation in a warm, soothing bath. The cost of creating a bathroom jungle varies according to the size and type of plants. But for around $50, you can pick up four sizeable plants to start building your tropical paradise.

There are plants that thrive in low-light conditions and can be suspended in baskets from the ceiling and plants that look terrific displayed in wicker wall-racks and pot-holders, a decorating technique that particularly suits Victorian-style bathrooms. For those who want a more formal, uncluttered look, a solitary weeping fig (*Ficus benjamina*) tucked at the side of the bathtub can add a very pleasing indoor-garden effect. The key to sustaining a successful bathroom jungle, however, is to frequently sponge-clean the leaves of your plants. Dust, talcum powder, hair lacquers and other sprays will coat leaves and block a plant's pores. Wiping leaves off with a damp cloth or sponge once a week will go a long way to keeping plants happy and healthy. One word of caution before beginning to turn your bathroom into a jungle: in the interests of harmony, make sure that everyone in the family is happy with what you have planned.

Here is a starter-guide to your basic bathroom jungle.

- The spider plant (*Chlorophytum*), with green-and-white striped leaves, is totally reliable. Suspended from the ceiling in a hanging basket, it will trail its baby plantlets over the sides and demand minimal attention.

55° to 70°F (13° to 21°C). They like the medium light of an east or west window, although the leaves will bleach if exposed to too much light, or darken if not given enough.

7. *Odontoglossum.* The name means "toothed tongue," and the most famous member of this group is the white *O. crispum.* They come in every color combination imaginable and the long, upright spikes can carry as many as 20 flowers for up to six weeks.

8. *Miltoniopsis.* Sometimes called the pansy orchid because of the pansy-like shape, these flowers are native to cool, moist environments in South America. They carry three to eight large flowers per stem, and as the plant matures, the blooms generally increase two to three times in size.

9. *Zygopetalum.* With a scent reminiscent of hyacinth or narcissus, these orchids produce seven or eight flowers that can last up to eight weeks. They come in greens, purples, raspberry and burgundy shades. Usually they bloom in late winter or spring, but mature specimens can bloom twice a year. They like average household temperatures of 65° to 75°F (18° to 24°C) and can be moved outside to the light shade of the patio in early summer to fall. They prefer the low light of a north-facing window sill to the medium light of an east or west window with sheers.

10. *Masdevallia.* These deceptively delicate-looking yet vigorous plants produce vivid yellow, red, white, electric purple or orange flowers. Some are solid-colored, while others are spotted, splotched or striped. Under normal growing conditions, these orchids bloom freely year round. They prefer cool to average household temperatures, but will tolerate warmer temperatures for short periods of time if there is increased air movement and humidity.

- The peace lily (*Spathiphyllum*) is another excellent choice. The large, soft green arrow- or heart-shaped leaves are certainly attractive enough, but this South American beauty also sends up stiff stalks that produce elegant, white, lily-like spathes. All it asks is that you keep the soil evenly moist, keep the temperature between 55° and 75°F (13° to 24°C), and wash the leaves occasionally to keep tiny insects away.

- Like the peace lily, *Anthurium* also has deep green foliage and thrives in warm, humid conditions, but instead of a plain white spathe, it can produce red, pink or coral spathes.

- The asparagus fern (*Asparagus densiflorus* Sprengeri group) has a graceful, bushy, trailing habit, while *A. plumosus* has slightly frothier, more compact foliage. Although not technically ferns, they are called ferns and are easier to grow than many ferns.

- Outstanding true ferns suitable for the bathroom include *Davallia canariensis* and *D. bullata* (hare's foot ferns), and *Adiantum raddianum* (Delta maidenhair fern). All are available at garden centers.

- For more meaty foliage, you won't do better than golden pothos (*Epipremnum aureum*), which you will mostly find wrongly labeled as *Scindapsus*. Reputed to be the easiest of all houseplants to grow, it has shiny, heart-shaped leaves splashed with yellow, and thrives in even the most neglected circumstance. Train it to climb or simply allow it to cascade or run where it will. Good varieties to look for are 'Marble Queen' and 'Satin'.

- For something novel, how about sticking a few air plants (*Tillandsia*) here and there? Native to Latin America, they are like tufts of grass and come with a glue stick so they can be attached to mirrors or pots. They are usually sold already fixed to a seashell, piece of coral or wood. Air plants get their nutrients from dust particles in the air. The only attention they require is to be lightly misted once a week.

- To really add a jungle-like feel to your bathroom, grow an urn plant (*Aechmea fasciata*), which has blotchy silvery leaves, or the prayer plant (*Maranta leuconeura*), which has highly decorative leaves that turn up like "praying hands" when it is dark. *Cymbidium* orchids, *Echeveria*, *Aloe vera* and *Dieffenbachia* are all also worth considering.

- If space is no problem, go the whole hog and find a spot for an Areca palm (*Chrysalidocarpus*), which grows to 5 to 7 feet (1.5 to 2.1 m). If space is tight, try a dwarf date palm (*Phoenix roebelinii*), which grows to 3 feet (90 cm).

Winter

Faery Songs

Shed no tear–O, shed no tear!

The flower will bloom another year.

Weep no more–O, weep no more!

Young buds sleep in the root's white core.

—John Keats

In the Garden

- Order seed catalogs.

- Go shopping for terracotta and ceramic pots and containers. Prices are at their best at this time of year.

- Bring holly and ivy indoors.

- Check greenhouse for insect attacks on plants being overwintered.

- Start bedding plants such as pelargoniums, marigolds, snapdragons, nicotiana, lavatera and salvia from seed indoors.

- Watch for wet snow that can weigh down branches and damage shrubs.

- Start drawing up plans for your vegetable garden and annuals you want to start from seed for summer color.

- Check dahlia tubers, fuchsias and pelargoniums stored in a frost-free place for any signs of rot or diseases.

3 Projects for Winter

1. Beat the crush and pick up the best of the new amaryllis. Put it in a pot slightly larger than the bulb. Only the top third of the bulb should be showing. Water and place in a bright window in a warm room. When flowers appear, move the pot to indirect light. Or pop hyacinths in a brown bag at the back of the fridge. Bring them out in November, and stand them on pebbles in water. White roots will quickly form. Flowers will appear in time for Christmas. (For more complete instructions, see page 179.)

2. Paperwhites are great fun for all ages to grow. Simply fill a container with colorful pebbles, marbles or stones. Place a few paperwhite bulbs on the top and add water to the bottom of the bulbs. Place in a warm room. They will bloom very quickly and have a fresh, sharp fragrance. If you like the flowers but not the scent, ask for the bulbs with light fragrance.

3. Raise coleus from seed. These plants are increasingly popular for their striking foliage color in the summer garden. Seedlings are interesting because they show the colors of mature plants. Simply sprinkle seed onto a lightly moistened tray of potting soil. Press the seeds down with your fingers but don't cover them. Coleus needs light to germinate. Cover the tray with plastic wrap and set it in bright, indirect light at 70°F (21°C). Seeds will germinate in two weeks. Once they have developed true leaves and look a little more substantial, transplant them into small pots (three or four to a pot) and keep them in bright light. They can be planted outside in a semi-shady area of the garden in May (see page 24).

- On a mild, windless day, spray fruit trees and roses with dormant oil and lime sulfur to kill lingering bugs and diseases.

- Beat the rush and get your lawn mower tuned up. Clean and sharpen tools.

- Check trees towards the end of winter. While they are still dormant, prune out dead, diseased or damaged branches. Disinfect your pruners in a bleach solution between cuts to avoid spreading disease.

- Buddleia, hardy fuchsia, hibiscus, honeysuckle and summer-flowering clematis can all be pruned in late winter. Cut buddleia and summer clematis back to 3 feet (90 cm) from the ground.

- Prune hydrangea. Remove dead flower heads and shorten stems to a pair of healthy buds.

- Prune back lateral and side branches of wisteria to within two or three buds.

- Watch for early signs of spring, such as the first snowdrops and crocus.

- As conditions permit, amend the soil in flower beds and borders by spreading a mushroom manure or other general-purpose organic fertilizer. Dig well-rotted compost or manure into the vegetable garden.

Beauty of the Winter Garden

Images dance in the head after a walk in the winter garden. Blood-red berries and leathery green leaves of English holly. Silvery frost on the steel-blue needles of a Colorado spruce. Clusters of tiny purple fruit, suspended like jewels on the wiry branches of a beautyberry bush. Black tufts of mondo grass against the crisp white bark of an elegant Himalayan birch.

The spring garden has its magic. It is the embodiment of youth and energy, optimism and strength, growth and health, hope and mystery. The summer garden is a party spirit—flamboyant, carefree, full-bodied, slightly out of control, ripe. The autumn garden is a place for quiet contemplation and calm introspection, a tranquil refuge where we consider the past and think about the challenges ahead. The mood of the fall garden is predominantly mellow and slightly melancholic.

The garden in winter is a place of stillness and peace. Many mistake it for death and decay but it is nothing more than a sleep with a promise of renewal in spring. Some turn their back on winter, calling it sullen and sad, a time when nature is frozen dead, the penalty of Adam, a season with icy fangs, churlish chiding winds, a time when silver arrows pierce the air and the naked earth is forced to crouch and shudder at the ice king's feet. Yet there is immense beauty to be found in the winter garden if we're prepared to look beyond the barren landscape to evidence what John Keats meant when he penned: "Weep no more–O, weep no more! Young buds sleep in the root's white core."

Above you, the low sky is the color of old silver dollars, polished marble and antique mother-of-pearl, while all around you graceful, skeletal branches of trees form complex patterns, making it hard to decide if trees look more beautifully clothed in the splendor of their summer foliage or naked and transparent in winter.

Colorful crops of berries light up every corner of the winter garden: white snowberries (*Symphoricarpos albus*), yellow holly berries (*Ilex aquifolium* 'Bacciflava'), pale green and pink berries of mountain ash (*Sorbus hupehensis* and *S. vilmorinii*). Then there are the resolutely festive red berries of the Washington hawthorn (*Crataegus phaenopyrum*), *Photinia davidiana*, *Cotoneaster*, *Pernettya*, and the prodigious bunches of orange *Pyracantha* berries. But what is more cheery than the bright purple clusters of *Callicarpa* berries, gloriously dotted against an untouched fall of new snow in a November landscape?

There are other colors, like the subtle flush of pink in the bark of the *Stewartia*, which seems more striking in winter. But few trees in the winter garden hold our eye quite like the polished mahogany-red bark of the paperbark cherry (*Prunus serrula*) or the pure white bark of a Himalayan birch (*Betula* 'Jacquemontii') or the peeling skin of the paperbark maple (*Acer griseum*). Elsewhere in the garden, long, open, sunny stretches are brightened by the scarlet sticks of Siberian dogwood (*Cornus alba* 'Sibirica') and the yellow twigs of its cousin, *Cornus stolonifera* 'Flaviramea'.

In the perennial border, we find the lovely remnants of summer. Brittle brown plumes of astilbe poke out of shallow snowdrifts like rusty relics. Bold, straw-like fountains of Chinese silver grass (*Miscanthus sinensis*) and feather grass (*Stipa gigantea*) and the fading plumes of pampas grass (*Cortaderia*) take on a ghostly elegance when clothed in hoarfrost. Hydrangeas desperately hold on to their fragile freeze-dried flower heads, and some rose standards still wave bouquets of half-opened buds that will crumble to dust long before the grass begins to grow again. Meanwhile, the color of blue grasses in terracotta pots on a subzero day looks like a slice of sky cut and saved from the days of summer.

Other evergreen plants give structure and form to the beds and borders. The bones of the garden are never more visible than in the bareness of winter. Yuccas, dwarf conifers, hardy ferns all refuse to give way to winter's cool jabs. On ice-cold days, rhododendrons slip into survival mode and dangle their leaves like schoolboys back from snowballing with their hands pulled inside the sleeves of their coats. A blast of arctic air withers the sturdy evergreen euphorbia into looking like it has just been dunked in a swimming pool.

A surprise to many people, there are flowers in the winter garden. The deliciously fragrant pink and white blooms of *Viburnum bodnantense* 'Dawn' are already claiming center stage. In the wings, the yellow and bronze witch hazels will soon team up with Christmas roses (*Helleborus niger*), followed by wintersweet (*Chimonanthus*) and the heady scent of winter daphne, *Camellia sasanqua* and winter jasmine. The variegated foliage of holly and two-tone cultivars like *Euonymus fortunei* 'Emerald 'n' Gold' and *Elaeagnus pungens* 'Maculata' is perhaps appreciated best in the bleak midwinter, a time when bi-tone foliage has fewer rivals. Mixed with hardy bird's foot ivies and high-contrast foliage like the black leaves of mondo grass (*Ophiopogon* 'Nigrescens'), euonymus and elaeagnus are elevated to a higher status in the winter garden.

If you are walking in a garden and you say to yourself, "This is a wonderful, peaceful garden, I would like it for myself," you realize there is nothing outrageous or too startling there to take your attention away.

—Rosemary Verey, British garden writer, lecturer and owner of Barnsley House, Gloucestershire

Even in the most practical gardens, there are usually plants that need winter protection. Tasmanian tree ferns or baby palm trees wrapped in sackcloth and tightly tied with string invariably end up looking like Egyptian mummies stacked for shipment. But even this image tells us that a day will come when the burlap will come off and the warmth of the sun will bring back life and growth.

A walk in the winter garden is a time to think of triumphs and losses, days of extraordinary beauty gone by, the enthusiasm of spring, the laughter of summer, the tranquility of fall. It is a time to remember Shelley's words: "If winter comes, can spring be far behind?" and an opportunity to meditate on something Bernard Shaw said: "Be like the sun and the meadow, which are not in the least concerned about the coming winter."

Turning Winter into Spring

Smart gardeners know how to get a jump on spring. They use their propagator boxes to start new plants indoors under lights during the winter months, and this gives them a head start the moment spring rises up. Winter is also a good time to make garden plans for the new year, and one of the best winter planning exercises is to think of interesting ways to get your children and grandchildren into gardening. To help get you in the mood, you can bring amaryllis and paperwhites into bloom or force base branches of forsythia to blossom by bringing them into your home.

Amazing Amaryllis

Amaryllis is a flower people either love or hate. Some find the large, super-fragrant blooms just too colorful and scented. Others love them with a passion and grow them every fall. It is certainly a flower that commands attention and forces you to have an opinion about it one way or another. If you've never tried your hand at growing these popular floral wonders, give it a go. You'll be surprised how easy they are to bring to bloom. There are four sizes: 10, 12 1/2, 14 and the mammoth 16-inch bulbs (23, 32, 36 and 40 cm), which produce three or four stems. Top varieties include 'Picotte' (white with red edge), 'Apple Blossom' (rosy blush), 'Liberty' (deep red), 'Star of Holland' (red with white center), 'Allure' (white with crimson edge), 'Double Queen' (rich velvet red), 'Green Goddess' (white with green center) and 'Aphrodite' (white with pink tips and bronze edges).

Here are some tips on how to get your amaryllis off to a good start.

- Plant the bulb in ordinary sterilized potting soil in a pot that is a little wider than the bulb. Only a third of the bulb should be above the rim of the pot. Make sure there are drainage holes at the bottom.

- Water thoroughly with lukewarm water immediately after potting. Keep the soil moist, but not wet, for at least a week. Try not to get water directly on the bulb stem (called the "nose").

- Place the pot in a warm room in a well-lighted spot. A south-facing window is the best location. Watch for the green shoots to appear.

- Fertilize regularly as soon as the plant starts to grow. Use regular houseplant liquid fertilizer or a slow-release fertilizer.

- Once the plant is flowering—which can take six to eight weeks—move it out of direct sunlight and into a slightly cooler spot where it gets some indirect light.

- Turn the pot regularly to keep the flower stalk from leaning. Remove the faded flower heads by cutting them off. When all the flowers have faded, cut the stalk off just above the bulb nose.

Now, some tips on how to care for your amaryllis so it will rebloom.

- After the flowers have faded, allow the plant to continue growing in a warm spot in the light. Water regularly to keep the soil moist but not wet.

- Over summer, you can sink the bulb in its pot into the soil outdoors or keep the bulb indoors in a bright spot with a southern exposure. Don't let it dry out.

- In September, stop watering and place the bulb (still in its pot) in a dry, cool place in light shade for 10 to 12 weeks. The temperature should be 55° to 60°F (13° to 16°C).

- In November or December, remove the bulb from its pot. Clean up the old foliage and any old roots, but leave plump, healthy roots intact.

- Repot the bulb in fresh soil. Initiate the growth cycle by placing the pot in a warm, bright spot. The amaryllis will bloom again in about eight weeks.

- If a bulb has been grown successfully for a few years, it will produce offset bulblets. You can either move the bulb to a larger pot with the bulblets left attached (this will give you a dramatic show of flowers) or you can carefully remove the bulblets from the mother bulb and put them into separate pots.

Forcing Paperwhites and Other Bulbs

Indoor fireworks were once popular in England. They were tiny, ignitable, miniature novelties that could be safely set off in a box on a tabletop for the amusement of children at Christmas. Paperwhites are gardening's equivalent of indoor winter fireworks. Simply give them a sip of water, stand back and watch them go off, sending up a rocket of green shoots, sending down a whirl of white roots, and exploding into a cluster of white flowers that fill the air with a spicy, pungent fragrance.

This is an ideal project to do with children, as the bulbs flower quickly—in less than six weeks. Simply put pebbles or marbles in a dish or pot, plant the bulbs on top and fill the dish with water to the bottom of the bulbs.

These bulbs are all forms of *Narcissus tazetta*. There are a few named varieties to try. 'Ziva' produces pure-white flowers on 14-inch (36-cm) stems and is the most heavily scented. 'Sheleg' is lightly scented and grows 16 inches (40 cm) high. 'Galilea' is shorter than the other two and takes a little longer to come into bloom. There are also two yellow forms— 'Chinese Sacred Lily', which has white petals with a butter-yellow cup and a soft, pleasant fragrance, and 'Grand Soleil d'Or', which has yellow petals with a bright-orange cup and pleasant scent.

Early winter is the time of year to start having fun tricking bulbs into blooming indoors to provide color and fragrance during the winter months. The common term for this process is "forcing," but that's not quite accurate. You're not really forcing a bulb to do anything it doesn't want to do—you're simply fooling it into thinking it has already gone through the cold, dark days of winter and arrived at the light and balmy days of spring.

You can buy pre-chilled hyacinth bulbs—labeled "prepared"—or you can buy regular hyacinths and pre-chill them yourself by popping them into the fridge in a paper bag for 12 to 14 weeks. There are special forcing jars (or glasses) designed specifically for growing hyacinths indoors. Simply fill the glass with water, sit the bulb on the top and leave it in a cool, dark place—perhaps an unheated garage or cellar—until the roots develop and the flower bud starts to appear. Then bring it back into a warm, well-lit room.

The pre-chilling period is important. If the bulb is not adequately chilled, it won't flower properly. What you'll end up with is a bunch of leaves and a wonky, mutated-looking flower. To keep the water from getting murky, add a piece of activated charcoal. This prevents algae forming.

The key to forcing bulbs indoors is to concentrate on getting them to root properly before you encourage them to put energy into producing leaves and flowers. The optimum temperature for promoting root growth is 48°F (9°C). Grape hyacinth (*Muscari*), crocus and dwarf iris (*I. reticulata*) should all be potted and then placed in a cool, dark spot (crawl space, cellar or unheated garage) for at least 8 to 10 weeks. The container must be twice as deep as the bulb is long, to give room for root development. The moment you see shoots appearing (top growth), bring them into a warm, bright room to promote flowering. Do this in early winter and you will get blooms from mid-January to early March. Don't forget to keep watering lightly each week.

Forsythia as a Tour de Force

You can also have fun "forcing" into bloom branches of natural spring-flowering shrubs such as forsythia, quince (*Chaenomeles*) and pussy willow (*Salix*). One of the easiest and most rewarding winter gardening projects, this will bring an exhilarating breath of spring freshness to your home. The sight of all those spring blossoms should also do a lot to rekindle your enthusiasm for the new gardening season just around the corner. There is no shortage of plant material suitable for forcing. Clipped branches of such trees as crabapple, cherry, dogwood, plum and pear will all produce wonderful pink or white blossoms when brought indoors.

Witch hazel looks great in a simple arrangement on a coffee table, especially when combined with a few twisted branches of Harry Lauder's walking stick (*Corylus avellana* 'Contorta') or a few branches of birch or Japanese maple (*Acer palmatum*). If you're lucky enough to have a pink-flowering *Viburnum bodnantense*, you will know how delightful it can be to cut a few stems and bring them indoors in January or February. But of all the spring-flowering shrubs, the easiest and most popular to force into bloom is forsythia. Placed in a blue glass vase, the twigs of delicate bright yellow flowers can look magical. Here's how to get the best results.

- Cut forsythia on a sunny day when the temperature is above freezing.

- Choose branches with swelling flower buds—slightly plumper than leaf buds—that appear just about to pop.

- Make sure you use sharp pruners. It is important to make a clean cut to prevent disease problems from infecting the bush.

- Take branches that are flush with a main artery-type branch. As you do this, try to shape the bush attractively, so that you are also pruning effectively as well as collecting branches for forcing.

- Once you get the branches inside, recut the ends on a slant and hammer the ends so that they look mashed. This helps the branch take up water to nourish the buds.

- Remove all the leaves from the bottom third of the branch before placing it in a vase of warm water. The tepid temperature of the water simulates warm spring rain and encourages the flower buds to break a little faster.

- Place the vase in a bright room where the temperature is 60° to 70°F (16° to 21°C). The warmer the room, the sooner the flowers will appear. You can speed up the process by recutting the stems and changing the water fairly regularly.

- Once the branch is in full flower, keep it out of direct sunlight. The blossoms should last two or three weeks. If you cut new branches at intervals you can create a sequence of flowers through March.

13 Ways to Get Kids Gardening

How do we make gardening fun for children? The garden can be a wonderful place to work alongside your children or grandchildren. Some of the best conversations happen when kids are busy digging or planting or harvesting vegetables without a worry in the world. But how can we lure them away from the high stimulus of video games and television and outside into the fresh air and sunshine of the garden? It can be a challenge, but parents have a couple of powerful points in their favor. First, children love being close to their parents and the garden is a great place to get close to the ones you love. And nature has its own special beauty, mystery and magic and is perfectly capable of sneaking up and surprising even the most worldly children with the simple joy of discovery. So here are 13 great ways to introduce kids to the fun of gardening. Some of these projects are designed for toddlers, others are intended for older children.

1. **Get some action plants.** The first step in getting children excited about gardening is to capture their imagination with the wonder of plants. Even children who profess no interest in gardening will be fascinated by the sensitive plant (*Mimosa pudica*) and the Venus flytrap (*Dionaea muscipula*). The leaves of the sensitive plant fold up the second they are touched. After a few minutes, they open again. The Venus flytrap has jaw-like leaves that snap shut when triggered. Both plants are available at garden centers.

2. **Play the name game.** Using radish seed, which germinates super-fast at 45° to 70°F (7° to 21°C) in four to six days, show children how they can write their name or draw a smiley face or make an X's and O's box in the soil. You can do this indoors, too, in a shallow tray filled with soil mix. Another name-project you can do is to scratch your child's name on the side of a green pumpkin while it is still growing on the vine. This is something Beth Richardson, author of *Gardening with Children*, did secretly for her 3- and 10-year-old sons. "Several weeks later, when it was time to pick the bright orange globes sitting in the back of the garden, I sent the boys out to see how many they could find. A few joyful shrieks later and they were running to tell me about the magic that had happened in the garden. The secret, says Richardson, is to cut no deeper than 1/8-inch (.3 cm) into the pumpkin rind. If you cut deeper it could rot or get infected. "Once the name has been etched, turn the pumpkin so that the part with the name on it is facing the sky or getting a good flow of air around it."

3. **Make a sweet-pea wigwam.** Tie together three or four 6-foot (1.8-m) bamboo canes or bean-poles to form a teepee-shape in an open, sunny corner in the garden. Plant sweet peas or scarlet runner beans around each of the canes. They will quickly grow to the top of the canes and can be encouraged to fill in the sides to create a fun hiding space. You can also make a secret hiding place by planting a series of tall sunflowers such as 'Giganteus' in a circle. For a smaller, more manageable sunflower, look for 'Teddy Bear'.

4. **Plant a vegetable pizza.** Make a circle and divide it into six wedges using radish seed or pebbles for marking the boundaries. Plant your six favorite vegetables inside each of the wedges. Lettuce, bush beans, peas and beets are all quick to mature, but if you really want to stick with the pizza theme you could go for onions, tomatoes, peppers, garlic, basil and oregano, all of which can be harvested and eaten on a real pizza.

5. **Sprout an avocado.** All you need is an avocado seed, three toothpicks and a jar of water. Jab the toothpicks into the pit so they are evenly spaced around the middle. Set the pit, big end down, on top of the jar. Fill the jar with water to cover the bottom third of the seed. Place the jar in a warm, shaded place. The seed will split open in a couple of weeks. A root will start to grow from the bottom and a stem will appear at the top. When this happens, move the jar to a sunny window sill. After the first leaves appear, put the seed into a pot of ordinary soil mix. The plant will grow into a small tree.

6. **Make a flower-food garden.** These are plants that have the appearance or aroma of food but aren't. Start with poached egg plant (*Limnanthes douglasii*) and cherry-pie plant (*Heliotropium*). Add *Melianthus major*, which smells like peanut butter when the leaves are rubbed, and a chocolate plant (*Cosmos atrosanguineus*), which has maroon flowers that smell like rich chocolate. Add the apple, peppermint and chocolate aromas of specialty mints, plus the oranges and lemons smell of scented geraniums. For conversation, grow a pineapple lily (*Eucomis*), which produces a flower that looks very much like a pineapple.

7. **Attract butterflies and hummingbirds.** Few sights in the garden are as enchanting as seeing a hummingbird hovering as it feeds at a fuchsia or spotting a butterfly as it flutters over a patch of phlox. To guarantee your children see these wonderful sights, plant plenty of fuchsia, foxgloves, petunias and tubs full of nicotiana, which will also add sweet fragrance to the garden at night. For butterflies, plant phlox,

verbena, zinnia and buddleia. They are drawn to sweet-smelling plants, so roses and sweet peas also lure them to the garden.

8. **Grow a pot full of strawberries.** Memories are made of this: eating sweet strawberries, freshly plucked from the plant. The plants are available from garden centers. Plant half a dozen in a strawberry pot—three on the sides, three at the top—and you'll have a bumper crop for picking.

9. **Grow animals.** To make a garden full of imaginative creatures, start with a few sheep with the soft wooly feel of lamb's ears (*Stachys*). Throw in a few gentle dragons (*Antirrhinum*) with jaws that really snap. For something a little creepy, grow some back mondo grass (*Ophiopogon*), which looks like a giant black spider on the ground. At the back, you could have a gaggle of geese with white nodding heads (*Lysimachia clethroides*).

10. **Make a crazy container of color.** In a half-barrel, sow an assortment of wild summer flowers: California poppies, bachelor buttons, clarkia, love-in-a-mist, marigolds, salvia, snapdragons, candytuft, cosmos, sweet peas, nasturtium, poppies, mallow and black-eyed susans.

11. **Bulb bounty.** The easiest bulb project going is to grow paperwhites in a dish of pebbles or hyacinths in water-filled forcing jars (see page 180). Enlist your children's help when planting things like summer hyacinths (*Galtonia*), clumps of gladioli, pineapple lilies (*Eucomis*), lilies—especially giant trumpet lilies—and dahlias. Seeing these ugly tubers and corms turn into beautifully colorful flowers is magical.

12. **Have a seed race.** For this you need six 4-inch (10-cm) plant pots and a small bag of soil mix. Label each pot and plant marigolds, pumpkins, radish, sunflower, beans and nasturtium. Water and place them in a sunny window. See which seed is the first to break through the surface or which grows faster. Seedlings can all be planted out in the garden.

13. **Plant a tree.** The beauty of this project is that your children can see the tree growing and maturing as they do. They also have the memory of planting the tree with you. Autumn is the perfect time for tree planting. If you plant a fruit tree, there is the added satisfaction of the harvest. All good memories.

Trees and Shrubs

In the barren days of winter, you can see clearly what your garden needs to give it more structure, what conifers to introduce for more visual interest and cohesion through the winter months, and what shrubs might bring color and fragrance to your garden. This is a good time to visit public gardens, where you can note the stars of the winter garden and make plans to bring this winter interest into your own yard.

Stars of the Winter Garden

- *Betula jacquemontii* (white birch). There are several trees with outstanding winter bark color—the paperbark maple (*Acer griseum*) with its peeling orange-brown bark; the paperbark cherry (*Prunus serrula*) with its polished mahogany-red trunk; and the arbutus tree with its reddish bark. But they all take a back seat in winter to the dazzling form of *Betula jacquemontii*, which has a pure white trunk and branches. It is outstanding when seen against a bright blue sky on a brisk January day. Hardy to at least Zone 6.

- *Callicarpa bodinieri* 'Profusion' (beautyberry). This produces outstanding clusters of small, pale purple berries. Hardy to Zone 2.

- *Camellia sasanqua* 'Yuletide'. One of the best of the winter-flowering camellias, this has fragrant, deep red flowers with yellow centers. Hardy to Zone 7.

- *Cornus alba* 'Sibirica' (Siberian dogwood). Also known as tatarian dogwood, this is considered the best in cultivation for its cheerful red stems, which are very eye-catching in the bare winter garden. Two other red-twig dogwoods—*C. sericea* (red osier dogwood) and *C. sanguinea* (blood-twig dogwood)—add winter color and interest, along with *C. stolonifera* 'Flaviramea', which produces greenish-yellow shoots when pruned and grown in full sun. All hardy to Zone 3.

- *Corylus avellena* 'Contorta'. A list of the stars of the winter garden would not be complete without a mention of "Harry Lauder's walking stick." In late winter its twisted branches are handsomely decorated with greeny-yellow lamb's-tail catkins. This is one of those plants that you never think of when planting your garden but always wish you had when you see it in bloom. Hardy to Zone 5.

- *Daphne odora* 'Aureomarginata' (winter daphne). This evergreen shrub produces extremely fragrant flowers in midwinter to early spring. The blooms are white with purplish-pink markings. It will thrive in a fairly sheltered spot close to the house, preferably near the entrance where its magnificent perfume can be appreciated. The rich green leaves have a golden-yellow edge to them. This daphne is special because it is not prone to viral infection, which many daphnes are. Hardy to Zone 7. The February daphne (*D. mezereum*) is also extremely fragrant, producing bright purplish-pink blooms in early spring. Hardy to Zone 5.

- *Erica carnea* (winter-flowering heather). These fuss-free plants flower from November to December; other varieties bloom from January to April. They are extremely useful for filling gaps in the winter border. One attractive combination is 'Springwood White' with 'Pink Spangles'. For pure foliage interest, look for 'Foxhollow' (yellow foliage with pink tinge) or 'Aurea' (golden foliage in spring). Hardy to Zone 5.

- *Hamamelis* x *intermedia* (witch hazel). Winter is witch hazel's moment of glory. It goes completely unnoticed all year, an insignificant deciduous bush lost in the corner of the shrubbery, but then it produces exceptionally fragrant, pale canary-yellow or coppery-red blooms on bare branches in winter. The two most popular forms are 'Jelena' and 'Diane'. The Chinese witch hazel (*H. mollis*) produces scented, pale yellow flowers. Top varieties include 'Pallida' and 'Brevipetala'. All hardy to Zone 5.

- *Picea pungens* 'Koster' (Colorado blue spruce). It is always exciting to see color in the garden in winter, and the blue Colorado spruce is one tree that can provide it. The blue needles of 'Koster' turn an exceptionally bright, metallic blue in winter. Hardy to Zone 2.

- *Sarcococca humilis* (sweet box). For about six weeks from the middle of January, this little evergreen bush produces insignificant white flowers that hardly merit a second glance. They do, however, perfume the air on mild days with the most delicious scent that suggests the sweetness of privet on the summer air. Hardy to Zone 6.

Christmas Rose

Helleborus niger (Christmas rose). This midwinter beauty is not a tree or shrub, but it is definitely a star performer in the winter garden. It has exquisite, nodding white flowers, about 2 inches (5 cm) across, with yellow centers. It's one of the most popular perennials with knowledgeable gardeners. However, the Christmas rose is a total contradiction in terms: It is not a rose at all, being more closely related to the buttercup family, and it rarely ever blooms at Christmas. Mostly flowering from late January to March, it has more in common with snowdrops and crocus as one of the first harbingers of spring than it has with festive plants like poinsettia. Still, the Christmas rose is one of the miracles of nature, a wonderful, cheery flower in the middle of winter. Hellebores prefer fertile soil, partial shade and dislike heat and intense sunlight. They sulk and flower poorly for a year after being divided. Hardy to Zone 3.

- *Skimmia* 'Rubella'. The dark evergreen leaves are aromatic and the dense clusters of bronze-red buds are so impressive that in Europe it's often sold as a winter houseplant. 'Rubinetta' is another variety with deep red buds. Hardy to Zone 7.

- *Viburnum bodnantense* 'Pink Dawn' (winter-flowering viburnum). Take a whiff of the powerful fragrance of these bright pink blooms and you'll think it's summer again. Hardy to Zone 7.

Captivating Conifers

Conifers fall into 10 main groupings—firs (*Abies*), true cedars (*Cedrus*), false cypress (*Chamaecyparis*), cypress (*Cupressus*), junipers (*Juniperus*), spruce (*Picea*), pine (*Pinus*), yew (*Taxus*), red cedar (*Thuja*) and hemlock (*Tsuga*). But the simplest way to make sense of conifers is to divide them into two key landscape groups—feature trees and dwarf specimens. They are all useful to create year-round structure, stability and textural interest. Conifers with blues and golden foliage add color and interest to the winter garden, while the weeping varieties provide graceful forms and focal points.

Here's a pick of the best conifers for your garden. They are all hardy to Zone 6 or better.

Feature Trees

- *Abies koreana* (Korean fir). A good pick for spacious gardens, this has a strikingly symmetrical shape, fragrant dark green needles and purple cones. It grows to about 35 feet (10.5 m) after 10 or 15 years.

- *Cedrus atlantica* 'Glauca' (blue Atlas cedar). A fairly slow-growing tree that can reach over 60 feet (18 m) at maturity. It has rich green foliage and tends to lose its formal, pyramidal shape once it has reached 16 feet (5 m).

- *Cedrus atlantica* 'Glauca Pendula' (weeping blue Atlas cedar). This has silvery-blue needles on long, weeping branches. It needs to be staked or it will crawl along the ground. It is best grown to about 12 feet (3.6 m), making an attractive feature in a garden.

- *Cedrus deodara* (Himalayan cedar). A beautiful weeping tree, but it needs to be placed in the right location. It starts out as an innocent-looking little tree but can grow quickly to 60 feet (18 m). The weeping branches have a very graceful appearance but the blue-green needles are quite prickly. 'Kashmir' is a new improved variety that is the hardiest of all the deodara cedars. It has blue-green pyramidal growth and a more pronounced weeping habit. It grows to 14 feet (4.3 m) after 10 years.

- *Chamaecyparis nootkatensis* 'Pendula' (weeping Nootka cypress). A medium-sized tree that grows slowly to 30 feet (9 m). Long, graceful, dark green branches hang loosely from a slender upright center for an elegant overall appearance.

- *Larix decidua* 'Pendula' (weeping European larch). This is a deciduous conifer with soft green weeping foliage that turns golden in October. Use it as a mounding groundcover or stake it for an upright specimen. It will grow as tall as you stake it. Without the stake, it makes a natural groundcover.

- *Metasequoia glyptostroboides* (dawn redwood, fossil tree). This deciduous conifer is a beautifully architectural big tree with an attractive branching structure and soft green, feathery needles that turn golden before they drop to the ground in fall. It grows at a moderate rate to more than 65 feet (20 m) at maturity.

Most gardeners are basically show-offs. After all, it's pointless to do all this work if you're not going to show the world—or at least the gardening cognoscenti—what you have created.

—Jill Stewart-Bowen, former president of Victoria Horticultural Society, British Columbia

- *Picea pungens* 'Hoopsii' (Colorado blue spruce, Hoop's blue spruce). The bluest of the spruces and one of the most desirable, this has stiff horizontal branches and dense, silvery-blue needles. It is relatively slow growing, reaching only 8 feet (2.4 m) after 10 years. Its growth can be somewhat irregular for the first few years, but the spectacular blue needles easily make up for this. Other popular forms include 'Fat Albert', a compact, slow-growing, upright pyramidal tree; 'Fastigiata', very narrow and with vivid blue needles; 'Globosa', a globe-shaped bush; and 'Moerheimii', a superb, dense, conical tree with dark blue needles.

- *Sequoiadendron giganteum* 'Pendulum' (weeping redwood). This weeping form of the familiar redwood has a twisted trunk and long branches that droop straight down. It grows to 30 feet (9 m).

- *Taxodium distichum* (swamp cypress). This is a deciduous conifer with bright yellow-green needles in spring that turn reddish-brown in autumn. It is totally happy growing in wet or well-drained acid soil, making it the perfect tree for swampy, damp ground. It has even been planted directly into water beside ponds. It grows 45 to 65 feet (13.5 to 20 m).

Dwarf Conifers

- *Abies balsamea* 'Nana' (dwarf balsam fir). Compact and slow growing to 3 feet (90 cm), this has green foliage. An ideal shrub for the rockery.

- *Chamaecyparis obtusa* 'Nana Gracilis' (dwarf hinoki cypress). Very compact, this grows to 4 feet (1.2 m) and has dark green foliage. It is a good choice as a feature plant in a Japanese-style garden.

- *Chamaecyparis pisifera* 'Mops' (goldthread cypress). This has bright golden foliage and grows into a compact, 3-foot (90-cm) shrub. Also look for 'Sungold', which grows 18 inches (45 cm) tall and 3 feet (90 cm) wide.

- *Chamaecyparis thyoides* 'Heatherbun'. Dense, globular, fairly fast growth to 5 by 4 feet (1.5 by 1.2 m) in 10 years. Extremely soft foliage with dark reddish-purple winter color is lovely to stroke (better than a cat).

- *Juniperus horizontalis* 'Blue Chip'. One of the best of the low-spreading, creeping junipers, this has exceptional steel-blue foliage and spreads to 3 feet (90 cm). *J. horizontalis* 'Wiltonii' is another good variety that forms a dense carpet of blue foliage. It can be used to cascade over walls. Other top names are 'Ice Blue', 'Blue Rug', 'Prince of Wales', 'Calgary Carpet', 'New Blue Tamarix' and 'Bar Harbor'. For something a little different, look for *J. horizontalis* 'Mother Lode', which has brilliant

Take Your Cedar for a Spin

Make your own cedar spiral, sometimes called a conifer twist. Here's a project you can do in spring.

- Start out with a bushy, 3- or 4-foot (90-cm to 1.2-m) pyramidal cedar. Look for *Thuja occidentalis* 'Smaragd', 'Holmstrup' or 'Brandon'. Make sure there are no holes in the foliage where you can see the main trunk.

- Put the plant in a place where you can walk around it comfortably. Place the pot on a platform so you don't have to crouch down. This will make it easier to clip away at the bottom part.

- Wearing gloves, put your hand into the bush and take hold of each individual branch before you cut it. This will allow you to see exactly what you are doing at each stage and to get an idea of what the bush will look like after the cut.

- You can use string or a piece of fine rope to wind around the plant from top to bottom. The guideline should wind around the bush at a 45-degree angle.

- Start at the bottom of the plant and cut the first sweep of the spiral, removing branches close to the main trunk. Take a little off at a time. When you get three-quarters of the way around, stop and move around to the other side. Continue pruning away, following the line of your sweep. The biggest mistake you can make is to merrily clip away without realizing the angle of the spiral has changed. Cut and check every minute or two to make sure you're right on track.

- The dense foliage that forms the actual spiral is called the "spin." The thickness of the spin should slowly decrease as you make your way up the bush. The secret is to keep looking around the corner as you prune.

- When the spiral is clearly formed, take hedging shears and thin down the bulk of the spin. Clean up the top and tip-prune the edges of the spiral to create a more bunchy effect. As you maintain your topiary, clipping away new growth to keep the shape, you will find the spiral shape will slowly become more pronounced.

gold foliage and is an excellent groundcover plant. Also consider 'Holger', which grows to 12 inches (30 cm) and spreads to about 6 feet (1.8 m). The new spring growth is yellow. Growing on top of the older blue foliage, it makes for an eye-catching two-tone effect.

- *Juniperus squamata* 'Blue Star' (blue star juniper). The best of the dwarf junipers, this has steel-blue foliage. It grows only 3 feet (90 cm) high and looks good year-round. *J. chinensis* 'Mint Julep' has bright mint-green foliage and *J. chinensis* 'Old Gold' has bright golden foliage and is slow growing to 3 feet (90 cm).

- *Picea pungens* 'Glauca Globosa' (dwarf globe blue spruce). Hardy to Zone 2, this has the bluest foliage of all the dwarf spruces and grows into a compact shape about 3 feet (90 cm) high.

- *Pinus mugo* 'Pumilio' (dwarf mugo pine). One of the most common evergreens used in low-maintenance schemes, rockeries and alpine borders, this offers excellent texture contrast. It is slow growing to 4 feet (1.2 m) but it can be kept lower and is fairly shade tolerant. *P. parviflora* 'Yatsubusa' is a very dense-growing dwarf shrub with silvery white buds that stand up like candles in the spring. It grows to about 3 feet (90 cm) in 10 years.

- *Thuja occidentalis* 'Rheingold' (Rheingold cedar). A popular dwarf conifer that provides striking color in the winter garden, 'Rheingold' grows to 4 feet (1.2 m). It's a perfect cone shape and has deep golden foliage. *T. orientalis* 'Aurea Nana' has even brighter golden foliage that slowly turns bronze-green in winter.

- *Tsuga canadensis* 'Jeddeloh'. This grows to about 6 feet (1.8 m) after 20 years. It has striking blue-green needles and a beautiful weeping habit. It's ideal for planting over banks and is very shade tolerant.

Your Best Bets for Hedging

Thinking about installing a hedge? Privacy is such an important element in a garden, but if walls or fences won't do the job of defining borders and providing the privacy you want, the task usually falls to a hedge of some sort. Hedging also gives a garden stability and structure throughout the seasons. There are different kinds of hedging—formal, informal, deciduous, evergreen. Even roses can be used to create a hedge if space is not too limited. Some gardeners mix plants to create a tapestry hedge.

Here's a guide to popular hedging plants.

- *Buxus sempervirens* (boxwood). This can be used for a low hedge, but it can also grow over 10 feet (3 m) high. A slow-growing dwarf form,

B. 'Suffruticosa', is ideal for defining a rose bed or herb garden or for simply dividing one part of the garden from another. *B. koreana* 'Winter Beauty' is a hardier form with blue-green foliage, also very useful for making parterres. 'Morris Midget' is a very compact form. All hardy to Zone 4.

- *Forsythia* x *intermedia*. One of the heralds of spring, this popular deciduous shrub can be used to create a striking hedge of bright-yellow flowers in March. Another one that is not tough enough for areas with super-cold winters. It grows to 10 feet (3 m). Hardy to Zone 5.

- *Ilex crenata* (Japanese holly). A member of the holly family, this has tiny black berries in winter, but it has all the appearance of a box-type hedge and can be clipped into a formal-looking, waist-high barrier. Hardy to Zone 5.

- *Ligustrum ovalifolium* (privet). This is a popular and attractive hedge in temperate areas because of its soft, glossy leaves. It can be sheared into a tidy shape. Not the right pick for extremely cold areas, where it is deciduous. Hardy to Zone 7.

- *Photinia* x *fraseri*. A good choice for mild-area gardens where the large, soft-green leaves stay evergreen all winter and the new leaves are an attractive red-bronze in spring and summer. Photinia can be left to grow 10 to 12 feet (3 to 3.6 m) high or pruned as low as 4 or 5 feet (1.2 to 1.5 m). Hardy to Zone 7.

- *Prunus laurocerasus* (English laurel). The main complaints about this plant are that it's too common and grows far too quickly so it requires a lot of maintenance. Left unpruned, it can reach 30 feet (9 m). Nevertheless, it is still a very popular form of hedging because of its big, glossy, evergreen leaves. Hardy to Zone 7.

- *Taxus baccata* 'Fastigiata Aurea' (golden yew). The new foliage in spring is golden-yellow and then turns green, retaining touches of gold on the edges of the needles. Like the variegated cedars, this is more useful as a feature plant, but it could be incorporated into a hedging scheme. It will ultimately reach 15 feet (4.5 m). Hardy to Zone 5.

- *Taxus media* 'Brownii' (Brown's yew). With a vase-shaped form, this is the perfect choice if you want a relatively slow-growing, formal-looking hedge in a shaded area. It grows to 8 feet (2.4 m) within a few years and can put on 12 to 16 inches (30 to 40 cm) a year. Hardy to Zone 5.

- *Taxus* x *media* 'Hicksii' (Hick's yew). A cross between English and Japanese species, this yew produces a narrow, upright bush with lovely, dark-green foliage that holds its color and requires minimal maintenance. It can take 10 years or more for it to reach 8 or 10 feet (2.4 to 3 m). Hardy to Zone 5.

- *Thuja occidentalis* 'Smaragd'. For the typical, average-sized home garden, this dependable cedar is an excellent pick. With a cleanly defined, pyramidal shape, this has rich emerald-green foliage that holds its color through winter. It can grow to 20 feet (6 m) if left unpruned. Other varieties of *Thuja* to consider for hedging include the dark green 'Nigra' and the narrow, bright green 'Brandon'. More unusual forms are 'Sherwood Frost' (creamy variegation) and 'Yellow Ribbon' (bright yellow), but these are generally not as popular as the more common green forms. Most people like their hedges green or blue-green. The gold and variegated varieties look good as feature plants, but they don't come highly recommended for hedging. The best hedging plant for home gardens in the country is 'Holmstrup' because of its resistance to deer—a big problem for gardeners in country locations. Hardy to Zone 3.

- *Thuja plicata* 'Excelsa' (red cedar). If you want privacy and you want it fast, there is no better plant than western red cedar. Hardy to Zone 5, 'Excelsa' grows 10 to 12 feet (3 to 3.6 m) high and has shiny, deep-green foliage that is particularly attractive in the relatively colorless days of winter. Another benefit of 'Excelsa' is that it is very easily pruned once established. Hardy to Zone 5.

- *Tsuga* (hemlock). There are two excellent kinds to consider—*T. heterophylla* (western hemlock) and *T. canadensis* (Canada hemlock). Western hemlock is ideal for coastal gardens. Its loose, finely textured, dark-green foliage has a fernlike quality that makes it a very attractive backdrop. Canada hemlock is more suitable for colder areas. Grows to 35 to 70 feet (10.5 to 21 m). Hardy to Zone 4.

- Other possibilities to consider include hardy hibiscus (*H. syriacus*), spirea, potentilla, barberry (*Berberis*), oleaster (*Elaeagnus*), holly (*Ilex aquifolium*) and *Viburnum tinus* 'Spring Bouquet' or *V. plicatum* 'Summer Snowflake'.

Deck the Halls

Dormancy is something plants do to survive winter and save energy for the new season. We can learn from that. After a busy spring, summer and fall in the garden, winter brings us a lovely opportunity to rest and recuperate. Nevertheless, we still have a chance for some horticultural fun and games around the festive season. There's holly and ivy to rediscover and poinsettia to decorate with. This is also a great time to experiment with winter containers at entrances, inside porches and in hallways.

Poinsettia: It Looks a Lot Like Christmas

The most popular flowering potted plant in North America—easily outselling chrysanthemums, Christmas cactus, cyclamen and florist azaleas—the poinsettia is more temperamental than most people know. Sensitive to changes in temperature and prone to disease and growth problems during cultivation, especially if overwatered or exposed to too much humidity, poinsettias require careful and diligent handling to bring them to maturity in time for Christmas.

The work of the growers starts in August. They take 3-inch (7.5-cm) cuttings and get them growing. By September, they pinch-prune the plants to make them bushier. Timing is everything. Too much growth hormone early in the process can ruin the crop. Too much humidity can leave plants unsightly and unsellable.

From the first of November to the end of December, millions of poinsettias are carried out the doors of garden centers, supermarkets and florists and into homes, offices, banks, churches and shopping malls. The U.S. Department of Agriculture estimates more than 60 million poinsettias are sold every year over the Christmas season. The majority—in fact, 80 percent of the world's poinsettias—get their start at the Paul Ecke Ranch in Encinitas, California. Thousands more are brought to market by the Ecke Ranch's biggest rival, Fischer, of Colorado.

The top reds are 'Freedom', 'Sonora', 'Cortez' and 'Peterstar'. Best of the whites are 'Cortez White', 'Annette Hegg', 'Sonora White' and 'Peterstar White'. Favorite pink and pink-speckled varieties include 'Pink Peppermint', 'Silverstar Pink', 'Jingle Bells', 'Flirt' and 'Monet'. With an eye on Generation Xers, the Ecke Ranch has introduced a red poinsettia called 'Winter Rose', which has rose-like bracts and a more erect shape.

Here are some tips on how to buy and care for your poinsettia.

- Never buy a wilted plant or one whose compost has dried out completely. Choose stocky, multi-branched plants.

- Don't buy plants that have been left standing outside a store on a cold, rainy day.

- Look for plenty of color with lots of buds still to open.

- Check leaves for signs of pests or diseases.

- Take your plant home in a warm car immediately after buying it. Don't leave it in a cold car while you go shopping for a couple of hours.

- Don't keep your poinsettia on top of the TV or stereo where it will be subjected to too much heat or in a hallway where it will be repeatedly exposed to cold air from outside. Many poinsettias die in these hostile locations. Plants need daytime temperatures of 64° to 70°F (18° to 21°C) and never lower than 60°F (16°C) at night.

- Don't overwater. Most plants need only a cup of water once a week. Overwatering will cause root rot and the plant will drop its leaves and die. Try to keep the soil moist at all times without being soaking wet.

- Light is not a big issue, but poinsettias flower best when they get about six hours of indirect light daily.

- Don't leave your plant in the paper protective sleeve for more than 48 hours. Poinsettias produce ethylene gas and if allowed to build up in the sleeve it will cause the leaves and bracts to droop.

- Don't leave your poinsettia trapped between curtains and a cold window overnight. This is almost certain to kill it.

Other Popular Plants for Christmas

Cyclamen, Christmas cactus (*Schlumbergera truncata*) and kalanchoe (*Kalanchoe blossfeldiana*) are also favorite plants at Christmas. Here are some tips on how to buy and care for them.

- **Christmas cactus.** These are good value because if cared for properly they will flower year after year. Most have pink flowers, although you may get lucky and find some with white blooms. Christmas cactus is native to the cool, mountainous forests of Brazil.

  Pick plants that have only one or two flowers about to open and with a lot more buds at the tips of shoots. Place it where it will get the most natural light but not in a spot where it is exposed to cold drafts or excessive heat. It needs a minimum temperature of 55°F (13°C). Let the soil dry out between waterings, then stand the plant in a saucer of water for 20 minutes. Pick off the individual blooms when they are finished. Repot the plant in spring.

- **Cyclamen.** A member of the primrose family, cyclamen are very popular indoor plants, especially useful for adding festive color during the holidays.

  Check for a large number of developing flower stems. Leaf stems should be short and stocky. Don't buy if the plant appears to be leggy. Water only from below. Feed once a week with half-strength liquid fertilizer. Keep at a temperature of 50°F (10°C) in good light. Turn the plant every other day. Remove flowers as they wilt by pulling them away from the base of the plant.

- **Kalanchoe.** These plants, with their diminutive flowers, are making a big comeback. You will find a wide variety of colors, including orange, white, yellow, pink, salmon and red.

  Look for plants with compact, thick-lobed, deep green leaves. Don't overwater. Drench the soil thoroughly and then allow it to become moderately dry before watering again. Feed every couple of weeks with a liquid fertilizer. Try to find a room where the temperature is a little cooler, around 50°F (10°C)—perhaps close to a window or in a hallway. Snip off dead flowers and repot the plant in spring.

The Holly and the Ivy

Ignored or rejected most of the year, these two plants are catapulted every December into the spotlight as traditional symbols of Christmas. At one time, ivy was associated with Bacchus, the Roman god of wine, and thought to provide protection against drunkenness. Holly was commonly used during the Roman winter festival of Saturnalia as a festive symbol of fertility and fruitfulness. When Christians transformed the festival into Christmas, they continued using holly as a decoration and gave another meaning to the red berries (said to have been originally yellow and turned red by Christ's blood) and the thorny leaves (said to represent Christ's crown of thorns). Today, holly and ivy decorations are as popular as ever.

Much of the holly used to deck halls at Christmas is grown at holly farms. Sprigs of bright red berries and the plain green leaves of classic English holly (*Ilex aquifolium*) are available at most garden centers. The best varieties for growing in the garden are 'Hedge Hog', 'J.C. van Tol', 'Siberia' and 'Argentea Marginata'. The blue hollies—

I. meserveae 'Blue Boy', 'Blue Prince' and 'Blue Princess'—all have blue-green leaves.

Holly always combines beautifully with varieties of English ivy (*Hedera helix*), especially vines that have been left to develop their distinctive yellowy seed clusters. Of the ivies, the most common—and popular—is English ivy, believed to have been brought to North America from Britain more than 200 years ago. The second most popular ivy is Persian ivy (*H. colchica*), slightly less hardy and always identified by breaking off a piece and sniffing it; Persian ivy smells of celery. An attractive holly-and-ivy display for table or hallway is easy to make by combining a few small pots of one of the tiny bird's-foot varieties of ivy, such as plain green 'Needlepoint' or variegated 'Glacier', with a few upright stems of English holly with red berries. For something equally effective, you could use variegated false holly (*Osmanthus heterophyllus* 'Tricolor') and add some wintergreen (*Gaultheria procumbens*), which has its own cheery red berries.

Your Guide to Christmas Trees

- Blue spruce (*Picea pungens*). Far too nice a tree to cut, this is available as a live tree. The needles are pointed and sharp, which means it's not the best tree if you have children or pets.

- Douglas fir (*Pseudotsuga menziesii*). The most popular and least expensive Christmas tree. It has aromatic fragrance, especially when freshly cut, and attractive, dense, upward-pointing branches. Some of the trees are produced through "stump culture," which allows more than one tree to be harvested from the stump of a single tree.

- Fraser fir (*Abies fraseri*). This tree is growing in popularity because of its attractive triangular form, upward-curling branches, and dark, blue-green needles with silvery undersides. It has a pleasant aroma and good needle retention.

- Grand fir (*Abies grandis*). The most fragrant of Christmas trees, this gives off a strong citrus aroma when the needles are crushed. It is easily distinguished by its sprays of lustrous, deep green needles with silvery-white undersides.

- Noble fir (*Abies procera*). One in three people now choose a Noble fir for their Christmas tree. This is the best variety if you don't want needles dropping everywhere. It has excellent needle retention and a pleasant aroma.

- Nordmann fir (*Abies nordmanniana*). An attractive tree very similar in appearance to the Noble fir, this is an ideal choice for a smaller room because it has a compact, narrow base. The broad needles are dark green on top with a gray stripe on the underside. It has good needle retention, but not quite as good as the Noble fir.

- Norway spruce (*Picea abies*). This has short, soft, bright-green, prickly needles and the traditional conical Christmas-tree look. It is usually only available as a live tree, which means it cannot be kept indoors longer than 10 days if it is to survive.

- Scots pine (*Pinus sylvestris*). A good alternative to the traditional Norway spruce. Its long needles, which are produced in bundles of two, give the branches a bushy appearance. The tree has good needle retention, but it sometimes grows crooked and fails to produce the desired Christmas-tree shape.

- White fir (*Abies concolor*). Popular on the east coast, this has long, silvery-green needles that give off a strong citrus smell when crushed. It has good foliage color, a pleasing natural shape and aroma, and good needle retention.

How to Care for Your Christmas Tree

- Once you've chosen your tree, keep it in a sheltered, unheated area such as a porch or garage to protect it from the wind and sun until you are ready to decorate it.

- Before you set up your tree, make a fresh, straight cut across the base of the trunk, about 1/2 inch (1.2 cm) up from the original cut. This makes it easier for the tree to absorb water.

- Locate your tree away from drafts and heat sources such as heating vents, fireplaces, radiators and television sets.

- Don't use outdoor lighting on your tree. Only use mini-lights, which generate minimal heat.

- Water daily. The tree stand should be rinsed with a capful of bleach and some water before inserting the tree. This reduces the growth of microorganisms that can block the tree's ability to take up water.

- Christmas trees don't appear to do any better when given distilled water or mineral water to drink. Plain old tap water is all that is needed.

- Keep the tree stand filled with water. A seal of dried sap can form over the cut stump in four to six hours if the water drops below the base of the tree, preventing the tree from absorbing water later when the tree stand is refilled.

Winter Containers: How to Brighten Your Entrance

There's no more welcoming sight to have by your front door over winter than a container full of colorful plants. It not only provides a cheery spectacle in the midst of winter's gloom, it can add a special, festive flavor to your main entrance. This doesn't have to be a difficult or complicated

Care of Live Christmas Trees

If you buy a live, burlapped or potted Christmas tree—Colorado blue spruce, Scots pine, Serbian spruce or Norway spruce—there are two important rules to remember.

1. Don't keep the tree indoors for longer than 10 days. The problem is not so much one of watering (important as this is) but one of accidentally waking the tree from its dormant or semi-dormant state and tricking it into putting on rapid new growth. The tree can die if after a warming spell indoors it is then put outdoors where it will go into shock when it discovers it is winter and not spring after all.

2. Always allow your live Christmas tree to gradually reacclimatize to the outdoors by first moving it to a cool room, then into a cooler garage or greenhouse before finally moving it fully outdoors.

task. You can simply take some purple ornamental cabbage (kale), add some silver-leafed dusty miller and fill in the gaps with a mix of winter pansies. Neatly assembled in a medium-sized pot, this dependable trio will provide color and foliage interest through to spring. The only problem—it is a rather lackluster combination, especially once you've seen what can be achieved with a little flair and imagination. Here's a look at plants that are perfect for the job.

Anchor Plants

An important part of planting a winter container is to decide on a structural feature plant to anchor the display. The size of these shrubs at maturity is not very relevant, as they are mostly moved into the garden once they have served their usefulness in the container. Here are a few reliable choices.

- *Choisya ternata* (Mexican orange blossom). This has handsome, shiny, dark green foliage that is aromatic when crushed. It is only hardy to Zone 7, so to look good all winter in colder climates it would need to be in a protected spot.

- Dwarf conifers. There is a good selection available, both globe and upright shapes. Look for *Chamaecyparis* (false cypress), notably *C. obtusa* 'Nana Gracilis' (dwarf Hinoki cypress), or *C. obtusa* 'Nana Aurea' (dwarf golden Hinoki cypress), which are both hardy to Zone 5. Also consider blue junipers (*Juniperus*) such as 'Blue Star', 'Berkshire', 'Hybernica', 'Blue Arrow' or 'Skyrocket', all hardy to Zone 3. A dwarf mugho pine (*Pinus mugo* 'Pumilo'), hardy to Zone 1, or a dwarf Alberta spruce (*Picea glauca* 'Conica'), hardy to Zone 4, would also serve the purpose.

- *Euonymus fortunei*. 'Emerald Gaiety' has crisp, gray-green and creamy-white variegated foliage and will ultimately grow into a compact bush about 3 to 5 feet (90 cm to 1.5 m) tall. 'Emerald 'n' Gold' has bright yellow and green variegated leaves and grows to 2 to 3 feet (60 to 90 cm). Its foliage has a pinkish tinge in winter. Other top varieties are 'Canadale Gold' (green with gold edges), 'Country Gold' (green with gold edges), 'Gold Tip' (green with gold markings), and 'Surespot' (green with yellow center). All are hardy to Zone 3.

- Evergreen azaleas and rhododendrons. Both of these make good centerpieces because of the attractive quality of the evergreen foliage. Gardeners in very cold areas should consider using one of the hardy Finnish rhodos or one of the Northern Lights Series of azaleas. (See Your Guide to Rhododendrons, page 37.)

- *Ilex crenata* (Japanese holly). This beautiful boxwood-like holly can grow to 5 or 6 feet (1.5 to 1.8 m), but it starts out small enough in a two-gallon pot and can be pruned to size. Hardy to Zone 5.

- *Nandina domestica* (heavenly bamboo). There are two outstanding dwarf forms—'Gulfstream' and 'Harbor Dwarf', both of which grow eventually to 24 to 36 inches (60 to 90 cm). They grow in partial shade to full sun and like moist soil. Hardy to Zone 6.

- *Pieris japonica* (lily-of-the-valley bush). There are a few dwarf varieties of this popular evergreen shrub—'Prelude', 'Little Heath' and 'Bisbee's Dwarf'. They grow to 3 to 4 feet (90 cm to 1.2 m), compared to the 5 to 6 feet (1.5 to 1.8 m) of the standard type. They all have attractive new growth and are hardy to Zone 6.

- *Viburnum.* There are three main kinds to consider—*V. tinus* 'Spring Bouquet', which is compact and upright with dark, green foliage and hardy to Zone 7; *V. bodnantense,* which produces fragrant, pink flowers on bare branches in late winter and is hardy to Zone 6; and *V. davidii,* which has blue-green, deeply veined, leathery leaves and dark blue berries and is hardy to Zone 7.

Accent Plants

- *Acorus gramineus* 'Ogon' (sweet flag). This ornamental grass has bright, yellow-striped leaves and keeps its lovely color and shape throughout the winter, making it a perfect choice for adding height and structure to combination plantings. Grows to 10 inches (25 cm). *A. gramineus* 'Variegatus' has white-green striping and is the perfect complement to mixed plantings in silver, pink-purple or blue. Grows to 12 inches (30 cm). Hardy to Zone 4.

- *Ajuga reptans* (bugleweed). There are three forms of crinkly-leafed bugleweed (*A. reptans*) in the fall-magic series—'Burgundy Glow', which has bright, variegated leaves containing a blend of scarlet, cream and green; 'Mahogany', an outstanding native German ajuga with shiny, short-stemmed, rich reddish-brown leaves; and 'Catlin's Giant', which has large, reddish-purple leaves with a metallic sheen. They grow to 6 inches (15 cm). Hardy to Zone 3.

- *Carex comans* (bronze form). This is a slender, upright grass from New Zealand with warm, bronze-colored stalks about 16 inches (40 cm) high. Hardy to Zone 5.

- *Erysimum linifolium* 'Variegatum' (wallflower). This bushy plant has creamy-yellow variegated leaves that are very frost resistant. The coloring is similar to *Acorus* 'Ogon' but it's more upright. It grows to 12 inches (30 cm). Hardy to Zone 7.

- *Euphorbia amygdaloides* 'Purpurea' (purple wood spurge). Like most of the other plants in this series, this won't be new to keen gardeners, but the idea of using it in a winter container display is a clever idea that many gardeners have yet to try. A superb perennial, 'Purpurea' is very frost-resistant, and has reddish leaves that turn purple in cold temperatures. Grows to 18 inches (45 cm). Hardy to Zone 5.

- *Festuca cinerea* 'Elijah Blue' (blue ornamental grass). This keeps its powdery blue color all winter. It will eventually grow to 18 inches (45 cm) high. Hardy to Zone 3.

- *Gaultheria procumbens* (wintergreen). This has small, oval-shaped, leathery, green leaves and bright red berries. Normally used as a groundcover, this is a favorite accent plant at the moment for dressing up a winter container. Grows to 6 inches (15 cm). Hardy to Zone 3.

- *Hedera helix* (ivy). There are numerous excellent hardy types that add color and foliage interest to a container. 'Glacier' has dark green leaves with creamy-yellow edges; 'Kholibra' has mottled green and yellow leaves; and 'Needlepoint' has dark birdsfoot-shaped leaves. They are all hardy to Zone 6. More tender but very attractive in containers is *H. canariensis* 'Glorie de Marengo', which has marbled leaves tinged with pink. It is hardy to Zone 8, so should only be incorporated into containers in very sheltered spaces.

- *Lamium galeobdolon* 'Hermann's Pride'. A well-known groundcover plant, this has shiny silver leaves with green veining. In a container, it will trail over the sides. It grows 8 to 12 inches (20 to 30 cm). Hardy to Zone 2.

- *Lavandula lanata* (wooly lavender). The most distinctive feature of this plant is its silvery-white leaves that are velvety to the touch and hold their color throughout the winter. Grows to 2 feet (60 cm). Hardy to Zone 8.

- *Ophiopogon planiscapus* 'Nigrescens' (black mondo grass). Native to Japan, this produces a spidery clump of thin, jet-black, strap-like leaves. Although hardly a cheerful color, it is a valuable contrast to the bright yellows of plants such as *Acorus gramineus* and *Lysimachia nummularia* (creeping jenny). It grows 6 to 8 inches (15 to 20 cm) high. Hardy to Zone 6.

- *Salvia officinalis* (common sage). 'Icterina' (also known as 'Aurea') has variegated golden-yellow and green leaves; 'Purpurascens' has lovely soft eggplant-colored leaves; and the leaves of 'Tricolor' are a mixture of white, purple, cream and pink. They grow 18 inches (45 cm) high and are hardy to Zone 6.

- *Santolina chamaecyparissus* (lavender cotton). Its soft, feathery, silver-gray foliage is delicate and fragrant and doesn't lose its color during the winter months. Grows to 12 to 18 inches (30 to 45 cm). Hardy to Zone 6.

- *Senecio cineraria* (dusty miller). The bright gray foliage of this very familiar plant adds light to any container, but especially to one in the dark days of winter. Grows to 2 feet (60 cm). Hardy to Zone 5.

- *Skimmia japonica* 'Rubella'. A slow-growing shrub with aromatic evergreen leaves and dense clusters of ruby-red flowers, it grows to 3 feet (90 cm). Hardy to Zone 7.

- *Viola cornuta* (pansies). Always popular for their cheery, dependable flowers, these come in a wide range of colors, but the ruby and burgundy tones offer a warmer welcome in the winter months than stark yellows and sky blues. They grow 6 to 8 inches (15 to 20 cm). Hardy in all zones.

Container Hints

- **Buy the best pot you can afford.** Frost-resistant and frost-proof pots are generally more expensive than ordinary clay, ceramic or terracotta pots. Plastic and fiberglass lookalikes are also available and can last for many years.

- **Good drainage is essential.** A 20-inch (50-cm) pot needs at least a 1-inch (2.5-cm) hole at the bottom. Use broken pieces of terracotta or stones at the bottom of the pot for drainage and cover this layer with landscape cloth to stop it from getting plugged up. Most large pots can be used without danger of cracking in reasonably well-protected spots close to the house. If in doubt, use a thin layer of styrofoam insulation or some pipe-insulating material from a plumbing store to line the inside of the pot.

- **Get the soil mix right.** Look for a mix with 10 percent pumice mixed in. If you can't find it, buy a small bag of pumice and add it to a regular bag of potting soil. The idea is to make the soil more porous so it drains better. Some soil mixes contain a lot of peat, which can make the soil boggy and lead to waterlogged pots.

- **Feed your pansies.** Spot-feed your winter pansies with a half-strength solution of 20-20-20 fertilizer and keep deadheading and pinching them back. Don't bother using slow-release fertilizer in the winter.

- **Be prepared to add new plants.** In spring, you will need to replace some of the plant material. The pansies and dusty miller can be changed for spring-flowering perennials and annuals.

Garden Design

What was wrong with your garden this year? Too much color? Not enough color? Perhaps you had plenty of plants but not enough structure. Could you use more hard landscaping, perhaps a new trellis or arbor, path or wall? Maybe you're looking for a major change, such as replacing a lawn with a traditional knot garden. Winter gives us the opportunity to walk the garden and come up with fresh ideas for next year. Knowing the elements that make a great garden will help bring those plans to fruition.

12 Steps to a Great Garden

1. **Have a vision.** Before you rush out to buy plants, stop and consider the kind of garden you want to create. Think about the big picture. Do you need an area for children to play? Where will you put the garbage cans? What paths do you need? If your garden is on a slope or hillside, perhaps you will want to grade it into terraces. If you know you don't have a good eye for design, hire a professional garden designer to draw up a plan for you. Look to other gardens for inspiration. You'd be surprised how many great gardens are simply copies or interpretations of world-famous gardens. Too often we simply build our gardens by following the shapes and lines left by a builder or the previous homeowner. It is easy to forget about imposing your own design and style. Look at your garden space as a blank canvas and don't be afraid to turn rectangles into circles or wavy borders into straight lines.

2. **Know your garden.** Walk your garden in all seasons in all weather. Get to know the shady areas, the damp spots, the frost pockets and the fast-draining, drought-prone areas. This is valuable knowledge that will enable you to build a better garden. If you have to improve drainage, for instance, you should do it before you try to install a lawn, shrub border or flower bed. View your garden from the inside of your home: a lot of great gardens have been designed so they can be seen at their best from a balcony, bedroom or living room window.

3. **Buy plants for specific places.** Don't just wander into a garden center and buy the first attractive plant to catch your eye. The key to successful gardening is to get a great plant in a good location . . . next to other right plants in right places. The most common garden error is to put shade-loving plants in sunny spots and sun-loving plants in cool damp places. You would be amazed how often it happens and it is almost always because the gardener has not taken the time to get in touch with the garden at the soil level. Since you have spent time getting to know your garden, you can shop with confidence for plants

for specific sites. Getting the right plant in the right place is the key to success. The greatest beauty in a garden is the healthiness of plants. Pests and disease descend on plants that are under stress, perhaps because they have been planted in the wrong spot. When buying trees, always ask about their height and width at maturity. You can get tall, column-shaped trees that don't get very wide, and wide-growing trees that don't get very tall.

4. **Feed your soil, rather than your plants.** It is such a shame to take time to pick out beautiful plants and then stick them in miserable, infertile soil. Most plants can't thrive and grow to maturity if they are trapped in lifeless, poorly drained soil. So before you plant anything, dig deeply and enrich the soil with well-rotted compost and mushroom or steer manure. That way you will get your plants off to a good start. Most plants need at least 18 inches (45 cm) of decent, fertile, well-drained soil.

5. **Think about the borrowed landscape.** This simply means being aware of the existing scenery around your garden. Look up and around and see what kind of landscape features you get for free from your neighbors. It could be a beautiful tree that flowers in spring or a view of a distant lake or sunny hilltop. Is there a flowering shrub that gives you a wonderful show or a scrambling vine that tumbles into your yard and fills the air with an intoxicating fragrance? If you are aware of these things, you can incorporate them into your own garden design. Many gardeners find that what visitors often admire most in their garden are trees and shrubs that are actually planted in neighboring gardens. Being aware of the borrowed landscape also means being sensitive to your neighbors and thinking carefully about how what you plant or take out will affect them. Gardeners with an eye for the bigger landscape picture are much more likely to create great gardens and inspire others to do likewise.

6. **Send a clear invitation.** Too many gardens don't invite you to stay. They seem to say "Come and look at the plants, but leave as soon as you're done." A well-positioned bench or group of chairs can send a friendly, welcoming invitation to sit and rest. If your garden doesn't do that, think about adding a simple bench or arbor-seat in a place that will call out to your visitors when they see it.

7. **Don't overlook scent.** Fragrance is the most frequently overlooked element in the garden, even though it is one of the most popular. Color is important, but delicious scents add an extra dimension to the pleasure of your garden experience. Make a list of plants that provide fragrance throughout the seasons and see if you can accommodate

them in areas close to porches and gateways where they will be most appreciated.

8. **Incorporate evergreens.** Evergreens provide year-long structure in the garden. They also provide background foliage for other plants. Low boxwood hedges can be used to define specific areas, such as rose beds and herb gardens. You can use a spiral-shaped conifer to create a focal point or a special accent at an intersection, or you can use two of them to flank a view.

All Tied Up in Knot Gardens

Did you tire of mowing your lawn last summer? Perhaps you should consider replacing the grass with a knot garden. Once you hear how effective knot gardens and decorative Renaissance parterres can be as beautiful, structural frames for displaying perennials, topiary, roses and herbs, I think you'll find the concept very appealing. These neatly patterned gardens not only look wonderful filled with colorful gravel, pebbles or flowers in summer, they provide an attractive, calming landscape scene in winter.

Knot gardens are basically simple geometric patterns formed out of crisply clipped, low boxwood hedges. The Italians in the 15th century were the first to take the straightforward formal parterre and have fun twisting it into elaborate, interlacing patterns. (*Parterre*, by the way, comes from the old French *par terre* and the Latin *per terre*, meaning "on the ground.")

Within a century, the idea had swept through Europe and caught on in a big way in Elizabethan England, where knot gardening became a celebrated art form, with gardeners using their imaginations to come up with all kinds of ornate designs. The French were also smitten with the idea, but they moved on from the basic Italian model to experiment with stunning designs of such intricacy that some were compared to the precision and delicacy of fine embroidery.

Flowers and shrubs were not planted inside the patterns in the beginning. Instead, compartments formed by the hedging were usually filled with "dead materials" such as sand, crushed tiles, lime,

plaster, pebbles, even coal dust. It wasn't long, however, before gardeners seized the opportunity to use the enclosed spaces for growing herbs, bedding plants, perennials, evergreens and decorative topiary such as boxwood cones and holly spirals. Today, some gardeners use the compartments to accommodate large terracotta pots filled with exotic plant material such as angel's trumpet (*Brugmansia*), *Dracaena* and *Phormium*. A modern misconception is that you need large amounts of space to do a knot garden. This is not true. You can install a very effective and elegant knot garden or parterre in a space no bigger than 10 by 10 feet (3 by 3 m). And if you don't like boxwood, you can follow the example of gardeners in the past and use lavender, hyssop, santolina or germander (*Teucrium chamaedrys*) for hedging.

At Barnsley House in Gloucestershire, an elaborate knot garden based on a 17th-century pattern has been built in a space measuring only 17 by 26 feet (5 by 8 m). The main lines are defined by box and germander, while domes of holly and variegated box are used to add interest and create height.

The beauty of a knot garden for today's gardeners is that it is intensely structural and relatively easy to maintain, which makes it an ideal replacement for an unwanted lawn area. A knot garden will also appeal to busy urban gardeners who want well-structured, manageable flower beds that are neatly contained within a permanent, low-maintenance landscape.

9. **Screen out eyesores.** Privacy and intimacy are so important to the romantic ambience of a garden, but eyesores can spoil the fun. Block out things you don't want to see by using trellises and arbors. Fences, hedges and walls are not always the best solution. If you are trying to screen out a house, for example, think about pleaching a row of small-growing trees instead of growing a tall hedge. The pleached trees can screen the eyesore while still leaving room underneath for an interesting planting at ground level. Gazebos, arbors and pergolas are other structures you can use to create privacy.

10. **Make good use of containers.** Pots and troughs, planters and urns are the little touches that make the difference between a great garden and a ho-hum garden. Statuary is trickier because it is more personal, but troughs and planters can help individualize your garden without making too strong a statement. You don't have to overdo it. A simple boxwood topiary ball or hydrangea or rose is often all that is needed. Use containers to bring fragrance closer to your sitting areas and to create a change of pace and points of interest for visitors exploring the garden. You can also use containers of potted plants to fill gaps left in the garden by perennials that have finished blooming.

11. **Share what you grow.** All expert gardeners know the best way to ensure that you have a plant forever is to give some of it away to a friend. That way, if your plant should suddenly die, you always have a friend who can give you back a replacement. The Victoria Horticulture Society has a marvelous motto: "Show what you grow, share what you know." Open your garden and let others see what you are doing. This is a great way to encourage and inspire others and exchange ideas. Gardening is all about sharing—sharing plants, sharing knowledge, sharing stories of successes and failures.

12. **Have fun when you garden.** The saddest thing is when new gardeners get serious and forget gardening is supposed to be fun. It is playing with plants. What tends to happen is that they get pushed and prodded by fanatical gardeners to become just as fanatical and . . . unhappy. Make a decision that if ever gardening stops being fun, you will stop what you are doing and do something else. Don't let gardening become a pain in the neck. If a plant dies, you can always get another one. If you make a mistake, don't be hard on yourself—that's how most people learn what works and what doesn't. Sometimes mistakes will turn out to be huge successes. You will always be making changes, moving plants around, even if they look fine, to try something new. The important thing is to have fun gardening.

Special Features for an Elegant Garden

Gardens are all about putting a diverse assortment of plants together in clever and creative ways in order to achieve beautiful, striking contrasts in foliage, form and color. There is, however, more to designing an above-average garden than simply filling up flower beds with perennials or planting graceful trees or designing lush shrubberies. While it is true that certain architectural plants, such as *Sedum spectabile*, *Euphorbia characias* or *Stachys lanata*, are useful in giving an ordinary border or flower bed some strength, texture and shape, for a garden to truly satisfy the eye it needs non-organic elements to give it stability and personality.

Here are a few classic garden features that great designers all over the world have repeatedly used to compose an elegant garden picture.

- **Arbors, pergolas and galleries.** Few structures in the garden are as attractive to the eye as an arbor covered with clematis or grape vines, or a pergola smothered in roses.

  Considered the quintessential element in any Elizabethan garden, the Egyptians, Romans and Italians loved arbors and the English like to think they invented them. The difference between an arbor and a pergola is subtle; it all comes down to a question of length. Arbors are usually thought of as short structures, 6 to 8 feet (1.8 to 2.4 m) in length, while pergolas are made up of a longer series of arbors forming an open-sided colonnade. Galleries are enclosed, arched, tunnel-shaped passageways covered with foliage. You don't see many of them any more, mainly because most gardens lack the space and most gardeners lack the interest. They were hugely popular in Victorian England. Arbors are by far the easiest of the three to install in the average-sized home garden. They can define an entrance, make a natural, pleasant transition from one space to another, or provide a secluded resting spot. They can even be expanded and used as an outdoor room for entertaining in summer.

- **Fences.** They do not make good neighbors, as poet Robert Frost is so often misquoted as having asserted. It is undeniable, however, that they do make life easier and serve an important purpose in clearly defining spaces. A high backyard fence, installed for privacy, should not be allowed to dominate the rest of the garden, but should be clothed with greenery as quickly as possible. Some fences, like the New England picket fence, have a classic look, evoking a country ambience, but many modern fences are necessary monstrosities that are best kept out of sight.

- **Gazebos or kiosks.** A quiet, enclosed, private place for sitting and having tea or entertaining, a gazebo is invariably used as a principal feature or focal point in the garden. Kiosks, on the other hand, are basically rain shelters used on large estates, places where people out for an afternoon stroll can take cover from a sudden shower. In the small home garden, kiosks can add a sense of mystery and structure as well as serving a practical use by providing space for storage. Square or octagonal, the most popular gazebo designs have decorative gothic touches or Moorish arches and mosque-like roofs.

- **Latticework and trellises.** Among the oldest types of garden enclosures, latticework and trellises are effective and inexpensive ways of hiding ugly areas of the garden by providing support for flowering and foliage plants. The Romans are credited with being some of the first to use trellises extensively. The look was refined over the years into a more sophisticated, decorative style for use against walls. Modern designs range from simple to elaborate geometric arrangements.

- **Birdbaths.** There are two reasons to put a birdbath in the garden: to stop the eye as it sweeps around the yard by providing a natural and attractive contrast to surrounding foliage, and to do the obvious—draw the flash and flutter of bird life into the garden, which makes the act of simply sitting and watching a heavenly pastime. At one time it was common practice to catch a bird and put it in a cage in the garden. In 18th-century Europe, caged birds were hidden to create the sound of a natural woodland setting. Birdbaths came into fashion as a more humane way to attract birds to the garden. A large, decorative birdbath set amid the lush foliage of hostas or dicentras or astilbe is a simple way to instantly create a romantic setting.

- **Bridges.** These have a symbolic value in the garden as well as structural usefulness: they represent transitions and the overcoming of obstacles in life. Gardens with natural brooks, streams or ponds should not overlook the opportunity for a small bridge. Humpback bridges are romantic, but even a simple, flat bridge can be inviting and attractive. The design and choice of material should be kept as simple and functional as possible. There is vague apprehension and intrigue involved in crossing a bridge, regardless of size, which adds interest and creative tension to a garden. Thomas Mawson, in *The Art and Craft of Garden Making*, says masonry bridges should be built from local stone and kept simple for "it is better to err on the side of plainness than to obtain an ostentatious result."

- **Fountains, ponds and water courses.** Considered by the Persians to be the most important element in the garden, water provides a soothing sound and attracts birds and butterflies, which add movement, interest and gaiety to the scene. In medieval gardens and courtyards, a fountain was often placed in the center as the principal decorative feature. Most gardens can accommodate water in one of its many forms: trickling, gurgling, dripping, spouting, still and mirror-like, or lively and spraying out from a statue or fountain. The sound of running water is often referred to as "white noise," useful for masking more disturbing sounds, such as the perpetual hum of traffic. Ponds will produce flies and frogs, and ponds with fish will bring in herons and raccoons, challenges to consider before digging the hole.

- **Furniture.** Stone seats and wooden benches, cast-iron chairs and tables all have a place in the garden. Teak is a wood favored by many gardeners but red cedar looks equally attractive. Decorative metal chairs with floral patterned cushions can look stylish on a brick patio. Small, flat stone seats or solitary wooden chairs look exceptionally attractive when squeezed in a small, secluded spot, lush with foliage, with just enough room for you and a friend or you and a book or just you.

- **Paths.** They have an infinitely more important job to do than merely provide a route between two points. Symbols of transition and connectedness, paths direct the eye and the foot to specific goals and help to define the overall structure of the garden. When leading someone down the garden path, make sure there is a reason for them to go. If a path leads to a dead end, put a seat or bench there, don't just let it stop like a dinner with no dessert. There should also be plenty to see en route: plant heavily on either side of a path and provide a reason for visitors to pause and examine a plant or piece of statuary. According to Katsuo Saito in *Japanese Garden Hints*, the rule for the correct width of a path is 6 feet (1.8 m) in heavily traveled public places and 1 to 1 1/2 feet (30 to 45 cm) in the home garden.

- **Pots and planters.** The solution to so many problem areas, a pot or half-barrel with an attractive plant in it can disguise awkward spaces and transform ugly corners into pleasant pictures. Large decks and patios can be shrunk to a more human scale by the use of varying sizes of pots, troughs and planters. The Greeks are credited with introducing containers into the garden, but the most lasting influence has been that of the formal Italian garden, which features fruit trees in ornamental containers to line paths and terraces. Glazed or colored pots look good in the garden, as do vases, urns or planters made of terracotta, wood, stone, lead, cast iron or concrete.

> *I think sometimes people get so wrapped up in their own problems and the problems of the world. I realize there are a lot of things out there that we really can't do as much about as we would like. For me, the garden is a special place to find peace and solitude.*
>
> —Nancy Vince, Maple Ridge, British Columbia, gardener

- **Statues and sundials.** Most of the world's great gardens seem to find room for at least one or two pieces of statuary and a sundial. Part of the idea is to give the mind a rest from flowers and foliage. Statuary is the horticultural equivalent of an intermission, a time to relax the concentration with a change of intellectual pace. Statuary subjects range from Greek gods and goddesses to oriental dragons and lions. Cherubs and children are popular but so are dogs, frogs, rabbits and birds, especially long-legged herons. Sundials, though fun and useful as focal points, especially in herb gardens, have generally been overtaken in popularity by birdbaths and fountains.

- **Weather vanes and whirligigs.** Old weather vanes on churches were mostly cocks designed to remind the faithful of Peter's denial of Christ "before the cock crowed twice." You can find a whole range of weather vanes—from trains, ships and foxes to witches, trumpet-blowing angels and a farmer hoeing a field. Whirligigs are somewhat related to weather vanes in that they are also wind-driven. But they are really garden toys or amusements featuring gardeners turning a pump handle or a chicken running for its life or a man perpetually sawing wood.

A to Z of Terms for New Gardeners

Acidic soil: Soil—perfect for rhododendrons, azaleas, heathers and hydrangeas—that has a pH of less than 6.5. *See also* pH.

Alkaline soil: The opposite of acidic soil, it has a pH of more than 7.5. Alkaline soil is also referred to as chalky, limey or sweet soil.

Annual: Hardy and half-hardy annuals are plants that complete their life cycle in a single season, going from seed to flower or fruit before dying.

Bare-root: A plant that has been dug up while dormant and packaged without soil around its roots. Mail orders from nurseries are mostly dispatched bare-root.

Bedding plants: Mostly annuals (although it can include biennials and tender perennials) that are "bedded out" in spring to provide summer color.

Biennial: Plants that complete their life cycle in two seasons, starting from seed and establishing leaves in the first year and flowering the following year. Examples are foxgloves, wallflowers and Canterbury bells.

Cambium: The green layer of living tissue just below the woody surface of a branch. A sign that your plant is still alive.

Carpet bedding: A style of planting, popular with the early Victorians, involving the tight planting of bedding plants to create intricate floral patterns.

Compost: Dark, blackish humus formed from the decomposition of organic matter. Can be used to enrich soil or as a mulch.

Cultivar: Short for cultivated variety, this refers to a plant selected from the wild or a garden and cultivated by controlled propagation to preserve specific characteristics.

Deadhead: Removal of faded flowers in order: 1) to maintain the tidy appearance of the garden; 2) to promote flower production by preventing seed development; and 3) in some cases, such as with delphiniums and lupins, to induce a second flush of flowers later in the season.

Dieback: The death of part of a shoot or branch caused by disease, water or nutrient deficiency, pest damage or incorrect pruning.

Division: A way of making more plants by dividing them into pieces, each with a root system or one or more shoots.

Dormant: Winter sleep for plants. Technically, it means there is little or no cellular activity. Plants go dormant to survive winter and save energy for the new season.

Drip line: An imaginary circle beneath a tree or shrub where water drips from the tips of the branches.

Espalier: The art of training a tree or shrub to grow flat against a wall, fence or trellis in a symmetrical pattern.

Fastigiate: A plant whose upward-growing branches create a columnar shape.

Forcing: Getting plants to flower out of season by manipulating temperature, humidity and light.

Frost pocket: An area of the garden where cold air is trapped during winter. Only tougher, more hardy plants can survive in frost pockets.

Genus: Genus is the name for a group of closely related species, and forms the first word in a plant's botanical name: *Lonicera*, *Fuchsia* and *Cotoneaster* are examples. A plant usually has three names: genus (first), species (second), cultivar (third), as in *Lonicera periclymenum* 'Serotina'.

Grafting: Propagating by taking the stem or bud of one plant and joining it to the root or stem of another.

Hardening off: Gradually acclimatizing a plant to a lower temperature in order to get it ready for planting in the garden.

Hardiness: Measure of a plant's ability to withstand extremes of cold and frost or other harsh conditions. *See also* Zones.

Heading back: Severely pruning back the main branches of a tree or shrub by a third to half.

Heeling-in: Temporarily planting a tree or shrub in a holding bed until you are ready to find a permanent home for it.

Herbaceous: Non-woody plants that die back to the ground in winter, then revive and grow again in spring.

Humus: Dark brown organic material formed from the decomposition of vegetable and certain animal matter. Humus enriches garden soil and gives it the life needed to nourish and sustain plants.

Hybrid: A new plant produced by crossing two or more different plants. Not all hybrids are improvements on the parents.

Insecticide: A chemical (liquid or powder) used to control or kill insect pests such as aphids and red spider mites.

Island bed: A flower bed, usually dominated by hardy perennials, that can be viewed from all sides.

Jardin de refuse: Polite way of describing temporary lodgings for plants you can't use, but can't bring yourself to throw away.

Juvenile foliage: New leaves that are different in their shape, size and color from the plant's more familiar adult foliage.

Knot garden: Popular with medieval English gardeners, who liked to weave low-growing herbs or boxwood hedging into elaborate, knot-like geometric patterns, sometimes with herbs or roses.

Layering: A method of propagation in which a supple branch of a plant is bent down and anchored below ground level until roots form and the newly established plant can be safely cut away from the parent.

Leaf mold: Decomposed leaves that can be used as a mulch or dug into the soil to create useful organic matter.

Loam: The best kind of garden soil for most plants—moderately fertile, composed of clay, sand and humus, with a texture that is neither too sandy nor too heavy.

Manure tea: Water in which compost has been allowed to soak to form a mild, fertilizing "tea."

Microclimate: Small area of the garden where the climate is different from the rest of the garden. When the microclimate is warmer, it means you can grow tender plants that require a climate with a higher zone rating.

Mulch: A layer of bulky organic matter usually placed around perennials to reduce moisture loss, inhibit weeds, improve soil and protect plants from frost. Good mulches include well-rotted manure, compost and leaf mold.

Native plant: A species that grows naturally in a certain location and that is not created by human cultivation.

Naturalize: Informal planting that mirrors nature's own relaxed style and design to create the impression that the plants are native.

NPK: Key plant-food ingredients of fertilizer: N for nitrogen, P for phosphorus and K for potassium. The numbers in fertilizer—for example 20-20-20—represent the percentage of each element in the mix. One way to remember what each does is to memorize "Little Red Flower" (L for leaf, fed by nitrogen; R for roots, strengthened by phosphorus; F for fruit or flower, promoted by potassium).

Oxygenator: A submerged water plant that helps keep ponds clean indirectly by releasing oxygen into the water.

Perennial: A plant with the ability to survive winter and live on for several growing seasons.

pH: Measure (1 to 14) of acidity or alkalinity of soil. Lilacs won't thrive in acidic soil; rhododendrons dislike alkaline soil. The lower the pH, the higher the acidity.

Pinching back: A way of encouraging bushiness in a plant by using your finger and thumb to pinch off growing tips.

Pollarding: Cutting back the main branches of a tree to within inches of the trunk to create a distinct globe effect once the new branches and leaves appear.

Pricking out: Careful removal of seedlings from the original seed tray into a roomier pot or growing space.

Rhizome: A horizontally creeping root system from which shoots and roots develop. A good example is bearded iris.

Rootbound: What happens when a plant has been left in a container too long, allowing roots to become tangled and choked.

Species: The second word in a plant's botanical name. A category of plants that are genetically similar, sharing at least one characteristic that sets them apart from all others. *See also* Genus.

Standard: A tree or shrub that is trained to grow a straight stem clear of branches.

Stock plants: The parent plants from which cuttings are taken for propagation purposes to ensure new plants are an exact clone.

Stress: A cry for help. Wilting or discolored foliage are two signs of stress, signals that a plant is not happy about its growing conditions. Stress can be caused by too much or too little sun, water or fertilizer.

Tanglefoot: "Tree paste" used around the trunk of a tree to make a sticky barrier against such insects as ants (which reduces damage done by aphids, mealy bugs and some scale insects), weevils, caterpillars and cutworms.

Tissue-culture: A high-tech way of propagating by "cloning" a plant, in which tiny pieces of tissue are grown in test tubes.

Top-dressing: Putting a thin layer of new soil or compost around plants or on lawns to improve the soil.

Topiary: The shaping of shrubs and trees into decorative forms.

Trace elements: The same thing as micronutrients—various minerals that plants need in small doses in order to grow.

Tuber: A fleshy root or stem (dahlia, for example) that stores nutrients for later use.

Tufa: Porous limestone rock ideal for growing alpine plants.

Umbel: A rounded, often flattened head of flowers produced at the top of a long stem. A good example is the flower head of an angelica plant.

Underplanting: Plants that have been placed beneath taller shrubs or trees, sometimes to provide leafy groundcover or seasonal color.

Variegated: Leaves that are spotted, streaked or edged with a different color from the main one.

Variety: A subdivision of a species, which grows true to its characteristics from natural propagation. Also called wild variety.

Vermicomposting: Making compost using worms.

Weed: 1) a plant growing in the wrong place; 2) a plant for which a useful purpose has not yet been found.

Wild garden: Informal planting style that attempts to imitate nature. Popular with avant-garde landscape architects, not with most homeowners.

x: The symbol that denotes that a plant is a hybrid between two or more species.

Xeriscaping: Method of landscaping with drought-tolerant plant material to dramatically reduce the use of water.

Zones: North America is divided into 10 climatic zones that are graded according to the average annual minimum temperatures. Zone 1 is the coldest (below –50°F/–46°C) and Zone 10 is the warmest (30° to 40°F/–1° to 4.5°C). Zone numbers are a useful guide when buying plants that can survive in the outdoors in the garden over winter.

Sources

It is difficult to compile a source list for a book such as this. So much has been taken in over the years of researching and writing gardening stories for *The Vancouver Sun*. The works listed here are constant sources of reference and have been particularly helpful in the compilation of this book.

Aden, Paul. *The Hosta Book*. Portland, Oregon: Timber Press, 1988.

Allen, Christine. *Roses for the Pacific Northwest*. Vancouver, B.C.: Stellar Press, 1999.

Austin, David. *English Roses*. London: Conran Octopus, 1993.

Bennett, Jennifer. *The Harrowsmith Northern Gardener*. Buffalo, New York: Camden House Publishing, 1993.

Brickell, Christopher. *Cavendish Encyclopedia of Pruning and Training*. Vancouver, B.C.: Cavendish Books, 1996.

Callaway, Dorothy J. *The World of Magnolias*. Portland, Oregon: Timber Press, 1994.

The Encyclopedia of Roses. Portland, Oregon: Timber Press, 1992.

Flowers by Color. Vancouver, B.C.: Raincoast Books, 1993.

The Gardener's Encyclopedia of Plants and Flowers. London: Dorling Kindersley, 1989.

Hessayon, Dr. D.G. *The Bulb Expert*. London: Transworld Publishers, 1995.

Hessayon, Dr. D.G. *The NEW Rose Expert*. London: Transworld Publishers, 1996.

Hiller's Trees and Shrubs. Holland: Hiller Nurseries, 1981.

Hole, Lois. *Vegetable Favorites*. Edmonton, Alberta: Lone Pine Publishing, 1993.

Lacey, Stephen. *The Startling Jungle*. Middlesex, England: Penguin Books, 1987.

Lancaster, Roy. *What Plant Where*. Vancouver, B.C.: Cavendish Books, 1995.

Lawson, Andrew. *The Gardener's Book of Colour*. London: Francis Lincoln, 1996.

Minter, Brian. *New Gardening Guide*. Vancouver, B.C.: Whitecap Books, 1998.

Noble, Phoebe. *My Experience Growing Hardy Geraniums*. Sidney, B.C.: Tri Investments, 1994.

Phillips, Roger and Martyn Rix. *Perfect Plants*. New York: Random House, 1996.

Phillips, Roger and Martyn Rix. *The Random House Book of Perennials*. New York: Random House, 1991.

Reader's Digest Encyclopedia of Garden Plants and Flowers. London: Reader's Digest, 1985.

Rees, Yvonne and Neil Sutherland. *The Water Garden*. Vancouver, B.C.:
    Whitecap Books, 1995.

Straley, Gerald B. *Trees of Vancouver*. Vancouver, B.C.: UBC Press, 1992.

Taylor, Patrick. *The 500 Best Garden Plants*. Portland, Oregon: Timber Press,
    1993.

Van Pelt Wilson, Helen and Leonie Bell. *The Fragrant Year*. Toronto: George
    McLeod, 1967.

Vertrees, J.D. *Japanese Maples*. Portland, Oregon: Timber Press, 1987.

Western Garden Book. Menlo Park, California: Sunset Publishing, 1992.

Woods, Christopher. *Encyclopedia of Perennials*. New York: Facts on File,
    1992.

Index

About the Author

Steve Whysall was born in 1950 in Nottingham, England. From 1968 to 1974, he worked as a reporter and editor for various newspapers in England, including the *Nottingham Evening Post, Bristol Evening Post* and *London Evening News*.

Courtesy *The Vancouver Sun*

He married and moved to Canada in 1975. For the last eight years he has written gardening columns for *The Vancouver Sun*. He lives in Burnaby, British Columbia with his wife Loraine, their daughter and two sons. Their English-style garden encircles their home and features a variety of the plants mentioned in this book.